Politics and Strategy

Politics and Strategy

PARTISAN AMBITION AND
AMERICAN STATECRAFT

Peter Trubowitz

PRINCETON UNIVERSITY PRESS

PRINCETON AND OXFORD

Library of Congress Cataloging-in-Publication Data

Trubowitz, Peter.
Politics and strategy : partisan ambition and American statecraft / Peter Trubowitz.
p.   cm.— (Princeton studies in international history and politics)
Includes bibliographical references and index.
ISBN 978-0-691-14957-8 (hardcover : alk. paper)—
ISBN 978-0-691-14958-5 (pbk. : alk. paper)
1. United States—Foreign relations—Decision making. 2. Strategic planning—
United States. 3. Geopolitics—United States. 4. Politics, Practical—United States.
5. Security, International. 6. Political leadership—United States. I. Title.
JZ1480.T78 2011
327.73001—dc22   2010039091

This book has been composed in Sabon

Printed on acid-free paper. ∞

Printed in the United States of America

10   9   8   7   6   5   4   3   2   1

For my parents

For a Prince should have two fears: one within, on account of his subjects; the other outside, on account of external powers.

—*Niccolò Machiavelli*

Contents

Tables and Figures

Preface and Acknowledgments

THIS BOOK IS ABOUT how political leaders manage conflicting geopolitical and partisan pressures in making grand strategy. It develops an argument about grand-strategy formation that incorporates ideas from the *Realpolitik* and *Innenpolitik* traditions in international relations – two of the most venerable approaches to the study of international politics. The book proposes a typology of grand strategy variants and develops a model that specifies the international and domestic conditions under which national leaders will choose one type of strategy over another. The model's predictions are tested using historical case studies, drawing heavily on the American political experience. My hope is that it will offer some insight into contemporary U.S. statecraft and the shape of things to come.

At various stages of the project, I have benefited from the comments, suggestions, and insights of colleagues and friends. I wish to thank especially Walter Dean Burnham, Mick Cox, George Gavrilis, William Hurst, John Ikenberry, Farid Kahhat, Charles Kupchan, Jeffrey Legro, Tse-min Lin, Michael Mastanduno, Nicole Mellow, Henry Nau, Jungkun Seo, Jeffrey Tulis, Robert Vitalis, and Bill Wohlforth. Parts of the argument were presented at the Center for International Studies at Tsignhua University in Beijing, the Centro de Investigación y Docencia Económicas (CIDE) in Mexico City, the Dickey Center for International Understanding at Dartmouth College, the Miller Center for Public Affairs at the University of Virginia, the Mortara Center for International Studies at Georgetown University, and the Woodrow Wilson School of Public Policy at Princeton University. I wish to thank those who organized these seminars. My students at the University of Texas at Austin have offered valuable feedback and constructive criticism. I am grateful to them, too.

I took my first, tentative stab at the book's central argument while a visiting scholar at the Centro de Investigación y Docencia Económicas (CIDE) in Mexico City in 2000–2001. I would like to thank Jesus Velasco and the División de Estudios Internacionales for making that opportunity possible. A Fulbright Fellowship at Beijing Foreign Studies University (BFSU) in 2002 and 2003 offered an invaluable comparative context for analyzing the sources of grand strategy, as did return visits to the Center for International Studies at Tsinghua University in Beijing during the summers of 2005, 2007, and 2010. I wish to thank Mei Renyi and Jin Li at BFSU and Yan Xuetong and Shi Zhiqin of Tsinghua, for their many kindnesses.

At Princeton University Press, I would like to thank Chuck Myers for his sound advice and encouragement, and for keeping us on a tight schedule. Deborah Tegarden's careful attention to detail during the book's production has been a windfall, as has Brian MacDonald's meticulous copyediting. In getting to the printed word, I also received a hand from the College of Liberal Arts at the University of Texas at Austin. I wish to acknowledge the College's support by providing much needed release time from the classroom in Fall 2009 so that I could complete a draft of the manuscript.

I have accumulated many debts in writing this book, but none is greater than the one I owe to my wife, Catherine Boone. She is as tough and exacting a critic as there is in the field of political science, and she is peerless as an editor. I have benefited enormously from her comments and suggestions about the book. Our two teenage sons, Josh and Sander, have also been enthusiastic participants in this venture.

CHAPTER ONE

Introduction

STATESMEN, PARTISANS, AND GEOPOLITICS

IN THE SPRING OF 1795, President George Washington faced an agonizing political choice. His special envoy to England, Chief Justice John Jay, had returned from London with a draft of a treaty that strongly favored the British. Revolutionary France's bid for empire in Europe had fanned tensions in Anglo-American relations, and Washington hoped to avert war. He sent Jay to London hoping to reassure London about American intentions and to head off the possibility of a conflict with Britain. But Jay came back with a treaty that was so pro-British that the president was viciously attacked by his partisan foes for a near treasonous deal with the former colonial power. Having delayed action on the treaty for some months, as long as diplomacy would allow, the president now had to decide whether to send it to the Senate for ratification. George Washington faced a strategic dilemma. If he threw his support behind Jay's treaty, the president risked destroying his fragile government from within, through paroxysms of partisan rage. If Washington shelved the treaty to quiet his political detractors, however, there would likely be war with England, which had the potential to destroy the nation from the outside. Geopolitics and domestic politics were two faces of the same coin: the president could not respond to one threat without weighing its impact on the other.

Washington's dilemma was especially acute, but his strategic conundrum was as old as statecraft itself. Political leaders have always had to deal with cross-pressures and trade-offs between geopolitics and domestic politics. This is because leaders face conflicting institutional incentives. One set of incentives is generated by the executive's role as statesman in world politics. The other is generated by the leader's role as chief of a ruling coalition or party on the home front. The tension inherent in this dual role is present in regimes of all types but is especially intense in democracies such as the United States. In democracies, where a leader's hold on power depends on popular support, leaders must respond to shifting geopolitical pressures while *simultaneously* competing to secure the political backing of not only partisans but also a decisive slice of the national electorate.

This book is about how leaders manage these conflicting institutional incentives at the broadest level of foreign policy—the level known as grand strategy. International relations scholars use the term "grand strategy" to refer to the purposeful and planned use of military, economic, and diplomatic means by states to achieve desired foreign policy ends, whether in peacetime or during wartime.[1] *Politics and Strategy* focuses on the determinants or sources of grand strategy: How do leaders select or choose their grand strategies? Why do some leaders pursue ambitious, costly grand strategies, whereas other leaders adopt narrower, cheaper ones? When do leaders respond assertively to check foreign threats, and when are they likely to rely on less confrontational means to deal with external challenges? International relations scholars do not yet provide satisfactory answers to these questions.

THE TWO FACES OF GRAND STRATEGY

Two general approaches dominate the study of grand strategy in international relations.[2] The first draws on the tradition known as *Realpolitik* or realism. It argues that grand strategies are determined by a country's geopolitical circumstances and especially by its position in the international system.[3] Scholars in the realist tradition stress international factors such as a state's relative material power (e.g., military strength, gross national product, population size), whether prevailing military technology favors the offense or defense in fighting wars, and the distribution of power among states in the international system (whether the system is multipolar, bipolar, or unipolar). These and other international constraints, realists argue, shape states' ambitions and possibilities, defining what strategies their leaders might reasonably expect to succeed in a world

---

[1] Though some scholars trace the basic idea back to Machiavelli, the term "grand strategy" was not used until the eighteenth century, when German military writers popularized it (Wheeler, 1993). Grand strategy originally referred to such things as military training, battle tactics, and campaign operations, or, for lack of a better term, "generalship." Gradually, it came to refer to the planning as well as the use of military resources. The scope of grand strategy was also broadened to include peacetime as well as wartime planning and economic and diplomatic resources in addition to military ones (Paret, 1986).

[2] A third, more recent approach, sometimes referred to as *Ideapolitik* focuses on the influence of national policy ideas (e.g., strategic culture). It shares some common features with *Innenpolitik*. However, *Ideapolitik* is sufficiently different to warrant treatment as a separate tradition of analysis. See, for example, Kupchan (1994); Johnston (1995); Katzenstein (1996); Kier (1997); Tannewald (1999); Finnemore (2004); Legro (2005); Dueck (2006); Samuels (2007); and Qin (2008).

[3] Realist literature on the topic is vast. See, for example, Spykman (1942); Knorr (1956); Luttwak (1976); Jervis (1978); Waltz (1979); Gilpin (1981); Posen (1984); Kennedy (1987); Walt (1987); Friedberg (1988); Snyder (1991); Desch (1993); Wohlforth (1993); Christensen (1996); Zakaria (1998); Van Evera (1999); Copeland (2000); Mearsheimer (2001); Gaddis (2005); Layne (2006); Schweller (2006); and Yan (2008).

that is fundamentally anarchical. These considerations determine leaders' foreign policy strategies and choices.

Realist explanations of statecraft differ sharply from a second approach that argues that grand strategy has a domestic face. Scholars in this domestic politics or *Innenpolitik* tradition point to pressures *within* states, rather than pushes and pulls from the outside, to explain leaders' choices. The domestic politics approach starts from the premise that societal interests (e.g., industrialists, bankers, merchants, interest groups) have a stake in whether a nation's foreign policy is expensive or cheap, offensive or defensive, or coercive or cooperative.[4] Leaders are thought to respond to these interests in setting grand strategy and choosing national priorities in international affairs. In *Innenpolitik* accounts of grand strategy, states' foreign policy choices are thus constrained, and perhaps even distorted, by societal interests and pressures. *Innenpolitikers* argue, for example, that the roots of the classic problem of "strategic overextension," in which a state's reach exceeds its grasp, lie on the domestic side: the combination of powerful economic interests and weak, ineffectual governing institutions allow narrow special interests to push political leaders into overly ambitious foreign policies.

In this book, I argue that this international-domestic distinction misses the essential dynamic that defines how leaders set grand strategy. The fact is that leaders take both geopolitics and domestic politics seriously, and they do so for a simple reason: to do otherwise is to risk their reputation as leaders and their hold on political power. It is clear that leaders who misread or ignore the interests of their domestic coalitions or parties risk losing power and office. But as Niccolò Machiavelli warned, the same is true for "princes" who misjudge their state's geopolitical circumstances and capabilities. They too risk political punishment by their partisan supporters and domestic publics. The unanticipated rise of a foreign challenger, the failure to take an old or new foe seriously enough, or the headlong pursuit of an ill-advised foreign adventure can seriously damage a leader's reputation and credibility, at home as well as abroad. Failure or defeat in international affairs throws open the door to domestic opponents and would-be challengers to the throne.

---

[4] The literature here is substantial and diverse. See, for example, Hobson (1902); Kehr (1930); Schumpeter (1955); Mayer (1971); Fischer (1975); Block (1980); Cain and Hopkins (1980); Olson (1982); Kahler (1984); W. Harris (1985); Davis and Huttenback (1986); Gourevitch (1986); Frieden (1988); Lamborn (1991); Rosecrance and Stein (1993); Fordham (1998); Solingen (1998); Trubowitz (1998); Lobell (2003); Newton (1996); Narizny (2007); and P. McDonald (2009). A few realist scholars in the defensive realist school also weigh the impact of domestic interests, most notably Snyder (1991) and Van Evera (1999).

STATESMEN AS STRATEGIC POLITICIANS

Politics and Strategy advances an argument about how leaders make grand strategy that centers on these distinct international and domestic sources of political pressure. It builds on a growing body of scholarly literature that sees leaders as strategic actors who choose their policies on the basis of political self-interest.[5] Leaders are motivated by a concern for their reputations as effective statesmen on the international stage, as well as by the need to strengthen the political coalitions that secure their claims to office. Grand strategy is thus Janus-faced: its formulation, I argue, has as much to do with leaders' ability to govern effectively at home as it does with guaranteeing the nation's security abroad.[6] In contrast to *Realpolitik* and *Innenpolitik* approaches that emphasize either the external or the internal face of foreign policy making, this book shows how geopolitics and party politics *combine* to produce grand strategy.[7] Shifts

[5] See, for example, Hechter and Brustein (1980); Bates (1981); Levi (1988); Lake and Powell (1999); and Bueno de Mesquita et al. (2003). On the general approach, see Frieden (1999).

[6] The idea that international and domestic politics are somehow interconnected is not new. Rosenau's (1969) efforts to catalog instances of what he called "linkage politics," Keohane and Nye's (1977) writings about "international interdependence," Katzenstein's (1977) work on the interaction of international politics and domestic structure in foreign economic policy, and Gourevitch's (1978) analysis of the international sources of domestic politics are some of the better-known efforts to connect these two domains. Perhaps the approach that is closest in spirit to the one I develop here is Putnam's (1988) "two-level" analysis of international negotiations. Putnam takes statesmen as strategic actors who are constrained by both domestic and foreign pressures: their choice of diplomatic tactics and strategies in international negotiation is constrained by what foreign leaders will accept, and by what their own domestic constituencies will ratify. He does not extend this intuition to the analysis of grand strategy and does not propose a theory of either geopolitical or domestic constraints.

[7] One variant of realism, neoclassical realism, does attempt to combine international and domestic politics. My approach differs from neoclassical realism in three important ways. First, neoclassical realists give pride of place analytically to the international environment; they rely on domestic politics to try to explain deviations from "the" national interest, which is dictated by international circumstance. My model takes realism as fundamentally underdetermining when it comes to defining the ideal choice point for national leaders—domestic interests shape definitions of a nation's long-term security objectives (see also Trubowitz, 1998). Second, neoclassical realists have no theory of domestic politics: they do not consider the competition and conflict between groups with different visions of the national interest, and shy away from arguments about domestic electoral and distributional conflicts over foreign policy. Neoclassical realist models typically operationalize domestic politics in terms of institutional structure, political culture, or elite values—factors to which *Innenpolitikers* (and I) assign little analytic weight. By contrast, in my model, electoral competition and distributional conflict are theorized as systematic influences on grand-strategy choice. Third, neoclassical realists do not ground their theories of grand strategy at the microfoundational level—that is, in the strategic choices of political leaders. As one neoclassical

in the parameters of strategic choice—be they international, domestic, or both—produce changes in grand strategy over time.

A nation's grand-strategy options can be described generically as varying along two distinct dimensions: the cost dimension and the ambition dimension. There are expensive, offensive strategies designed to alter the international status quo, such as expansionism, and cheaper offensive means, such as blackmail. There are also costly defensive strategies designed to maintain the status quo (e.g., so-called defensive or just wars) and relatively inexpensive ones, such as appeasement. Examples of each option abound in the international relations literature. Napoleon's expansionist drive in the early nineteenth century was a costly, offensive strategy aimed at changing the status quo—of shifting the balance of power in France's favor. There are also examples of cheap revisionist strategies (e.g., blackmail, subversion). John Mearsheimer (2001) characterizes Germany's repeated attempts in the run up to World War I to subordinate its European rivals, Britain, France, and Russia, as a strategy centered on intimidation. Edward Luttwak (2009) describes the Byzantine Empire's sustained reliance on covert operations and subversion as a cheap strategy aimed at consolidating its imperial gains. An example of an expensive, status quo strategy is Franklin Delano Roosevelt's intervention into World War II to check and balance against German and Japanese ambitions. A classic example of cheap status quo strategies is Neville Chamberlain's famous decision to conciliate Adolf Hitler over the Sudetenland in Czechoslovakia. What connects the various incentives and constraints that produce these divergent foreign policy choices is national leaders' political self-interest. Faced with different international and domestic circumstances, leaders tend to invest in the grand strategy that best serves their desire to hold on to political power.

At the core of *Politics and Strategy* is a model of executive choice. Which type of strategy a leader will choose depends on two main considerations, I argue. The first has to do with the international security situation and, especially, the presence or absence of a foreign challenger. How compelled leaders are to invest time, energy, and resources in foreign policy depends partly on how much "room for error," or what I call "geopolitical slack," the international environment affords. Executive choice also depends on a second factor: how much a leader benefits domestically from investing material resources in "guns" as opposed to "butter." National leaders have a strong incentive to invest in public poli-

---

realist (Rathbun, 2008, 315) points out, neoclassical realists "explicitly juxtapose" their approach to work cast at the microfoundational level. Instead, they start from the classic realist assumption that leaders seek to promote the national interest. On the neoclassical realist approach, see Rose (1998) and Lobell, Ripsman, and Taliaferro (2009).

cies that appeal to their partisans. In democracies, they have strong incentives to play to their own party's electoral strengths. One implication is that leaders' willingness to pursue ambitious, expensive foreign policies depends on whether their coalitions or parties have a sizable political (electoral) stake in investing national wealth in military strength, as opposed to domestic welfare.

This approach to the incentives and pressures shaping executive choice generates a series of hypotheses for explaining variation in the types of grand strategies that leaders choose and for tracking changes in a nation's grand strategy over time. These hypotheses are tested using case study analysis. The main cases developed here are twelve American presidencies—from George Washington's to Barack Obama's—that were intentionally selected to maximize cross-case variation on the two causal variables: geopolitical slack (measured by the presence or absence of a clear foreign challenger) and coalitional or party preference (measured by party support for investing in "guns" versus "butter").[8] I ask whether there is a systematic relationship between the values on the causal variables and the predicted outcomes—that is, the type of grand strategy in which each president invests.

The chapters that follow show that these international and domestic variables go far in explaining presidents' choices in the domain of grand strategy. Presidents vary widely in terms of foreign policy ambition and in terms of how far they are willing to go in investing domestic resources to achieve those ends. The variance in grand strategy is explained by the amount of geopolitical slack presidents enjoy and by the intensity of their party's preference for spending on guns as opposed to butter. Presidents who hold office when the nation faces a clear geopolitical threat will respond, but how heavily they will rely on military power (as opposed to alternative, cheaper means) depends greatly on their party's preference on the guns-versus-butter trade-off. Conversely, very different levels of geopolitical slack can produce grand strategies that are broadly similar in terms of cost or expense. This can happen when presidents are responding to similar sets of domestic political incentives.

America's history and political system make it exceptionally useful as a laboratory for testing theories about how leaders choose their grand strategies. Because America's international position has varied greatly over the course of its history, it is possible to assess how variations in the level of a state's international security shape and constrain presidential choice in the domain of foreign policy. Partisan differences over foreign

---

[8] In the concluding chapter, I extend the argument to non-American cases. I show how this model of executive choice can help explain the grand strategies of China's Hu Jintao and Russia's Vladimir Putin.

policy are also often stark in America's two-party system, with one party committed to ambitious and expensive strategies and the other party preferring narrower, less expensive options. Moreover, party preferences change over time. Republican and Democratic sensitivities to the costs of grand strategy have varied considerably, even over the course of the twentieth century. By comparing presidents from different parties under similar geopolitical circumstances, it becomes possible to assess how changes in party control of government influence foreign policy choice.

Politics and Strategy focuses on presidents of differing talents, persuasions, and experience. Some of the presidents analyzed here are widely considered to be among America's greatest leaders. Others are remembered mostly as disappointments or worse, failures—as presidents who overreached or underperformed. The analysis shows that, in the foreign policy arena, most of the presidents we examine acted in expected ways most of the time—they chose grand strategies consistent with their geopolitical and partisan circumstances. The theory helps to explain why both realism and *Innenpolitik* overpredict expansionism and to qualify (or disqualify) theories of grand-strategy choice that focus on state "strength," political ideology, or leaders' personal qualities. But some presidents do not behave as predicted, and this can be just as revealing, theoretically. The empirical analysis points to areas where we need more refined theories of how resource constraints and popular opinion may affect leaders' ability to deliver the strategies their partisans prefer, of how international shocks can affect policy preferences inside leaders' coalitions, and of how leaders assess risks, both domestic and geopolitical, of nonstate challenges such as terrorism. My hope is that this book provides a theoretical basis for addressing these questions in more nuanced and empirically grounded ways.

GRAND STRATEGY PAST AND PRESENT

Understanding how leaders choose their grand strategies is not merely of historical and theoretical interest. It also offers some much-needed perspective on the challenge of balancing geopolitics and domestic politics today. Scholars and practitioners debate whether "unipolarity" increases or reduces the likelihood of continued U.S. engagement with the world, and especially its willingness to lead. Although neither of America's two major parties favors a strategy of disengagement, withdrawal, and isolationism, they do disagree sharply about over *how* America should engage the world. Should the country's leaders seek to capitalize on America's huge power advantages to revise the international system in ways that better serve U.S. interests, or should they rely on strategies of self-restraint and international collaboration in hopes of preserving the status quo? If the past is any guide, the outcome of this "great debate" will depend on whether one party is able to impose its preferences decisively by breaking the current political stalemate and establishing control over the machinery of national government.

Unipolarity also poses new challenges for leaders of other states in the international system. Early predictions that unipolarity would cause China, Russia, and other states to actively "balance" against the United States have not fared well. Some analysts attribute the absence of hard balancing against America to the huge power disparities favoring the United States. For so-called secondary states, the risk of punishment for balancing against the "unipole" is said to be too high; the power gap between America and the rest is simply too great. Other scholars attribute the absence of balancing against U.S. power to America's continued willingness to provide international public goods and to play by the existing rules and norms of international order. As long as the United States is acting in accordance with international mores, they argue, other states have less reason to resist or challenge America's authority. *Politics and Strategy* suggests that the debate so framed is missing a critical factor in the calculus of "secondary states."

Today, America's potential rivals have little incentive *domestically* to try to shift the balance of international power to their advantage. China's leaders are preoccupied with economic development; Russia's are busy consolidating power. The analysis presented here suggests that for these leaders, cost is the decisive determinant in responding to unipolarity. The practical realities of holding on to power in China and Russia today give their leaders strong domestic incentive to avoid costly grand strategies to check American power. For the international relations analyst, the critical task is judging how long this confluence will last. That requires a method for determining when leaders will find it in their political self-interest to actively balance against concentrated power and when they will not. This book takes the first steps toward developing a model to explain how such choices are made.

CHAPTER TWO

Grand Strategy's Microfoundations

GRAND STRATEGY REFERS TO THE PURPOSEFUL use of military, diplomatic, and economic tools of statecraft to achieve desired ends. Scholars often define these goals in terms of national security, power, or wealth, but the ends can also refer to other valued goods such as national honor, prestige, and profit. In this book, I argue that grand strategy can also be viewed as a means by which national leaders strive to maintain or strengthen their hold on executive power. In making this assumption, I do not mean to suggest that leaders deliberately eschew or devalue the principles of "good" statecraft. Indeed, I argue that it is precisely because leaders are interested in holding on to power domestically that they *must* take the country's security and welfare seriously. Leaders, I argue, have a political stake in thinking about whether and how geopolitics can *help* them domestically. Just as importantly, they must consider how it might *hurt* them—how adverse international developments might weaken their hold on power.

This chapter develops the theory of executive choice of grand strategy in three stages or parts. First, I construct a framework for describing variation in the outcome of interest, or grand-strategy orientation, and build upon long-standing schemas for characterizing state's grand strategies to construct four "ideal types" of grand strategy. Next, I propose a way to think theoretically about how leaders choose (forge) grand strategy. I draw upon literatures in the *Realpolitik* and *Innenpolitik* traditions to propose a model of political incentive that incorporates both geopolitical and partisan constraint and that yields a matrix consisting of four different configurations of pressure and counterpressure. Then, with these elements in place, I lay out the theory of geopolitical or partisan "cause" and grand-strategy "effect" that is examined in the case studies. In spite of its coarseness, this "first cut" theory captures cross-case variations in grand strategy and the forces that shape it that have been recognized by scholars ever since Niccolò Machiavelli described the dos and don'ts of statecraft in *The Discourses* and *The Prince*. I conclude the chapter with a discussion of the research design and the layout of the book's empirical chapters.

VARIATIONS IN GRAND STRATEGY

All definitions of grand strategy assume that selection of the means of statecraft is not accidental, inadvertent, or simply fortuitous. Leaders choose or design their grand strategies, even if other factors, including dumb luck, determine the strategy's ultimate success. Purposefulness does not necessarily mean that leaders always work from an explicit, fixed, long-term plan, or that leaders characterize their guiding philosophy or approach to statecraft in precisely the terms that scholars would use in their retrospective analyses. What concern us here are *patterns* of consistent strategic behavior across a series of events, places, and policies. What means or strategies do leaders rely on consistently to deal with the international challenges or opportunities they face? Does their behavior change in predictable ways as international or domestic circumstances shift? To explore these questions, it is necessary to consider the types of grand strategies leaders can employ, and how these differ.

Revisionist and Status Quo Strategies

Grand strategies can be compared and contrasted in terms of both ambition and cost. By ambition, I mean whether a strategy is designed to alter or to maintain the status quo: whether its purpose is, in Hans Morgenthau's (1948, 21) words, to "increase power" or "keep power." Arnold Wolfers (1962) drew a similar distinction, distinguishing between "revolutionary" and "status quo" foreign policies. More recently, John Mearsheimer (2001) has cataloged grand strategies as means for "gaining power" or "checking aggressors."[1] What these and similar analytic distinctions have in common is the recognition that grand strategies can be revisionist or status quo in ambition. Leaders can design grand strategies in efforts to shift the international distribution of power in their favor. Alternatively, leaders may seek to prevent other states from turning the balance against them.

War itself, the most lethal or destructive of foreign policy tools, can be the centerpiece of either revisionist or status quo grand strategy. Wars of conquest are expansionist and revisionist. They are fought to gain power. Coercive military force is used to seize foreign lands, subjugate their peoples, and expropriate resources. Wars of conquest can turn into protracted and expensive defensive operations as states try to defend what they have seized from other powers or quell popular resistance movements. Still, wars of conquest are in the first instance efforts to change the status quo and gain power and wealth. By contrast, defensive wars are fought to preserve the existing distribution of power. Sometimes referred to as "just wars," defensive wars are fought to check aggression, not gain power, even though they may result in territorial gains or a more

---

[1] Mearsheimer focuses on great powers, but, as I show, smaller states use many of the strategies he catalogs.

favorable military balance, or both. Preemptive wars are a special case of defensive wars (Reiter, 1996). Preemptive wars seek to forestall a shift in the balance of power by strategically attacking before an adversary does. They too are driven by fear rather than profit. They are thus defensive, even though the defender is the first to use force. Like other defensive wars, preemptive wars can result in territorial gains, a more favorable military balance, or both.

Expansionism, which may or may not involve war, is a revisionist grand strategy par excellence. It is designed to acquire more power and influence by extending a nation's geopolitical reach and political control beyond its borders. Frequently, it involves the use of war (wars of conquest), though states often try to extend their territorial frontiers and geopolitical reach through intimidation or blackmail, without actually using military force. Blackmail involves the use of coercive threats (as opposed to force) to cause a favorable shift in the distribution of power. A famous example is Hitler's threat of war against Britain and France in his attempt to wrest control of the Sudetenland in Czechoslovakia in 1938. Expansionism can take different institutional forms. The classic form is imperialism, where states rely on formal methods of colonial control over foreign nations, their peoples, and their resources. But there are less formal methods of expanding political interests abroad such as the creation of spheres of influence, annexation, protectorates, and military bases (Zakaria, 1998).

Leaders can also attempt to gain power at a rival's expense using "divide and rule" stratagems or what Mearsheimer (2001) calls "bait and bleed" and "bloodletting" strategies.[2] Bait and bleed and bloodletting are less coercive than blackmail, relying more on guile and double-dealing than outright intimidation. Subversion is another inexpensive offensive stratagem that leaders may employ. Luttwak (2009) argues that the Byzantine Empire conducted subversion on a strategic scale, relying on espionage and covert operations. On the battlefield, field commanders weakened their opponents by relying on gifts and promises to win over an opponent's garrison chiefs and foreign allies. Beyond the battlefield, Byzantine leaders sought to "recruit and reward lesser dynasts, officials,

---

[2] Bait and bleed and bloodletting are attempts on the part of a state's leader to exploit opportunities for gain that can arise when two rival states are poised to go to war against each other or are actually engaged in hostilities. A bait-and-bleed strategy involves a state's efforts to fuel tension between rival states on the verge of war against each other in hopes that, by fighting, they will exhaust and weaken themselves, thus creating possibilities for the state that instigated the war through baiting tactics to expand its power. Bloodletting seeks to achieve the same end by fueling and prolonging an existing war between rivals. Both are essentially "divide and rule" strategies that attempt to gain increased power and influence through other states' misfortune.

and subordinate tribal chiefs to serve the empire in preference to their sovereigns, for whatever reason, from personal resentment, jealousy, or greed to enthusiasm for the Christianity of the true orthodox church" (Luttwak, 2009, 63).

Binding is another stratagem leaders can use to strengthen their state's international position. Like blackmail, bait and bleed, and bloodletting, it does not rely heavily the use of military power. It is usually used by the leaders of great powers eager to "lock in" (Ikenberry, 2001, 54) their state's international advantages after winning a war, but to do so without assuming the substantial enforcement costs of maintaining imperial rule.[3] Ikenberry argues that Franklin Roosevelt and his successor, Harry Truman used such a binding strategy to lock in the huge material advantages the United States gained as a result of the devastating effects of World War II in Europe and Asia. Weaker secondary states (e.g., Britain, West Germany, Japan) were offered increased security, access to the huge American market and U.S. investment capital, and opportunities to participate in the institutional bodies and counsels (e.g., World Bank, NATO) that issued edicts and policies concerning their interests. In exchange, these secondary states follow agreed-upon principles and institutional processes that conferred international legitimacy on America's plans to reshape the international order. The binding arrangement made enforcement of U.S. power easier and guaranteed a steady stream of benefits to American business through increased trade and investment.

Many grand strategies are status quo–oriented in nature. Balancing is perhaps the best-known defensive grand strategy, though scholars disagree about how frequently leaders actually rely on it (P. Schroeder, 1994a). Balancing involves efforts to prevent another state from upsetting the status quo—from increasing its share of power at the "defending" state's expense (Waltz, 1979; Walt, 1987; Jervis and Snyder, 1991). One form of balancing involves a leader's efforts to build up his state's military capabilities. International relations scholars call this "internal balancing" because a leader is relying on the state's own resources to deter a potential aggressor or to defend against the foreign aggressor should deterrence fail. A leader can also try to check a threatening state by pooling resources with other states through the formation of alliances.[4] This is called "external balancing." Balancing against foreign threats frequently involves some combination of internal mobilization and alliance forma-

---

[3] As Schweller (1997, 70–71) notes, binding can function as a defensive strategy, too. Facing a rising power, leaders can offer incentives (e.g., diplomatic recognition, access to markets, membership in international institutions) to make challenging the existing international order a less attractive option.

[4] Offensive alliances such as the 1939 Molotov–von Ribbentrop Pact between the Soviet Union and Germany are rare and short-lived. On the infrequency and instability of offensive alliances, see Walt (1997, 159).

tion, though typically, leaders do attach greater weight to one strategy or the other. Unlike war, which can be revisionist or status quo in nature, balancing is a defensive strategy.

Appeasement, buckpassing, and bandwagoning are also status quo strategies.[5] Appeasement refers to efforts by a leader to conciliate or "buy off" a potential aggressor by making unilateral diplomatic and economic concessions (Gilpin, 1981; Rock, 2000; Ripsman and Levy, 2008). Buckpassing is also a strategy that leaders sometimes use in hopes of gaining increased security. In this case, a leader relies on some other state to check the potential aggressor, while keeping his own country on the sidelines. Buckpassing assumes that there is some other state that is willing (or simply unable to avoid) the costs of deterring and defending against the potential aggressor (Posen, 1984; Christensen and Snyder, 1990). Bandwagoning is a strategy by which leaders willingly subordinate their states and themselves to the stronger power, seeing little hope of diffusing the threat posed by the foreign challenger, and seeing political security or profit in collaborating directly with it (Walt, 1987; Labs, 1992; Doyle, 1993).[6]

One other status quo strategy, retrenchment, warrants attention here. Retrenchment involves scaling back existing foreign commitments or military capabilities, or both (Huntington, 1988; Kupchan, 1994). Like the other status quo strategies, it is designed to maintain a state's international position rather than to improve it. Unlike other status quo strategies, however, retrenchment can occur in the absence of a threatening foe. Retrenchment aims at reducing the size and cost of a nation's geopolitical footprint. Often it is a response to strategic overextension (Kennedy, 1987; Kupchan, 1994). Many great powers have found themselves in such a fix, but smaller states can also pursue retrenchment strategies. One important reason they do is to reduce the cost of the nation's foreign policy. This brings us to grand strategy's second dimension.

Expensive versus Cheap Strategies

Grand strategies also differ by cost, and the differences between strategies in terms of cost can be substantial. Wars of conquest, imperialism, and

---

[5] Most international relations scholars view bandwagoning as a defensive strategy. However, as Schweller (1997) notes, leaders sometimes bandwagon with other states to exploit opportunities to acquire additional territory, markets, or resources—that is, they can bandwagon for offensive or revisionist purposes. Schweller calls this "bandwagoning for profit." I follow standard usage here.

[6] Bandwagoning is similar to appeasement in that it involves unilateral concessions to the threatening state. However, bandwagoning differs in one important respect. Leaders that bandwagon with a foreign power do so because they see no hope of diffusing the threat and possible profit in conceding sovereignty to it. Appeasers believe that the threat can be diffused or checked by making diplomatic concessions that preserve their own sovereignty and that usually come (at least in part) at some other state's expense.

internal balancing are comparatively expensive. Building an army takes time and money, which can be hard to extract from a resistant populace or legislature (Lamborn, 1983; Morrow, 1993). Military spending can also limit a state's ability to satisfy important social welfare goals. (This is the "guns versus butter" trade-off.) Other strategies, such as appeasement or buckpassing, are considerably cheaper. They require little in the way of taxation or conscription because they rely disproportionately on the use of diplomacy as a tool of foreign policy. This is even true of isolationism. While isolationism, variously defined as nonexpansion or nonengagement, involves less (absolute) activism on the diplomatic front than appeasement or buckpassing, rarely does isolationism mean diplomatic inactivity, let alone closure to the outside world (Nordlinger, 1995). Even Japan's extreme, wrenching inward turn in the 1630s did not result in out-and-out closure. Japanese isolationism meant greater internal political control for the new Tokugawa leadership, thanks in part to the use of resources garnered from ending Japan's imperial ambitions in Korea (Samuels, 1996, 33–35, 79–84; Legro, 2005, 125–27).

Generally speaking, the cost of grand strategy depends on the weight attached to military power relative to diplomatic means, how intensively costly strategies are implemented, and how long the costly means are sustained. Some status quo stratagems can be very costly, a result that is especially transparent in the case of internal balancing, which involves the build-up of domestic military capability. International relations scholars usually consider internal balancing more effective and reliable than external balancing (e.g., Morrow, 1993; Mearsheimer, 2001). External balancing means reliance on allies, but allies can be undependable and diplomatic commitments, in the absence of the military capacity to enforce them, can strain credibility. Internal balancing may be more rational, but it is also more costly. Wealth must be taxed, requisitioned, or expropriated, and such extraction is generally unpopular, often more obviously so in democracies.

Revisionist strategies also vary by cost. Imperialism and war are costly. They also eat up domestic resources that could be invested domestically to achieve ends other than build-up for war (Gilpin, 1981; Kennedy, 1987). Some international relations scholars argue that in the long run, war and imperialism can pay off if conquerors are able to extract wealth from defeated states by imposing taxes and confiscating property (Milward, 1977; Lieberman, 1996; Mearsheimer, 2001). Other international relations scholars disagree, arguing not only that wars of conquest are costly to wage but also that the high costs of maintaining empire in the long run often make imperialism a losing venture (Van Evera, 1999). We do not need to resolve this issue here to recognize that whatever their benefits, wars of conquest and imperialism are strategies that are much more

		Ambition	
		Revisionist	Status Quo
Cost	High	➤ Imperialism ➤ Wars of conquest ➤ Spheres of influence	➤ Internal balancing ➤ Preemptive war
	Low	➤ Blackmail ➤ Subversion ➤ Binding	➤ Appeasement* ➤ External balancing ➤ Buckpassing

* Other well-known strategies in this cell include bandwagoning, isolationism, and neutrality.

Figure 2.1. Grand strategies by ambition and cost

expensive to mount and sustain than blackmail, divide and rule, or subversion. The cheaper revisionist strategies are not necessarily cost free, however. Coercive threats are more likely to succeed if the state has the military capacity to make good on them, and divide and rule can involve giving each side weapons that it can use against the other. Nevertheless, these revisionist strategies are less expensive than imperialism and war.

We now have a way of describing variations in *types* of grand strategies. Grand strategies can be broadly classified in terms of their ambition and cost: whether they are revisionist or status quo in purpose, and whether they are expensive or cheap to employ. Figure 2.1 categorizes grand strategies in terms of these dimensions of variation. The purpose is not to provide an exhaustive list of strategies but rather to identify basic types, recognizing that the strategies listed in each cell can also differ among themselves in terms of cost and scale of commitment to purpose. Leaders also often combine elements of strategies within a single cell of figure 2.1. In the 1930s, for example, Britain's leader Neville Chamberlain pursued a low-cost, status quo–oriented grand strategy: he made unilateral diplomatic concessions to Hitler (appeasement), while also pressuring France to assume responsibility for deterring possible German expansionism (buckpassing).

America's presidents have used most of these grand strategies at one point or another in the nation's history. Contrary to many received theories of changes in U.S. grand strategy over time, the choice of strategy does not vary simply by era (prebellum versus postbellum in the nineteenth century, nineteenth versus twentieth century, Cold War versus post–Cold

War), by partisan affiliation, or by geopolitical circumstance. I argue that much of the variance in grand strategy is explained by variations in the amount of geopolitical slack presidents had to work with, combined with variation in the intensity of the dominant party's (coalition's) preference for guns as opposed to butter. The argument holds even in times when a stark realist account claims to offer greatest purchase in explaining foreign policy choice—that is, when America has faced a clear and present foreign danger. In these instances, presidents have a very strong incentive to respond to international threat, yet how they respond (which *type* of grand strategy they choose) depends greatly on their party's interests and priorities. To understand why, we need to look more closely at how international and domestic circumstances combine to pressure and cross-pressure leaders.

A MODEL OF EXECUTIVE CHOICE

In the field of international relations, analysts study grand strategy without studying leaders. While many scholars write about the sources of grand strategy, few systematically explore the role that political leaders play in setting national priorities and choosing among competing strategic options.[7] To some extent, this reflects a widely held view that, although individuals do matter from time to time, it is not possible to generalize about their behavior—to predict, for example, when a leader might opt to appease a foreign challenger rather than "balance" against the threat, either alone or with allies. Most scholars settle for simply arguing that either geopolitics or domestic politics is more critical in understanding foreign policy. This book shows that this debate is unproductive and that it distorts our understanding of international relations. I seek to show that by developing a theory of foreign policy incentive and constraint that operates at the level of the political leader, it is possible to take into account both *Realpolitik*'s concern with security and geopolitics and *Innenpolitik*'s emphasis on domestic interests and politics. This allows us to generate predictions about grand-strategy choice that improve upon those of both realism and *Innenpolitik*.[8]

---

[7] Two important exceptions are Jervis (1976) and Khong (1992).

[8] Following the analytic strategy proposed by rational choice theorists, I adopt the simplifying assumption that leaders are strategic politicians. In my model, leaders prefer the option that will maximize their hold on power by allowing them to avoid foreign policy disaster and strengthen their domestic coalition. The model does not require the analyst to know a particular leader's personal or "ideal" preferences when it comes to foreign policy. (For example, the theory does not require us to know whether a leader was warlike, or whether he or she had a deep personal vision of world order.)

Geopolitical Slack: Security as a Variable

The idea that statesmen worry first and foremost about national security is central to realism. Contemporary realists do not provide microfoundational grounding for this claim about the importance of security concerns, but it is possible to do so.[9] The claim can be grounded in the strategic interests of the statesman. Statesmen have a very compelling reason to take world politics seriously. It is their fear of failure. In the sixteenth century, Niccolò Machiavelli identified the essence of this political danger: rulers who overestimate their states' power relative to that of others "are guilty of error and are blameworthy."[10] Leaders who misjudge their states' geopolitical circumstances and capabilities often do pay a stiff price. In the modern world, they rarely pay with their lives, but the political costs of strategic failure can be high. Military defeat often results in removal from office, especially if the costs of war, in blood and treasure, have been high (Goemans, 2000). Minimally, the weakened leader is vulnerable to domestic opponents and would-be challengers.

International relations scholars have written extensively about the geopolitical ramifications of success and failure in statecraft.[11] Does military success in one area translate into foreign policy success in other areas? Does failure to deter expansion in one place invite tests of resolve in other places? Many realists think the answers are yes.[12] Hans Morgenthau argued in *Politics among Nations* (1948) that states that develop a "low reputation for military power"—an unwillingness to mobilize and use it, even in self-defense—only tempt other states to press their advantage and thus, ultimately, to encourage aggression. Realists from Morgenthau to Mearsheimer have argued that Britain's unwillingness to stand up against Nazi Germany's early predations in Mittleuropa only whetted Adolf Hitler's appetite, resulting in Germany's bid for hegemony on the European continent and beyond. By contrast, states that establish a "reputation for unchallengeable power" are less likely to have their authority and power threatened. It is said that imperial Rome's utter ruthlessness in crushing its enemies on the battlefield helped buy the empire centuries of stability and prosperity.

Whether the geopolitical effects of success and failure are actually so interdependent and cumulative is hard to determine, but leaders surely have *a political self-interest* in acting as if they are. Leaders know what

[9] For an illuminating discussion of "individualist realism," its roots in Machiavelli's writings, and its implications for grand strategy, see Doyle (1993).

[10] Machiavelli (1966, 23).

[11] See, for example, Schelling (1960); Jervis (1970); Axelrod (1984); Keohane (1984); Mercer (1996); and Press (2007).

[12] See, however, Slater (1993).

history teaches: that strategic failure abroad often results in political blame at home. In ancient Greece, where "reputation was everything" in foreign policy, Athenian leaders were acutely sensitive to the possibility of blame for their conduct of statecraft, as well as the promise of praise and accolades (Strauss, 1986, 33). Foreign policy success was "highly valued within Roman society and conferred immense *personal* prestige on anyone who could accomplish it" (Mattern, 1999; emphasis in original). Failure had its consequences, too. Word of military defeat often produced panic and fury among Rome's citizens. Concern about protecting a far-flung empire was also essential to British domestic politics in the nineteenth and early twentieth centuries. The party out of power was quick to seize on foreign setbacks to weaken the party in power. "Positions of power at home rested on imperial foundations. In this way the empire was a crucial asset in the domestic war of position—a 'national' interest above party" (Bright, 1985, 239).

Worries about the domestic costs of failure have also weighed heavily on America's leaders, sometimes inordinately so. Harry Truman suffered a vicious domestic backlash after the "fall of China" in 1949. During the Cold War, successive presidents, Republican and Democratic alike, so feared a domestic political backlash for "losing a country to communism" that they attached value to places of little intrinsic geostrategic interest (Garofano, 2002; Mueller, 2005). Foreign policies that were justified in terms of international commitments often also had a great deal to do with protecting an administration's domestic political credibility and closing off a possible avenue of attack by opponents.[13] Credibility abroad and credibility at home were conflated.[14]

For national leaders, foreign policy success matters. How pressing this performance constraint is, I argue, depends on how much slack there is in the external environment. The term "slack" refers to a country's position and room for maneuver in an international system in which power is distributed unevenly. It is measured by the intensity of the threat(s) a

---

[13] Vietnam was a classic example (Gelb, 1971), but there were others (G. Goldstein, 2008). Today, some analysts fear that U.S. leaders are repeating the same mistake in Afghanistan, and for the same *domestic* reason: the fear of domestic political blame for failure (Mearsheimer, 2009).

[14] Reflecting on Johnson's strategy toward Vietnam, McGeorge Bundy, the national security adviser to presidents John Kennedy and Lyndon Johnson, captured the connection. "LBJ," Bundy said, "isn't deeply concerned about who governs Laos, or who governs South Vietnam—he's deeply concerned with what the average American voter is going to think about how he did in the ball game of the Cold War. The great Cold War championship gets played in the largest stadium in the United States and he, Lyndon Johnson, is the quarterback, and if he loses, how does he do in the next election? So don't lose. Now that's too simple, but it's where he is. He's living his own political survival every time he looks at these questions" (G. Goldstein, 2008, 98).

country faces from foreign challengers. Leaders have geopolitical slack when their country faces no immediate threat to its physical security and when the possibility of a rapid and adverse shift in the distribution of power is relatively low. Leaders have little geopolitical slack when the reverse is true—that is, when security is scarce and their state is exposed and vulnerable to foreign intimidation and aggression. Leaders who are compelled by geopolitical pressures to hedge against the risk of foreign policy failure (and the threat of second-guessing by domestic rivals) have less slack than those who hold office when security is plentiful (when no state poses a serious challenge to the nation's security).

As intuitive as this definition of geopolitical slack is, it is not without complications. For one thing, foreign threats are not always unambiguous. As realists have long argued, it can be difficult to distinguish a revisionist state with aggressive aims from a status quo state with defensive intentions. Threat assessment is an art, not a science. Moreover, the process of divining foreign threats is frequently incremental, fragmented, and contentious (Jervis, 1976; Friedberg, 1988; Wohlforth, 1993). Sometimes a potential challenger's capacity to project power cannot be determined quickly or definitively. Domestic policy disputes over the scope, severity, and immediacy of foreign threat are not uncommon. Defining threats in geopolitical terms also leaves little room for consideration of other types of international threat that might not weaken a state's international position but may involve a security risk, along with the risk of domestic blame and political humiliation for the statesman caught off-guard. Today, terrorism does not pose a threat to America's geopolitical position, but presidents cannot afford the political cost of ignoring it.

In this study, I take a practical approach to these complications. I treat geopolitical slack as a continuum involving varying degrees of risk of domestic blame. At one end are situations where the threat of a shift in the balance of power is unambiguous—where leaders face a "positive probability that another state will either launch an attack or seek to threaten to use military force for political reasons" (Wallander and Keohane, 1999, 25). Security is scarce: the risk of foreign aggression and thus domestic blame is high. These leaders have little geopolitical slack. They have very little room to discount a challenger's ability or intention to alter the status quo militarily. Leaders in this situation have a strong incentive to move proactively to check the challenger and to avoid international developments such as "falling dominos," "turbulent frontiers," or "military gaps" that their publics might blame them for and that their domestic adversaries might exploit.

At the other end of the continuum are leaders who face no geopolitical rival and no proximate threat of foreign attack, because no state has the intention or the capability to launch a military attack against it to win territorial or political concessions. Leaders in this situation have less need to worry about strategic failure. They have less need to fear blame for leaving the nation strategically exposed and vulnerable to foreign aggression. These leaders enjoy high geopolitical slack. When international constraints are looser, they are freer to entertain grandiose arguments about "national greatness," "manifest destiny," or "spreading civilization" or, alternatively, to heed the skeptic's warnings about the dangers of "strategic overextension," loss of sovereignty, or turning into a "garrison state."[15]

Most of the cases examined in this book lie at one or the other end of the geopolitical slack continuum. Most of the cases center on either presidents who had little geopolitical slack and recognized the situation as such, or presidents who held power when the country did not face a geopolitical challenger and security was plentiful. In between these extremes lie more ambiguous cases where the potential military challenge is less real or immediate, or where nonstate actors are the source of danger. A gray-area case examined in this book is that of George W. Bush. On Bush's watch as president, the United States faced no peer challenger. The threat of military attack against the United States by another power was low, as was the risk of political intimidation and blackmail. Still, geopolitical slack did not mean that Bush could safely discount the risk of strategic failure. Journalistic accounts indicate that worries about a second September 11–style attack, and the likelihood that Bush and his administration would be blamed for it, weighed heavily on the president and his principal foreign policy advisers (Suskind, 2006).

The theory of executive choice thus treats security as a variable. Leaders can have more or less geopolitical slack, depending on whether security is scarce or abundant. Although this is a departure from some strains of realism, many realist scholars do assume, explicitly or implicitly, that security is variable.[16] Some realists, for example, argue that disproportionate power gives states a freer hand internationally and increases the likelihood that they will expand. Having little to fear, hegemonic states are more easily seduced by domestic ideologies favoring expansion (Krasner, 1978). Other realists argue that intense international pressure heightens fears of strategic exposure and strategic encirclement and

---

[15] Which of these arguments becomes the dominant "narrative" depends greatly on domestic politics—that is, on whether investing in military power serves a leader's coalition's interests.

[16] Realists are divided on how stark the security dilemma is. In the absence of a clear geopolitical threat, defensive realists argue that prudent leaders will avoid expensive balancing or expansionist strategies. Offensive realists, by contrast, predict expansionism. For a good discussion of the differences, see Mearsheimer (2001, 17–22).

that this can lead leaders to overreact and create self-fulfilling prophe-cies (Jervis, 1976; Kupchan, 1994). Today, realist scholars debate how the United States will (and should) respond to "unipolarity": whether American primacy increases or reduces the likelihood of continued U.S. engagement with the world, and especially whether primacy increases or reduces America's willingness to lead (Ikenberry, Mastanduno, and Wohlforth, 2009). Here, too, security is taken as a variable.

An analysis of geopolitical slack does not conflict with these realist arguments. Like theirs, my argument is a structural one: it weighs the effects of the presence or absence of an international challenger on lead-ers' choices. But a state's international situation, considered alone, is underdetermining. The analysis presented here improves on realism by developing a systematic theory of domestic political pressures and coun-terpressures. Leaders' choices in the domain of grand strategy depend greatly on domestic politics and on domestic institutions. While all lead-ers are attentive to geopolitical slack, there is reason to think that leaders of democracies may be more sensitive to the prospect of international risk and failure than leaders of autocratic regimes. Democracies are more politically open, and their leaders are more accountable to their nation's citizens. In democracies, political opponents are better able to scrutinize leaders' foreign policies and heighten public awareness of their shortcom-ings. Put another way, in democracies it is very easy (low cost) to make leaders pay a political price for their strategic lapses (e.g., intelligence failures) and foreign policy blunders.[17]

This dynamic is clear in the case of the United States. In the United States, the fragmentation and decentralization of power make it com-paratively easy for the party out of power to make political hay out of presidential mismanagement and incompetence. Presidents are therefore especially attentive to how much "freedom for maneuver" and leeway for error they have (Neustadt, 1990, 76). In statecraft, presidents who forget this principle often suffer politically, both electorally and in terms of their ability to persuade others, including members of their own party, to ac-cept their leadership policy agenda. Jimmy Carter learned this the hard way in the late 1970s. Widely believed to have misjudged and underes-timated the threats posed by Soviet Russia and Islamic fundamentalism,

---

[17] Some scholars also argue that because democratic leaders depend on a larger base ("winning coalition") of political support than autocratic leaders, their political success depends more on the provision of public goods such as security. As a result, democratic leaders cannot compensate as readily for foreign policy failure by doling out private goods such as government subsidies, tax breaks, and business contracts to buy off political sup-porters who might otherwise "switch horses" midstream and defect to a political challenger. See Bueno de Mesquita et al. (2003).

the president's public approval plummeted, leading many Democrats to distance themselves from Carter. This contributed to Teddy Kennedy's decision to challenge Carter for the Democratic presidential nomination in 1980. Although geopolitics was not the only cause of Carter's fall from public grace (an economic recession was equally damaging), it surely helped catalyze unusually strong opposition to a first-term president (Skowronek, 2008, 86–92).

Presidents thus have *self-interested* reasons for behaving as realists predict and thinking in geopolitical terms. When geopolitical conditions are unfavorable, and the risk of strategic failure and domestic blame is great, leaders will look for ways to minimize their political exposure by trying to check, contain, or diffuse potential threats.[18] Preemptive war is one possible response, but internal balancing, external balancing, appeasement, and buckpassing are more common responses to foreign challenges. When security is scarce, which strategy, or mix of military and diplomatic means, will leaders rely on? International relations theorists have tended to focus on external and war-related considerations (see e.g., Glaser, 2010). Is the threat time urgent (Morrow, 1993)? Are suitable allies available (Walt, 1987)? Does geography favor the challenger (Jervis, 1978)? The analysis here departs from realist logic in arguing that a more critical determinant of grand strategy is whether investing in military power as opposed to diplomacy serves a leader's domestic political interests.

What strategies will leaders prefer when security is abundant, and geopolitical slack is high? When security is abundant, one might expect leaders to devote more attention to problems at home. In the United States, for example, expectations of a domestic "peace dividend" ran high shortly after the Soviet empire collapsed and the Cold War ended. Yet history offers no shortage of examples of leaders who invested heavily in military power and used it when there was no immediate external imperative to do so. No nation's security seemed more plentiful in the late nineteenth century than America's. Yet during this period the United States turned away from many pressing domestic needs and transformed itself into a major military power and used that power to conquer and colonize the Philippines and Cuba. Knowing how much geopolitical slack leaders have tells us something about the type of grand strategy a national executive will favor, but his or her actual choice will depend on domestic as well as international circumstances.

---

[18] Leaders can also respond domestically by trying to inoculate themselves against blame-generating situations. For example, U.S. presidents frequently resort to presidential commissions and other bipartisan mechanisms to make it harder for the party out of power to exploit blame-generating opportunities (Wolanin, 1975). On blame-avoiding strategies more generally, see Weaver (1986).

Coalitional Preferences: Guns versus Butter

If the idea that statesmen worry first and foremost about security is central to realism, then *Innenpolitik*'s central thesis is that leaders are preoccupied with domestic interests and politics. This approach traces its origins to early twentieth-century accounts of British imperialism and German *Weltpolitik*. Vladimir I. Lenin's (1939) theory of colonialism and economist Joseph A. Schumpeter's (1955) theory of imperialism are classic examples of the *Innenpolitik* genre. So are contemporary theories of "diversionary war" and interest-group politics, which argue that leaders adopt expansionist foreign policies to deflect public attention from domestic problems (e.g., a bad economy, political scandal) or to secure the support of powerful domestic groups (e.g., industrialists, military services). As these examples suggest, *Innenpolitik* is less a single theory than a family of theories, each stressing a different, specific domestic variable in the explanation of statecraft. What ties these theories together is the common assumption that leaders think about grand strategy in domestic political terms.

In this book, I draw on three different strands of *Innenpolitik* to explain leaders' grand strategies. The first strand includes various interest-group theories that collectively view military build-ups, wars of conquest, military alliances, and other tools of statecraft as means that leaders use to distribute income toward their core domestic constituencies. A second strand includes diversionary war theories that focus on how leaders use military build-ups, "war scares," and expansionism to deflect public attention from their domestic failures or to divide and weaken their domestic political opponents. A third cluster of *Innenpolitik* arguments focuses on the relationship between grand strategy and revenue constraints: how the availability of state resources influences and shapes leaders' foreign policy choices. I argue that how intensively leaders invest the government's resources in military power (guns over butter) depends on how much it pays domestically to do so in each of these areas.

1. SOCIETAL INTERESTS AND GRAND STRATEGY

Leaders not only are statesmen; they also head up domestic coalitions, and coalition members' support depends in part on the leader's ability to deliver valued goods to their constituents. Even Machiavelli, who famously counseled the prince to make himself feared rather than loved, understood that a base of popular support was a valuable political asset (Whelan, 2004). Modern-day leaders do many things to gain that support. Leaders set national priorities, using public policy to direct governmental resources to their supporters and to strengthen their party's claim to power. They also work for policies that create jobs, distribute contracts, provide subsidies, and channel investments into projects. To retain elected office in democratic political systems, leaders formulate party platforms and public policies that are broadly responsive to the group interests and voting blocs that form the backbone of their political parties.

Although they differ on which societal interests matter most, all *Innenpolitik* scholars view grand strategy as means that rulers use to distribute income toward their domestic political supporters and to consolidate their hold on power.[19] In contrast to realists, who focus principally on the geopolitical advantages and disadvantages of investing in military power, *Innenpolitikers* emphasize its domestic benefits *and* costs: how militarism and war making privilege military contractors, arms merchants, and military staffs; how leaders use militarism and foreign crises to cover up their domestic failures and outmaneuver their political opponents; and how organized interests that benefit more from investing in domestic public goods lobby for less costly grand strategies such as isolationism, laissez faire, or autarky.

In the United States, the distributional benefits of investing in guns over butter have often varied geographically. In general, federal spending has a significant impact on regional growth and development; military spending may just be the most obvious case of this. Military spending played a major role in shaping patterns of regional growth during much of the Cold War (ÓhUllacháin, 1987; Markusen et al., 1991; Hooks, 2003), and the same is true for other periods of American history when military expenditures increased dramatically (Trubowitz, 1998). Various locational factors (including the availability of skilled labor, industrial specialization, local tax structures, and strategic characteristics) give some regions advantages as "sites" for military production, military bases, and military fortifications. Regions that stand to reap the largest rewards from military spending in terms of jobs, profits, and growth are more likely to favor foreign policies that put a premium on military power. Other parts of the country pay the "overhead costs" of an expansive grand strategy while receiving a disproportionately smaller share of the rewards. Citizens in these regions are more apt to see costly, ambitious, foreign policies in "guns-versus-butter" terms.

Societal interests can also benefit *indirectly* from government investment in ambitious grand strategies.[20] Wars of conquest are generally

---

[19] See, for example, Hobson (1902); Kehr (1930); Mayer (1971); Davis and Huttenback (1986); Fordham, (1998); Solingen (1998); Trubowitz (1998); Lobell (2003); and Narizny (2007).

[20] Some *Innenpolitik* theorists argue that the economic sectors that are the most competitive in international markets are the least likely to support grand strategies that require heavy investments in military power (e.g., expansionism, internal balancing). The logic is

thought to have been of great economic advantage to republican Rome, filling state coffers and enriching individuals of all ranks. War was especially rewarding for the aristocratic landowning class that benefited from huge slave markets supplied with conquered peoples from all around the Mediterranean (W. Harris, 1985). Similarly, in the nineteenth century, Britain's military commitments and expenditures in defense of a far-flung empire provided an "imperial subsidy" for England's foreign investors and commercial elites who worried about the risks of investing in India, Egypt, and other colonies (Davis and Huttenback, 1986). Political analysts view imperial Germany's pursuit of naval power in the late nineteenth and early twentieth centuries in a similar light. They write of mercantile elites who saw naval expenditures as a way of committing the empire to a programmatic policy of industry and international trade, while cutting the legs out from under their agrarian opponents (D'Lugo and Rogowski, 1993).[21]

Innenpolitik scholars tend to focus on how "imperialist groups" gain from expansionism, but of course not all domestic interests benefit from militarism and war making. Organized interests that have no stake in the international economy, worry about expansionism's redistributive effects, or fear increased state power might be used against them have little to gain from increasing the nation's war-making capacity. In late nineteenth-century America, the southern plantation class opposed northern efforts to ratchet up the government's war-making potential, partly out of worry over how political elites in the northern industrial core would use that increased military power (Bensel, 1984; Fry, 2002). For such interests, foreign expansionism was considered an onerous tax (and a generous subsidy for interests that would benefit from greater military spending). In general, leaders who represent interests focused on the home market are likely to prefer grand strategies that make fewer demands on national resources. This is why agrarian interests in imperial Germany saw little advantage in an arms build-up in the late nineteenth century (D'Lugo and

---

that militarism increases the risk of conflict and war, and thus threatens trade and profits. This line of reasoning goes back to Cobden (1868) and Schumpeter (1955), and sometimes it squares with the facts. Yet in many instances, the most dynamic, internationally competitive sectors strongly favor expensive, militaristic grand strategies. Instead of viewing military spending as unnecessary and imprudent, these sectors often see it as a means to expand, stabilize, and protect access to critical international markets.

[21] Similar commercial interests and pressures have shaped American grand strategy. After World War II, elected officials from parts of the country that stood to reap a disproportionate share of the benefits from rebuilding the world economy after one of history's most devastating wars and longest depressions were the ones most willing to invest government resources in defense spending, forward defense and alliances (e.g., NATO), and even military intervention (Fordham, 1998).

Rogowski, 1993), and why midwestern and western agrarian interests in the United States resisted calls for military build-up during the 1930s (W. Cole, 1983).

The same logic influences leaders whose core constituencies depend disproportionately on the production of domestically oriented public goods (butter) and goods destined for domestic market. In America in the 1890s, Republican Party leaders viewed federal expenditures as a means to dispose of budget surpluses, create jobs, and guarantee profits at a time when the United States did not face a geopolitical challenger (Bensel, 1984). During the 1930s, Democratic constituencies in the Great Plains and Mountain West that benefited disproportionately from federal spending on domestic New Deal programs were the ones that opposed intervention in the mounting European crisis (Trubowitz, 1998, 159–64). Today, with important constituencies such as organized labor preferring butter to guns, Democratic presidents in the United States feel the pressure of this constraint (Kupchan and Trubowitz, 2007). Isolationism may not be possible or even desirable given international conditions, but leaders who head such domestic coalitions are invariably drawn to cheaper grand strategies.

Just as leaders are reluctant to implement economic policies that directly threaten the interests of their core constituencies, they are indisposed to pursue security strategies that harm the constituencies they depend on. Of course, domestic coalitions are not monoliths; they are better seen as composites of blocs of interest groups and voters. Groups within a coalition may or may not share the same views about whether a nation's strategy should be coercive or conciliatory, expensive or cheap, offensive or defensive, or focused on defending the homeland as opposed to protecting overseas possessions. Common sense suggests that when domestic coalitions are more united over grand strategy, their leaders will find it easier to forge a coherent, internally consistent grand strategy. When coalitions are rent with conflict over foreign policy choices, leaders have a hard time designing coherent grand strategy.

2. GRAND STRATEGY AS A PARTISAN WEDGE

Innenpolitik reminds us that leaders are attentive to grand strategies' distributional consequences. Yet leaders also can derive other types of domestic benefits from foreign policy. Political leaders who find their hold on power threatened by internal crises or by domestic challengers can sometimes use foreign policy to improve their situation. The classic version of this idea is diversionary war or "scapegoat" theory (Levy, 1989). It argues that leaders use foreign crises, international threats, and nationalist appeals to deflect popular attention from their domestic failures to sustain their government's legitimacy. Leaders of democratic regimes are thought to be especially prone to such "gambling for resurrection" (Downs and Rocke, 1994) because they are more accountable to mass opinion than autocrats.[22] They are less able than autocrats to compensate for domestic failure by doling out private goods (e.g., rent-collecting opportunities, political office), and they find it more difficult than autocrats do to suppress domestic dissent and unrest with violence (Bueno de Mesquita et al., 2003).

Gambling for resurrection, however, is not the only (or even most common) way democratic leaders use foreign policy to strengthen their hold on power. Leaders often use foreign policy as a means to *divide* and polarize their publics rather than to rally and unify domestic opinion (Kaufmann, 2004; Snyder et al., 2009; Trubowitz and Seo, 2010). In the lingua franca of contemporary American politics, such partisan tactics are known as "wedge politics." As E. E. Schattschneider (1960) and William Riker (1986) made clear, in the United States divide-and-rule stratagems are as old as party politics itself. In two-party systems such as the United States, parties that cannot compete successfully on one issue invariably try to change the national debate by introducing a second crosscutting issue that divides the opposing party. Schattschneider (1960, 71) referred to this strategy as "the substitution of conflicts." Riker referred to such domestic maneuvers as "heresthetics." The classic example was the Republicans' injection of slavery into the national debate in the 1850s. In contrast to economic issues such as the tariff that tended to unite Democrats, slavery badly divided the party along North-South lines. Recognizing this, Republicans looked for ways to put the slavery issue on the national agenda. In Schattschneider's terminology, in the 1850s Republicans used the conflict over slavery to displace the conflict over the economy.

Leaders often use foreign policy in the same way. In the nineteenth century, U.S. presidents often antagonized Britain or "twisted the British Lion's tail" to appeal to swing voters, especially in West where national leaders found it hard to mobilize support among constituencies who resented unequal terms of the trade with merchants and industrialists concentrated in the eastern seaboard states (Stout, 1963). In the 1890s William McKinley and the Republicans used military power against a

---

[22] Empirical support for diversionary war or scapegoat theory is mixed. Some studies indicate that democratic leaders are more apt to manufacture foreign crises and employ military force during economic recession or depression. Other studies conclude that there is no systematic relationship. See, for example, Stoll (1982); Ostrom and Job (1986); C. Morgan and Bickers (1992); Lian and Oneal (1993); Gelpi (1997); Dassel and Reinhardt (1999); DeRouen (2000); and Tarar (2006).

declining Spanish empire not only to extend American influence in Latin America and Asia but also to divide and weaken the Populist movement, which resented Republican economic policies that benefited the big urban-industrial centers in the Northeast (Trubowitz, 1998; Logevall, 2002; Phillips, 2003). George W. Bush also weighed the partisan benefits of the "war on terrorism" in deciding to launch a "preventive war" against Iraq in 2003 (Snyder, Shapiro, and Block-Elkon, 2009). Bush and Republicans used the specter of war as a wedge issue to turn the 2002 congressional contest with the Democrats away from economic issues, where Democrats were widely judged by voters to be more capable. National security questions divided the Democrats badly and played to a long-standing Republican strength in this area among moderate and independent voters.

Wedge politics involves framing issues to divide the opposing coalition, either by appealing to its core constituencies or by peeling away "swing" voters and groups who might otherwise align with it. They are "positional" or polarizing issues that leaders use strategically to exploit latent cleavages in the opposing party (Stokes, 1963). I argue that presidents whose parties are unable to compete effectively on "bread and butter" issues such as the economy are more likely to look for ways to inject a second, crosscutting issue into the political process to move party competition onto the more favorable terrain of national security. Whether leaders can use national security (guns over butter) for such purposes depends partly on whether the opposing party is electorally vulnerable on the issue—whether the issue divides the opposition and appeals to moderate, swing voters. As I show in the case studies, it also depends on presidents' international circumstances and especially on how much geopolitical slack they enjoy. Presidents who can safely discount the possibility of awakening a dormant foreign rival have less to fear from ratcheting up international tensions by playing the "security card" at home.

3. RESOURCE CONSTRAINTS AND GRAND STRATEGY

"Strategy," the famous American strategist Bernard Brodie (1965) wrote, "wears a dollar sign." Because states' resources are limited, leaders must decide how much military power is enough and whether to rely on strategies that make fewer demands on the government's resources. They must also consider whether and how those decisions might affect what they hope to achieve domestically. Generations of political economists have described this trade-off in stylized terms as the choice between guns and butter. Leaders must decide whether to invest the state's resources in military build-up (guns) or to invest in domestically oriented policies and programs (butter). As a practical matter, the trade-off is rarely as harsh and unbending as modern economic texts portray it to be. Leaders can and often do invest in both guns and butter, relying on increased taxes or large budget deficits to reduce the severity of the trade-off.[23] Still, the guns-versus-butter distinction is a useful reminder that leaders do not make grand strategy in a fiscal vacuum.

In making grand strategy, a leader's political latitude is affected by the availability of resources to invest in military power and the factors that affect this: economic growth (Choucri and North, 1975; Kennedy, 1987; Barnett and Levy, 1991), administrative capacity (Hall and Ikenberry, 1989; Mastanduno, Lake, and Ikenberry, 1989), and domestic support for or opposition to the extractive policies that finance military spending (Lamborn, 1991; Stein, 1993; Solingen, 1998). In times of plenty, conflicts over national priorities and budget outlays ease, and domestic politics becomes less zero-sum. Leaders who hold power at a time of economic crisis, by contrast, have fewer resources at their disposal and are thus more constrained. Diversionary war theory predicts that it is precisely under these conditions that leaders are most likely to resort to coercive diplomacy or war. Sometimes these predictions hold up. Yet, as I show in the case studies, presidents faced with economic crises and tight resource constraints often do the reverse: they look for ways to mollify foreign rivals (appeasement), "outsource" the demands of security to other nations (buckpassing), or scale back foreign commitments and military expenditures (retrenchment). For these leaders, the political hurdles to the mobilization of resources for investment in military build-up were too high. Support within their own party for expansionism was weak, and the public was anxious about the high economic costs of foreign adventurism (i.e., higher taxes, increased inflation, higher interest rates).

Popular attitudes about taxes and nontax opportunity costs are thus important indicators of how much domestic latitude leaders have in making grand strategy.[24] In the American context, attitudes about taxation and conscription are particularly important because of the nation's

---

[23] This partly explains why empirical evidence of the trade-off between defense and welfare is inconsistent. Some studies point to a trade-off (e.g., Johnson and Wells, 1986; Kamlet and Mowery, 1987; Pampel and Williamson, 1988; Gifford, 2006). Others (Hicks and Misra, 1993; Huber and Stephens, 2001) find little evidence of a trade-off. Some scholars treat the guns-versus-butter trade-off as an "opportunity cost" (Russett, 1969; Mintz and Huang 1991; Heo, 1999; Melman, 2001). They argue that military spending absorbs resources that would otherwise be available for private consumption and productive investment. Prosperity and economic performance suffer. Others argue that military spending stimulates economic growth by enhancing aggregate demand, absorbing surpluses and regulating unemployment, promoting employment, and protecting and expanding foreign markets (e.g., O'Connor, 1973; Griffin, Devine, and Wallace, 1982; McNair et al., 1995). See Friedberg (1989) and Chan and Mintz (1992) for a useful review of these and related issues.

[24] Concrete measures of "public sacrifice" (Christensen, 1996, 26) must be tailored to the political and economic systems of particular countries.

antistatist tradition (Friedberg, 2000) and the centrality of fiscal policy to party competition and presidential politics (Witte, 1985; Skowronek, 1997; Gerring, 1998).[25] I argue that in the United States, the more anxious the public is about taxes and conscription, the higher the domestic political hurdles are to mobilizing military power, and the more restrained presidents are likely to be in setting grand strategy and national priorities. Even leaders who preside over coalitions that benefit from foreign expansionism will be more reluctant to invest in such policies if they are significantly at odds with public opinion at large or if they stand little chance of success internationally. Conversely, leaders who misread the international situation or the domestic "mood" by investing too little in guns can be attacked by political opponents for not doing enough to protect the nation.

Leaders thus have *self-interested* reasons for behaving as *Innenpolitik* scholars predict and for thinking about grand strategy in domestic political terms. When their domestic coalitions benefit from investing in military power, when they can use national security as a partisan wedge to divide and weaken their domestic opponents, and when the fiscal constraints on military mobilization are manageable, leaders are most likely to pursue the expensive foreign policies that are featured in many *Innenpolitik* accounts. These are the leaders who are most likely to build up their militaries to deter potential foreign aggressors, and to use the military to seize geopolitical opportunities. They are also the most likely to indulge in "myths" of expansionism (e.g., "weakness invites aggression," "the best defense is a good offense") and to engage in big stick diplomacy and power projection.

But what should leaders do when their political coalitions worry about the domestic opportunity costs of militarism and expansionism, and when their publics are worried about the financial trade-offs in terms of popular domestically oriented government programs? As I show in the chapters that follow, under these conditions leaders gravitate toward strategies that are comparatively cheap, even when international opportunities for foreign expansion arise. These are the presidents who warn of the *domestic* dangers of excessive militarism and expansionism ("corruption," "atavism," "despotism") and remind the public of the domestic opportunity costs of foreign ambition in terms of "productive investment," "social equity," and "lower taxes." They favor grand strategies that place less of a financial burden on society. This has often been the case in American history when security is plentiful, but it has even been true in some periods of high international tension.

---

[25] The United States instituted an all-volunteer military in 1973.

		Geopolitical Slack	
		Scarce	Abundant
Party Preference	Guns	Scenario I: Balancing ➤ Internal balancing ➤ Defensive war	Scenario II: Expansionism ➤ Expansionism ➤ Imperialism ➤ Wars of conquest
	Butter	Scenario III: Satisficing ➤ Appeasement ➤ External balancing ➤ Buckpassing	Scenario IV: Underextension ➤ Retrenchment ➤ Isolationism

Scenario I: International security is scarce; party prefers guns to butter.
Scenario II: International security is plentiful; party prefers guns to butter.
Scenario III: International security is scarce; party prefers butter to guns.
Scenario IV: International security is plentiful; party prefers butter to guns.

Figure 2.2. Strategic choice scenarios and associated grand strategies

DETERMINANTS OF GRAND STRATEGY

We now have the pieces in place to describe the determinants of grand strategy. The outcome we are trying to explain is variations in *type* of grand strategy, as described in figure 2.1. I argue that leaders' choices are explained by the prevailing configuration of geopolitical constraint and party pressure. The combinations of international and domestic incentive depicted in figure 2.2 constitute the basic configurations of pressure and cross-pressure that national leaders confront in their dual roles as statesmen and party leaders.[26] These circumstances do not dictate the precise strategy the executive will choose, but they do limit the types or range of grand strategies that a rational leader will be willing to authorize, mobilize resources for, and invest in when deciding where to place his or her own political capital.[27] As we have argued, grand strategies differ

---

[26] I henceforth use "party" and "coalition" as synonyms, except where a distinction is drawn deliberately. The theory should hold in both democracies, where coalitions are organized into political parties, and autocracies that do not have multiparty political systems.

[27] This typology does not distinguish grand strategies on the basis of whether they employ multilateral or unilateral diplomacy. Multilateral diplomacy can be employed as part of any grand-strategy type—it can go in any of the four cells in figure 2.2. Leaders can rely on multilateral diplomacy either to promote a multipronged revisionist strategy (e.g., imperialism) or to bolster a status quo balancing strategy, or to implement a strategy of retrenchment through burden sharing. During the Cold War, U.S. presidents often relied on

in terms of their comparative cost and the degree to which they are a response to geostrategic threat or opportunity. A leader can be expected to design grand strategy that protects or strengthens his or her position as head of state.

Balancers:
  Security Is Scarce; Guns over Butter

Scenario I describes the situation of leaders who have little geopolitical slack and whose parties gain from investing in military power (the upper-left quadrant in figure 2.2). In this scenario, leaders hold office when their nation faces an international challenger: either a rising power is actively seeking to extend its geopolitical reach at their nation's expense, or there is an established power whose military strength or economic dominance poses a potential threat to the nation's sovereignty or well-being. At the same time, these leaders preside over a domestic coalition that reaps benefits from policies that involve investing government resources in military power and other tools of statecraft (e.g., foreign bases, government procurement of military hardware, military aid to third parties). Economic and political interests within the leader's coalition prefer guns to butter and see national security not only as a way of enhancing external security per se but also as a means for economic gain, political advancement, or party building.

For these leaders, security is scarce. They cannot afford to discount the risk of strategic failure because the danger of second-guessing by their domestic opponents is too great. They must find ways to reduce the nation's strategic exposure and vulnerability to possible military attack, economic coercion, and political intimidation. Fortunately for these leaders, the high cost of investing in military power is not an issue. Indeed, they benefit politically from this form of investment. Efforts to mobilize military power enjoy broad support within the leader's coalition, while also signaling to the larger public a strong commitment to deterrence and defense. Under these conditions, geopolitical pressure and domestic imperatives are reinforcing.

---

multilateralism to balance against Soviet power, but on many occasions, they opted to act unilaterally rather than multilaterally (Leffler, 2004). Sometimes these choices are driven by cost considerations. In the security realm, alliances can help reduce the costs of balancing, especially for leaders who head up domestic coalitions that strongly prefer butter to guns. Alternatively, multilateralism can be part of a larger, more expensive grand strategy that great powers can use to reassure other countries about their willingness to work with others and abide by international rules and norms. This means that the "unilateral" versus "multilateral" distinction is not always decisive (or useful) when comparing and contrasting grand-strategy types.

Leaders in this scenario are likely to design high-cost grand strategies to safeguard the status quo. Active balancing against the threat—"internal balancing," or the build-up of military capabilities—is the most common response.[28] In extreme circumstances (i.e., when an attack is imminent), leaders are likely to resort to preemptive war. Whether a leader in this situation will prefer active balancing to defensive or preemptive war cannot be deduced from geopolitical slack and partisan preference alone. At this lower level of abstraction, other factors come into play (e.g., whether foreign attack is imminent; whether geography favors the defender).[29] Historical context is thus crucial in explaining whether leaders will prefer active balancing to defensive war. The theory of executive choice predicts what *type* of grand strategy leaders will favor, not which specific strategy he or she will choose. The theory does predict that leaders facing these geopolitical and partisan incentives are *un*likely to rely on cheaper, less reliable, "second-best" grand strategies. Leaders in scenario I experience little cross-pressure: domestic incentives reinforce international ones.

Expansionists:
Security Is Plentiful; Guns over Butter

The international environment is not only a source of danger and political blame. It can also be a source of opportunity for profit and political gain. Leaders who hold the reins of power when security is plentiful (when there is no geopolitical challenger and the international distribution of power favors their state) have less need to worry about guarding against foreign intimidation and aggression. In the absence of a geopolitical threat, leaders are freer to consider how grand strategy might help them consolidate power at home, and whether they should seize international opportunities to project power and influence abroad. Whether they will do so depends in large measure on whether expansionism pays domestically.

In the hypothetical scenario II (upper-right quadrant), leaders have a powerful incentive to seize opportunities to pursue expansionist policies. Because their coalition favors guns over butter, investing in military power pays partisan dividends for these leaders. Under these conditions, we can anticipate that leaders will face strong partisan pressure to build

---

[28] These leaders may also seek allies as a supplement to (as opposed to a substitute for) investing in firepower. Allies can add geopolitical value by expanding a state's defensive perimeter ("defense-in-depth"), by denying a challenger strategically valuable real estate ("forward defense"), and by forcing a potential enemy to spread its forces along multiple geographic fronts.

[29] Actively balancing can also be self-defeating if the state's resource base is insufficient to sustain a heavy investment in firepower.

up the nation's military capacity and project its power abroad, and that they will find arguments for expansionism, imperial projects, and wars of conquest more compelling. If the leader's domestic coalition is divided over the wisdom of conquest in particular cases, the leader in scenario II may favor less expensive revisionist strategies such as blackmail or subversion to secure territorial and other gains. Often arguments in favor of such efforts will be cast in defensive terms: arguments about creating "buffer zones," protecting strategic "choke points," or "guaranteeing access" to strategic materials may find receptive audiences. But in contrast to scenario I (and scenario III, discussed next), leaders in this scenario are responding to opportunity rather than threat. Geopolitical as well as domestic circumstances are ripe for expansionism.

How *assertively* leaders in this scenario pursue expansionism depends on a range of contingent and contextual factors that are not captured in figure 2.2. The precise contours of grand strategy will depend on whether geography and technology favor expansionism or, alternatively, favor states that would defend against it. The size of a state's economy also shapes the scope of a state's ambitions. Small or even middle-sized states cannot muster the same resources for expansionism and warfare that large, populous ones can, although scenario II does predict that, given international opportunity and domestic incentives to pursue expansionism, the small state will seek to extend its reach to an extent commensurate with its means. The theory of executive choice proposed here argues that when a leader faces the configuration of geopolitical and domestic incentives sketched out in scenario II, he or she will ratchet up military spending, define the nation's interests more broadly and assertively, and seize strategic opportunities to extend the nation's geopolitical reach. Expansionist interests and weak neighbors make for a potent combination.

Satisficers:
Security Is Scarce; Butter over Guns

In the hypothetical version depicted in scenario III (bottom-left quadrant), leaders face a potential aggressor. In this respect, their situation is similar to the one that leaders confront in scenario I: security is scarce and the risk of domestic blame for miscalculation is great. However, investing in military power is politically costly for leaders in scenario III. Their party prefers butter to guns, and their supporters are reluctant to prioritize foreign policies that put a premium on military power and the ability to project it abroad. Powerful elements within the party or coalition prefer to promote domestic consumption directly, via government expenditures in domestically oriented programs or, indirectly, by cutting taxes. In short, these leaders are under great pressure to invest at home. Doing otherwise runs the risk of losing the backing of their partisans, who might throw their support to a political competitor within the party.

In contrast to leaders in scenario I, leaders in scenario III are severely cross-pressured. In scenario III, leaders have a need to actively hedge against the risk of strategic failure abroad, but this conflicts with the practical realities of holding on to power within their domestic political party or coalition. While a robust strategy of internal balancing offers the best guarantee of success when it comes to national security, that strategy is not within reach domestically. These leaders are pressured to rely on grand strategies that do not place a heavy burden on domestic resources, that attach greater weight to diplomacy than force, and that still offer some prospect of limited success (or at least of avoiding humiliation, capitulation, or war). Faced with conflicting geopolitical and partisan incentives, we can expect these leaders to confront security threats by pursuing suboptimal or second-best strategies: to seek to bolster security on the cheap. These strategies are less ambitious and are less likely to successfully deter the foreign challenger than active balancing would. But they have the virtue of being much cheaper.

Leaders caught in this classic dilemma of statecraft can respond in several ways. They can form defensive alliances with other threatened states (external balancing). Appeasement, buckpassing, and bandwagoning are other common responses. Despite obvious differences, these strategies share two key features: they are undertaken in response to a threat, and they are comparatively cheap. They all seek to preserve the status quo at low cost.[30] How do leaders decide which of these second-best strategies to employ and whether to employ two or more in combination? Here too geopolitical slack and partisan preferences are insufficient to deduce the answer. One must weigh additional international and domestic factors. Are there suitable allies? Are there multiple foreign challengers that together pose a danger of strategic encirclement? Is there another state to pass the buck to? Does public sentiment reinforce or conflict with the party's preferences for butter? Would collaboration with the enemy appeal to members of the leader's coalition? In explaining why leaders sometimes favor appeasement over external balancing, figure 2.2 suggests that we must thus also consider why appeasement is preferred to other cost-containment strategies such as buckpassing and bandwagoning.

---

[30] In the case of bandwagoning, preserving the status quo can mean simply holding on to power, even at the expense of the state's sovereignty. See Doyle (1993).

Underachievers:
  Security Is Plentiful; Butter over Guns

Satisficing strategies are not the only type of strategy leaders can use to contain costs. When the international environment poses little threat, leaders can contain costs by eschewing expansionist foreign policies—by opting to *not* exploit opportunities to extend their nation's geopolitical reach. This is the predicted outcome in scenario IV (lower-right quadrant in figure 2.2). Here, leaders enjoy geopolitical slack, but have little incentive to invest in military power. International circumstances are permissive and allow for expansionism, but scenario II–type expansionist strategies do not serve the leader's political self-interest. Whatever promise international opportunities might hold, leaders in this scenario will shun these possibilities if pursuing them requires a heavy investment of government resources. This is because these leaders benefit more from investing those resources and their own political capital in domestic policy. Their partisan supporters prefer butter to guns. These leaders have no partisan incentive to emphasize security at the expense of domestic needs. And because security is plentiful, they have little pressure or reason to do otherwise.

Isolationism is one possible response to this combination of geopolitical and partisan incentives. But there are others. To the extent that they feel compelled by domestic political pressure to do something to increase the nation's military power, these leaders will stress less costly defensive means (e.g., coastal defense, military fortifications) over more expensive, offensive power projection. In general, these leaders will be preoccupied with internal matters and reluctant to seize opportunities to extend their country's geopolitical reach. In cases where the state already has a large geopolitical footprint and sizable armies defending foreign possessions, we would expect leaders in this situation to look for ways to reduce military costs, by either scaling back foreign commitments or cutting military budgets, or both. This is retrenchment. Retrenchment does not preclude the possibility that leaders will seek to capitalize on opportunities but predicts that they will do so only at little expense (e.g., by relying on diplomatic rather than military means).

In general, we expect leaders in this hypothetical scenario to minimize foreign entanglements and eschew opportunities to extend the nation's geopolitical reach because doing so involves large domestic "opportunity costs" for their domestic coalition. In this respect, leaders in scenario IV differ sharply from leaders in scenario II. In scenario II leaders behave the way many realists predict: they pursue expansionist policies when international opportunities to expand arise. However, whether leaders actually seize these international opportunities depends on whether it pays domestically to do so. Frequently, it does not. In scenario IV, leaders of nations that are strategically overextended will find it in their political self-interest to reduce military commitments and capabilities. (Leaders in scenario II are more likely to maintain existing commitments and avoid cost cutting in capabilities.) By the same logic, leaders of rising *economic* powers who find themselves facing the incentives identified in scenario IV are likely to underreach and "punch below their weight."

RESEARCH DESIGN AND OUTLINE

The book's core chapters describe and explain patterns in executive choice of grand strategy over the course of U.S. history. Scholars who use European history to formulate and test theories of grand strategy have not exploited the advantages of using the U.S. case as a laboratory. Until very recently, European statesmen rarely experienced what American leaders have sometimes been able to take for granted: geopolitical slack, or what the historian C. Vann Woodward (1960) once called "free security." A focus on the U.S. case allows for more systematic consideration of how variations in levels of "geopolitical slack" shape grand-strategy choices. Meanwhile, in the American two-party system, it is possible to track changing coalitional preferences over time. Historically, domestic consensus over grand strategy (and foreign policy more generally) is rare in the American context. Partisan rivalry and conflict is obvious, and it is the norm.[31]

The case studies presented in chapters 3–6 perform three functions. First, they show that the grand strategies that have been modeled as ideal types in figure 2.2 are recognizable in the real world. Second, they allow us to consider in greater detail whether, and to what extent, variation in geopolitical slack and partisan incentives produces the expected effects on a national leader's choice(s) in the domain of grand strategy. Third, the cases were selected and paired to control for rival theories of statecraft. The rivals considered here are explanations that give pride of place either to international security and power (*Realpolitik*) or to domestic interests and politics (*Innenpolitik*). If presidents facing comparable geopolitical conditions embrace different grand strategies or, alternatively, if presidents facing comparable partisan (domestic) incentives adopt dissimilar strategies, then neither strictly *Realpolitik* nor *Innenpolitik* theories can

---

[31] On partisanship and U.S. statecraft, see Greenville and Young (1966); Waltz (1967); Hogan (1992); Nincic (1992); Small (1996); Logevall (2002); Shefter (2002); Trubowitz and Mellow (2005); Narizny (2007); Craig and Logevall (2009); and Zelizer (2009).

explain grand-strategy choices. Both patterns of variation are found in the cross-sectional and longitudinal analyses that follow.

Each of the empirical chapters is organized around one of the scenarios described in figure 2.2. In each chapter, I compare the design of U.S. grand strategy across three presidencies that are drawn from different eras in American history. The chapters show that presidents facing similar configurations of international and domestic constraint opt for the same type of strategy and that presidents facing very different international and domestic incentives gravitate toward different types of strategy. These comparisons and contrasts generate support for the theory of executive choice of grand strategy that is laid out here. Moreover, by showing that these patterns hold up across presidencies despite changes in the nation's size, level of development, and governing capacity ("state strength"), we are able to discount some alternative explanations of variation in U.S. (and by extension, other countries') grand strategies.[32] The cases also show that in different historical periods, U.S. presidents acted consistently in response to the kinds of geopolitical and partisan incentives that are specified in our model. Their grand-strategy choices are thus unlikely to be due to their personal ideological visions, other personal idiosyncrasies, or length of tenure in office.[33]

---

[32] I control for changes in country size, economic development, and state strength by pairing presidencies on the dependent variable—that is, by grouping presidents by the type of grand strategy they adopt as opposed to the historical period in which they hold the presidency. I group presidencies by three broad time periods. The first period runs from the Founding up to the Civil War. During this period, the United States was on the "periphery" of the world economy, providing raw materials and investment opportunities for the core European economies (Wallerstein, 1979; Keohane, 1983). The federal government's role in society was limited, at least by European standards (Skowronek, 1982). So were the size, scope, and function of its military establishment (Deudney, 1995; Pollack, 2009). The second period runs from the Civil War to the onset of the Great Depression. During this period, the United States emerged as a major economic power, surpassing Great Britain as the world's leading industrial producer by the end of the nineteenth century (Kennedy, 1987) and by the beginning of the Roaring Twenties, surpassing Britain as the world's leading source of capital (Frieden, 1988). If the United States did not develop a full-fledged European style "fiscal-military state" (Brewer, 1989, xvii), then the Civil War, rapid industrialization after the war, and Progressive Era regulations did vest greater power and authority in the executive branch (Bensel, 1990). Beginning in the late nineteenth century, the federal government became more active, militarily as well as diplomatically, in promoting economic activity overseas (Rosenberg, 1982). The third period runs roughly from the New Deal era to the present. The United States is now at the core of the world economy. World War II and the ensuing Cold War spurred an era of unprecedented governmental activism in foreign (and domestic) affairs and the creation of an extensive, permanent peacetime military establishment (Koh, 1990; Pollack, 2009).

[33] The case studies also control for length of tenure in office, which is a variable that Quandt (1986), Gaubatz (1991), Potter (2007), and others identify as a key determinant of leaders' foreign policy choices. Some of the presidents examined here served one term;

The empirical chapters work deductively to ascertain values on the main independent variables and then ask if the hypothesized effects appear as predicted. We isolate events, crises, and episodes that provide clear circumstantial evidence of links between cause and effect. This approach, which is focused on the political leaders as the pivotal strategic actor, requires specific knowledge about particular presidencies: the international circumstances a president confronted, the partisan dynamics and rivalries that he had to contend with, and the foreign policies that he devised. Political scientists and historians have generated large literatures on individual presidencies, as well as on the evolution of the U.S. position in the international system and partisan dynamics over time. I rely heavily on these sources in characterizing levels of international threat, party preferences for guns and butter, the politics of strategic choice, and the characteristics of grand strategies.[34]

In each case, I draw upon substantial scholarly literatures and primary source data to determine values on the two causal variables (geopolitical slack and party preference) and the dependent variable (grand strategy).[35] Assessments of slack can vary depending on whether one is looking at "objective" measures of national power or leaders' *perceptions* of power. To control for this, I relied heavily on cases in which there is little ambiguity about how to code the slack variable—that is, where there is considerable agreement among historians and political scientists about the geopolitical situation facing the country and about how political leaders sized up international pressures at the time. In a few cases, the situation is less clear-cut, and political analysts are divided over how scarce security was during a given presidency. (For example, in the case of George W. Bush, there is debate over how much analytic weight to attach to the threat of terrorism and whether terrorism rises to the level of a geopolitical threat, given U.S. primacy by objective military and economic measures.)

---

others served two terms; and one, Franklin Delano Roosevelt, served multiple terms. Popular wisdom holds that in their second terms, presidents are more concerned about their personal legacy (their "place in history") than their party's interests. The implication is that second-term presidents are freer to buck their party's preferences and public opinion in setting grand strategy and establishing national priorities. In reality, presidents become lame ducks before the halfway point in their second term (Light, 1985), and, as a rule, second-term presidents are generally less popular than they are during their first term. As a result, second-term presidents may be more, not less, dependent on their party for securing the legislative backing and financial support needed to implement their foreign policy agenda.

[34] Where data on public opinion are available, I draw directly upon it; in other cases, I rely on secondary accounts that use newspaper editorials of the period as a "proxy" for public attitudes at large (e.g., Owen, 2000).

[35] In the cases of Bill Clinton and George W. Bush, I rely on journalistic accounts to supplement those by international relations and presidential scholars. In these cases, we do not have the advantages of historical accounts based on archival sources.

Similarly, party preferences regarding guns and butter are sometimes hard to divine from secondary accounts and the historical record. Parties may be divided over whether guns or butter should receive pride of place. Less commonly, parties may be willing to invest in *both* guns and butter. However, one bloc *inside* the party usually has the upper hand, and this is reflected in secondary literatures that draw on congressional deliberations, party platforms, and contemporary newspaper and media accounts. Partisan preferences should also be evident in patterns of congressional roll call voting. I therefore develop measures of party support and cohesion to gauge the strength of party support for key policies or elements in each president's grand strategy.[36] These indicators cannot tell us whether the president's choice of strategy was a direct response to his party's policy preferences (this is because lawmakers are often casting votes in response to presidential initiatives), but they can tell us whether the president's grand strategy is in or out of step with his party's foreign policy preferences.

Leaders who enter office facing strong international threats, and who have strong domestic backing to respond assertively to such threats, can be expected to do so. These leaders are expected to pursue the balancing responses described in scenario I of figure 2.2. Because these cases constitute "easy tests" for the theory advanced here, the chapters that follow do not offer an extended treatment of this scenario. Instead, we turn to harder tests of the theory, which are likely to give the best theoretical leverage on its predictions and to challenge rival theories and conventional wisdoms. The chapters focus on scenarios II, III, and IV of figure 2.2. The conclusion of the book offers a brief discussion of scenario I cases.

---

[36] In each of the main case studies, roll call votes were selected to measure levels of party support and party cohesion for key policies. Party support refers to the average level of support the presidents' foreign policies received from members of their own party and from the opposing party. The measures range from zero to one hundred, with higher values indicating greater party support. Party cohesion refers to the level of party unity—the extent to which party members take the same position in support of (or opposition to) a president's foreign policies. I use the Rice index, a measure of party cohesion or unity, to gauge party cohesion. The index ranges from zero to one hundred, with higher values indicating greater cohesion. For each presidency, I identified three key "litmus test" foreign policy issues that were either elements of the president's grand strategy or issues that members of Congress used to challenge the president's strategy. I then identified roll votes that revealed each Congress member's position on each foreign policy issue. Votes were coded as support for (or opposition to) the president's policies on the basis of accounts in the secondary literature (primarily historical) and, where publicly available, congressional roll call data sets (e.g., Policy Agendas Project; Project Vote Smart) compiled by other analysts. The specific votes were culled from roll call data available at Voteview.com, a source of congressional votes that is widely used by scholars of American politics. Party support and party cohesion scores reported in the case studies were computed by the author.

Chapter 3 focuses on leaders who adopt satisficing strategies (scenario III). These are presidents who have little geopolitical slack and are under intense domestic pressure to invest resources at home. All three responded as predicted: they sought security on the cheap. Two of them—George Washington and Abraham Lincoln—pursued a strategy of appeasement to deal with a threat posed by Britain. The third, Franklin Roosevelt, during the 1936 to 1940 period, experimented briefly with appeasement and then with buckpassing in response to Hitler's Nazi Germany. In each case, the basic outline of the story was the same: the president faced a serious geopolitical threat and presided over a coalition that had little interest in responding militarily. Cross-pressured, Washington, Lincoln, and Roosevelt opted for second-best strategies. In contrast to realists, who treat appeasement as a response to international pressures, I show that appeasement is a product of international *and* domestic constraints.[37] Leaders are most apt to rely on appeasement (or other satisficing strategies) when the need to provide increased security internationally conflicts with imperatives of governing domestically. Under these circumstances, leaders must provide security on the cheap.

Chapter 4 takes up the reverse scenario, when security is plentiful and militarism pays domestically (scenario II). I show that this combination of geopolitics and party politics gives presidents a powerful incentive to expand the nation's military capabilities and seize opportunities to project power abroad. James Monroe, William McKinley, and George W. Bush all faced these incentives. Each president defined the country's security interests broadly, greatly expanded the nation's military capabilities, and seized opportunities to extend the country's geopolitical reach. Despite the obvious differences over time in the nation's relative size and power, all three presidents saw little strategic downside or risk. Monroe, McKinley, and Bush had considerable geopolitical slack. Moreover, a foreign policy that put a premium on power projection offered each a means to strengthen his party's hold on power, as well as his own hold on the presidency. By themselves, the cases are not inconsistent with realist accounts that emphasize the importance of international position in explaining expansionism, or *Innenpolitik* accounts that view societal interests as the driving force. However, when compared and contrasted to the cases taken up in chapter 5, it becomes clear that realist and *Innenpolitik* explanations of expansionism are underdetermining.

Chapter 5 focuses on the combination of international and domestic conditions that cause leaders to underreach in world politics (scenario

---

[37] These cases also highlight the limits of purely *Innenpolitik* explanations. Each of these presidents held office at a time of domestic tension (in Lincoln's case, civil war), yet did not resort to foreign war as a panacea.

IV). Leaders are most apt to underreach when they have geopolitical slack and there is little partisan advantage in investing in military power. This is because under this combination of international and domestic incentives, presidents have little to fear geopolitically, and much to gain domestically, from investing resources at home. I develop this argument through an analysis of the decisions and actions of Martin Van Buren, Herbert Hoover, and Bill Clinton. In each case, security was relatively abundant; opportunities to expand the nation's interests were plentiful. Yet all three had to contend with powerful constituencies in their parties that opposed foreign expansionism and that saw greater advantage in domestic priorities and policies. I show that Van Buren and Hoover behaved as predicted. The Clinton case is more mixed than my theory of executive choice predicts. Yet when viewed in the context of chapter 4, these cases offer considerable support for the argument that whether leaders favor expansionism depends on whether foreign ambition pays domestically. If not, leaders who have geopolitical slack are likely to underreach internationally.

The concluding chapter offers brief treatments of three cases of scenario I determinants of grand strategy. These are the cases of Harry Truman, John Kennedy, and Ronald Reagan. Each president relies on internal balancing to check a potential aggressor. The cases highlight in broad brushstrokes the political logic of internal balancing: pressures of an external threat combined with domestic political support for military build-up produces the canonical, internal balancing grand strategy that figures so prominently in realist theories of state behavior.

Figure 2.3 summarizes the analysis presented in the chapters that follow.[38] Presidents are clustered in the figure by predicted grand-strategy *type* and their associated grand strategies. This is the dependent variable. The values on the two independent variables, geopolitical slack and party preference, are coded. Because party preference (registered here as preference for guns over butter) is a composite variable, the values on each of its subcomponents (e.g., distributive benefits) are coded as well. The main cases that make up chapters 3, 4, and 5 are followed by three shadow cases (taken up in the concluding chapter) in gray. The theory performs better in cases in which the values on the independent variables are unambiguously high or low than in cases in which presidents faced ambigu-

---

[38] The concluding chapter includes three additional "mini-cases": short accounts of Russia's Vladimir Putin and China's Hu Jintao, and a schematic analysis of grand strategy under Barack Obama. I use the non-American cases to show how the model of executive choice can be extended to nondemocratic settings, and to consider why "secondary powers" are not balancing against American power in the current period. The Obama case provides a basis for speculating about the future of U.S. grand strategy.

Leader	Geopolitical Slack	Party Preference: Guns over Butter			Predicted Strategy Type	Grand Strategy
		Distributive Benefits	Electoral Advantage	Fiscal Constraints		
Washington	No	No	No	Tight	Satisficing	Appeasement Neutrality
Lincoln	No	No	No	Tight	Satisficing	Appeasement
FDR[1]	No	Weak	No	Tight	Satisficing	Appeasement Buckpassing
Monroe	Yes	Yes	Yes	Loose	Expansionism	Sphere of influence
McKinley	Yes	Weak	Yes	Loosening	Expansionism	Imperialism
G. W. Bush[2]	Weak	Yes	Yes	Loose	Expansionism	Offensive war[3] Big stick
Van Buren	Yes	No	No	Tight	Underextension	Isolationism
Hoover	Yes	No	No	Tight	Underextension	Retrenchment
Clinton	Weak	No	Weak	Loosening	Underextension	Selective engagement
Truman	No	Yes	Yes	Loosening	Balancing	Containment
Kennedy	No	Yes	Yes	Loose	Balancing	Containment
Reagan	No	Yes	Yes	Tightening	Balancing	Containment

[1] Before Pearl Harbor attack.

☐ Case studies   ▓ Shadow studies

[2] After September 11 attacks.

[3] Some analysts characterize the war in Iraq as defensive or preventive war.

Figure 2.3. International and domestic incentives that shape grand strategy

ous signals and cross-pressures. What is essential here is not whether the theory of executive choice of grand strategy predicts outcomes in every case; it cannot. The more relevant test is whether it predicts and explains outcomes better than stand-alone realist or *Innenpolitik* theories. The analysis that follows suggests that it can.

CHAPTER THREE

Why States Appease Their Foes

FEW GRAND STRATEGIES ARE MORE MALIGNED, and more poorly understood, than appeasement. Ever since Britain's Neville Chamberlain unsuccessfully sought to mollify Adolf Hitler in 1938 by allowing Nazi Germany
to annex the Sudetenland region of Czechoslovakia, appeasing foreign
adversaries has been considered foolish, capricious, and even cowardly.
Winston Churchill famously compared appeasers like Chamberlain to
"one who feeds a crocodile, hoping it will eat him last" (Treisman, 2004,
345). Many international relations scholars have echoed Churchill's
harsh judgment (e.g., Morgenthau, 1948; Waltz, 1979; Mearsheimer,
2001). Yet, as I show in this chapter, the decision to appease a potential
aggressor is rarely the reckless, muddled choice that appeasement's critics
make it out to be. I argue that statesmen opt to appease foreign adversaries for hardheaded, pragmatic reasons. For them, appeasement is a means
for reconciling conflicting geopolitical and partisan goals.

THE APPEASEMENT PUZZLE

In this chapter, I argue that statesmen are most likely to pursue a strategy of appeasement when they are severely cross-pressured: when the
demands for increased security conflict sharply with what they are trying to achieve domestically. Appeasement involves efforts to "buy off" a
potential aggressor by making diplomatic and economic concessions. The
definition assumes that leaders have little geopolitical slack.[1] They hold
power at a time when security is scarce; they cannot safely discount the
risk of war. As I show here, however, these same leaders are also highly
constrained domestically. Economic resources are often scarce and leaders are under great pressure from their partisans to invest those resources
domestically. Caught between a rock and a hard place, cross-pressured
leaders seek security on the cheap. Appeasement is one common response
to this classic dilemma of statecraft.[2]

---

[1] Indeed, one of the main criticisms of appeasement is that such concessions only whet
the adversary's appetite for additional concessions. See, for example, Mearsheimer (2001).

[2] Buckpassing and bandwagoning are other responses that cross-pressured leaders sometimes favor. In the case studies, I explain why appeasement was preferred to buckpassing
and bandwagoning.

I develop this argument through an analysis of the grand strategies of George Washington in the 1790s, Abraham Lincoln during the Civil War, and Franklin Roosevelt before the outbreak of World War II. I show that each president grappled with the same basic political problem: how to reduce the risk of war with decidedly limited means. Each confronted a potential aggressor—in the case of Washington and Lincoln, it was Britain; for Roosevelt, the potential aggressor was Germany. None could afford the political risk of ignoring the danger.[3] At the same time, domestic politics created strong pressure to find an inexpensive way to reduce the nation's strategic exposure. Washington led a faction (the Federalists) eager to avoid war and to devote government resources toward domestic ends. Lincoln led a wartime coalition whose unity in the fight against the South depended partly on preventing foreign intervention in the war. Roosevelt led a party whose preoccupation with domestic recovery meant investing in butter, not guns. In the context of the tug of war between foreign and domestic priorities, appeasement emerged as a rational alternative to other possible strategies.

In making this argument, I go beyond recent scholarship on the logic of appeasement. Some scholars agree that appeasement can be rational, though only under certain, highly constrained *international* conditions (Mearsheimer, 2001; Treisman, 2004; Layne, 2008; Ripsman and Levy, 2008)—that is, when leaders face multiple foreign threats. In this view, appeasement is the product of a logic of "triage," or choosing between primary and secondary threats. In this chapter, I find some evidence to support this argument. However, I show what realists call "conserving enemies," or minimizing the number of enemies, is not the only, or even the most important, reason that leaders turn to appeasement. In each of the cases examined here, the president viewed appeasement less as method of strategic "triage" than as a means to gain added security at an acceptable *domestic* price. The critical choice, I argue, was not between primary and secondary foreign threats but between conflicting geopolitical and domestic imperatives.

These cases also provide a good test of *Innenpolitik* theories of grand strategy. In each case, the president's hold on political power was threatened by domestic instability; indeed, in Lincoln's case, by civil war. The temptation to use foreign policy to divert public attention from domestic troubles was great, and opportunities to do so were at hand. Yet as I show in this chapter, Washington, Lincoln, and Roosevelt refrained from the politics of diversionary war. Moreover, they did not reflexively adopt foreign policies favored by their core constituencies. In the absence of geopolitical slack, each president had to balance the demands of domestic coalition building against the need to avoid foreign policy failure. Geo-

---

[3] In all three cases, the U.S. faced multiple threats. I focus here on the primary challenger.

political cross-pressure sometimes dictated choices that ran against the narrow interests of their supporters.

George Washington and the Appeasement of Britain

When revolutionary France declared war on Great Britain in 1793, George Washington was in a difficult position. War in Europe threatened American diplomatic, security, and economic interests. For the United States, international security was scarce. Complicating matters greatly for Washington was his domestic predicament: he presided over a coalition composed of two factions—the Republicans and Federalists—who were deeply divided over how to respond to the crisis. The United States was still formally allied to France by virtue of its 1778 Revolutionary War alliance, and the Republican faction backed France's cause in Europe. However, the young American republic's prosperity was critically dependent on British trade and finance. London was demanding that Washington do nothing that might hamper its war effort against France, and the Federalists in Washington's coalition urged the president to align America's interests squarely with Britain's. Forced by events to choose between these two sides of his domestic political base, Washington carefully but firmly "tilted" U.S. policy toward Britain.

Following many historians of this era, I code Washington's grand strategy as appeasement.[4] While Washington insisted that his policy was one of strict neutrality between Britain and France, and while he never formally renounced the alliance with Paris, the president studiously avoided actions that would provoke a confrontation with Britain. Indeed, from his initial declaration of neutrality in 1793, to his decision to submit the controversial Jay Treaty with Britain for Senate ratification two years later, to his valedictory Farewell Address in 1796, Washington repeatedly appeased Britain's demands at France's expense. The centerpiece of Washington's strategy was the Jay Treaty, by which the president acquiesced to London's demand by effectively renouncing America's claim to freedom of the seas.

---

[4] See, for example, Flexner (1974); F. McDonald (1974); Ellis (2004); Harper (2004); and Henriques (2006). Some historians view Washington's strategy as neutrality rather than appeasement. However, given the many concessions Washington made to Britain at France's expense, appeasement seems more apposite. In any event, the difference is not essential for my argument. Appeasement and neutrality are both inexpensive status quo strategies that cross-pressured leaders may turn to when they have little geopolitical slack, and military expansion does not pay domestically.

The Jay Treaty grew out of a crisis provoked by Britain's strategy for containing and defeating France.[5] Britain financed the ground operations of its continental allies (Russia, Spain, Prussia, Austria, Portugal, Sardinia, and Naples) and, at the same time, used its formidable sea power to deny France much-needed supplies from America (Harper, 2004, 130). In the summer of 1793, London announced by order-in-council edicts that it would no longer allow neutral shipments of wheat, corn, and flour to cross the Atlantic. These were the very staples of American commerce with its then ally, France. By early 1794, the Royal Navy had seized more than 250 U.S. merchant vessels, and America's lucrative trade in the West Indies had been brought to a virtual standstill. London's harsh edicts hit America's port cities especially hard, but it was not long before the nation's farmers also felt the impact of Britain's hammer blow (Ferling, 2009, 325–26). Cries for retaliation and a second war of independence against England rang out.[6] Angry members of Congress urged Washington to slap an embargo on British imports and to sequester debts owed by private U.S. citizens to British creditors. Fearing such actions would antagonize London and risk war, Washington searched for a diplomatic solution to the crisis. In the spring of 1794, he sent Chief Justice John Jay to London to negotiate "a friendly adjustment of our complaints" and to signal the United States' "reluctance to hostility" (Ferling, 2009, 327).[7]

Washington achieved his main goal: Jay's negotiations averted war (Elkins and McKitrick, 1993, 412). The resulting treaty heavily favored England, offering London major concessions in return for no new gains by the United States.[8] Under the terms of the treaty, the United States acquiesced to most of Britain's demands regarding belligerent rights and the cutoff of food shipments to France, effectively abandoning Ameri-

---

[5] On the general history of the Jay Treaty, see Bemis (1962) and Coombs (1970).

[6] To many Americans, this was but the latest in a series of high-handed British economic policies since the 1783 Treaty of Paris that had given America its independence. London continued to occupy many frontier posts in U.S. territory in violation of the terms of the 1783 treaty. The British army used those posts to funnel arms from Canada to Indian tribes to slow the advance of American settlers and protect British fur-trading interests in the region.

[7] Washington also favored fortifying the main U.S. ports and increasing the size of the army—defensive measures that were unlikely to elicit a reaction by London. The president also allowed a toothless version of the Republicans' original embargo proposal to pass into law.

[8] Historians have long argued that Jay was too pliant an envoy and that a tougher bargainer could have gained concessions from London. Perhaps, but the resulting treaty reflected the huge power differentials between Britain and the United States at the time. Washington recognized that there were real limits to what the United States could reasonably expect from the negotiations.

cans' cherished principle of "free ships, free goods" (Wood, 2009, 197).[9] In return, Britain agreed to fulfill the terms of the Treaty of Paris that it had signed ten years before (by vacating the forts between the Ohio River and the Great Lakes). Britain's sole concession of substance was to agree to pay compensation for the damage inflicted by the Royal Navy to American property. From London's standpoint, this was a small price to pay for American acquiescence, and for transforming the United States into a "passive ally" in its war with France (Bowman, 1974, 219). On the issues that concerned most Americans—the impressment of American seamen and gaining access to British West Indian ports—the Jay Treaty offered little or nothing.[10] Although Washington recognized that the treaty amounted to appeasement, he did not hesitate to push ahead with ratification.[11]

Why did George Washington appease the British? The answer lies in the configuration of international and domestic incentives he faced. Realist accounts of the period make clear that Washington had little geopolitical slack (Sofka, 2000, 2001; Mearsheimer, 2001, 250–51).[12] The United States was strategically exposed, hemmed in on three sides by the British and Spanish empires, and vulnerable to "a pincer movement up and down the Mississippi and Ohio River systems" (Flexner, 1974, 281).[13] Washington worried most about British power. In part, this was because Britain continued to occupy military posts on American soil and used its forward position to incite Indian warfare against American settlers in the Northwest.[14] More fundamentally, it had to do with Britain's command-

[9] Most notably, the treaty adopted a broad definition of contraband, allowing Britain to seize enemy food as contraband. Under the terms of the treaty, the United States also agreed to repay pre–Revolutionary War debts—a major British demand.

[10] Under Article XII of the treaty, Britain agreed to open its West Indian ports to American ships less than seventy tons. At the time, the smallest American merchant vessels were usually six times that size (Ferling, 2009, 341).

[11] As Washington noted upon reviewing the treaty, there were "no *reciprocal* advantages in the treaty" and the "benefits are all on the side of G. Britain" (Ferling, 2009, 341).

[12] See also Whitaker (1964); Flexner (1974); Elkins and McKitrick (1993); P. Schroeder (1994b); and Harper (2004).

[13] At the time, Britain held Canada. Spain owned the entire west bank of the Mississippi, the Gulf Coast, and all of Florida. As Flexner points out, France's declaration of war in Europe ironically strengthened Britain's geopolitical leverage over the United States by leading the King of Spain to form a defensive alliance with the King of England. France's enemies thus surrounded the United States on three sides.

[14] Since American independence, neither Britain nor Spain had respected U.S. boundaries in the Mississippi Valley. As mentioned, the British continued to occupy military posts on U.S. territory. London's interest in those posts was driven mostly by its desire to regain control of the Northwest Territory's profitable fur-bearing forests and, to a lesser extent, to recover prewar debts owed to British creditors, which was a key provision of the 1783 peace treaty between England and the United States. London tried to make American settlement

ing presence on the high seas. The Royal Navy was the largest and most powerful in the world: it could have its way in American coastal waters.[15]

America was thus too weak and too strategically exposed for George Washington to ignore London's demands or to actively balance against it by aligning with France. Geopolitics alone, however, cannot fully explain why Washington sought security through appeasement, or why he did not select an alternative strategy to reduce the nation's strategic exposure, such as honoring America's treaty commitment with France, joining other maritime states to form an Armed Neutrality League to protect commercial shipping from British depredations (Bemis, 1918), or building up the nation's military capabilities in response to British threats (internal balancing).[16] In weighing his options, Washington had to consider how those geopolitical choices would affect his domestic priorities.

Washington's considerable strengths as commander in chief cannot be viewed in isolation from the pressures on Washington the politician. He was a gifted statesman who was completely at home in the world of *Realpolitik*. But the nation's first president was also fiercely ambitious and politically astute (Burns and Dunn, 2004; Henriques, 2006; Ferling, 2009), and he understood that the government's success depended critically on the success of the economy (Ferling, 2009, 289–92).[17] Washington's economic strategy, devised by Alexander Hamilton, rested fundamentally on international trade and on what economic historian Douglass North

---

of the region risky by inciting Indian warfare and providing arms to the Indian nations sandwiched between British Canada and the United States. Spain also continued to operate on American soil, or at least in territory that the United States claimed was its own. And, like Britain, Spain used the Indians strategically to pursue its objectives. However, because Britain's grip on the Indians was considerably stronger than Spain's, Washington's ability to solve the "Indian problem" was more dependent on decisions made in London than in Madrid. On Madrid's strategic interests and policies, see Whitaker (1964).

[15] Indeed, as Forrest McDonald (1974, 149) puts it, "a dozen of His Majesty's ships of the line could have rendered the United States impotent with a blockade and made a profit in the doing."

[16] Bandwagoning with Britain against France, as Alexander Hamilton urged, would have reduced U.S. exposure in the Northwest by putting an end to British arms and aid to the Indian insurgency. The "grand bargain" with Spain that Thomas Jefferson advocated might have accomplished much the same end in the Southwest. Jefferson argued that Madrid would cede the Mississippi to the United States in return for an American commitment to maintain Louisiana's independence against Britain.

[17] Washington's thirst for public approbation was matched only by his "inordinate sensitivity to criticism" (Henriques, 2006, 41). As Henriques observes, "While eager for power, Washington feared failure." Indeed, it was largely for these reasons that Washington was ambivalent about the presidency, agreeing to take command only when drafted. As the hero of the Revolution, Washington had little to gain by way of fame and glory and much to lose should the new government falter. The risks were considerable. After all, the country's first attempt at self-governance after the Revolution had failed.

(1961) famously characterized as export-led growth. Under Hamilton's plan, exports to Europe would stimulate the growth of production in the United States, while duties on European imports would finance the development of economically essential infrastructure (e.g., roads, canals, ports).

Washington's great domestic political gamble was that this economic strategy would work, and it paid off handsomely. As early as 1793, Americans were getting their first taste of economic recovery and a hint of "the years of unparalleled prosperity" to follow (North, 1962, 53). To be sure, those benefits were not equally shared. Shipping, banking, insurance, and construction interests in the northeastern seaports that were the bedrock of Hamilton's Federalist coalition in Congress benefited disproportionately from an export-led strategy aimed mostly at British markets (Adams, 1980). Southern farmers, the core constituencies of Republicans Thomas Jefferson and James Madison, were the principal losers. The region's farmers stood to gain more from a strategy that forced London and Paris to compete for American goods and that cut out British "middle men" to give U.S. farmers direct access to the continental European market, where most of their produce was ultimately consumed (Buel, 1972).

Although Washington attempted to position himself above the partisan fray, his decision to back Hamilton's scheme for economic development was telling. The president's policy preferences were much closer to the Federalists' than to the Republicans; and they grew stronger as the crisis in Europe deepened. Presidential scholars James MacGregor Burns and Susan Dunn (2004, 115) write that gradually but unmistakably Washington "fell into the conservative Federalist orbit."[18] The president's views were especially close to the Federalists' on matters of "high politics," where the risks to his reputation and hold on power were greatest. Republican leaders were increasingly frustrated by Washington's tilt toward Britain. They concluded that he was using foreign policy to strengthen the position of the Federalists. Thomas Jefferson's assessment of Washington's decision to back the Jay Treaty was that "a bolder party-stroke was never struck."[19]

Jefferson got it right: there is no question that Washington's efforts to appease Britain found greater support among Federalists and delivered greater payoffs to this faction. As table 3.1 indicates, on security and commercial policies favorable to London, Federalists voted in favor of

---

[18] Other historians who have poured over Washington's foreign policy record echo their judgment. See DeConde (1958); Bowman (1974); Kohn (1975); and Harper (2004).

[19] This is how he explained it to James Madison (Bowman, 1974, 226).

TABLE 3.1.
Federalist and Republican support for George Washington's foreign policies,
1789–1797

	Appease Britain		Deter Piracy		Stabilize Frontier	
	Party support	Party cohesion	Party support	Party cohesion	Party support	Party cohesion
Federalists	78%	67%	79%	60%	78%	56%
Republicans	20%	71%	21%	62%	28%	56%

Roll call voting in the U.S. House of Representatives from the 1st through
4th Congress. Number of roll call votes: appease Britain (17); deter piracy (12);
stabilize frontier (28).

pro-British policies nearly 80 percent of the time.[20] Republican opposition to Washington's policy of appeasement toward Britain was equally intense, with support averaging just 20 percent.[21] Like most foreign policy votes during this period, these "partisan" divisions over how to deal with Britain reflected the stresses of sectionalism (Bell, 1973, 17–31). Eighty percent of those voting for the critical Jay Treaty in Congress, for example, came from the Federalist strongholds of New England and the Mid-Atlantic region. Nearly three-quarters of those voting against the treaty came from southern states, where Republicans held sway (Sharp, 1993, 133). Faction cohesion in voting was high. Overall, Federalists voted together 67 percent of the time on matters concerning U.S. relations with Britain; Republicans voted together more than 70 percent of the time.

These same battle lines shaped debate over Washington's response to the secondary challenges posed by Barbary piracy in the Atlantic and by an Indian insurgency in the Ohio Valley. Federalists strongly favored building a small fleet of ships to deter attacks on American shipping by the Barbary states of North Africa—Algiers, Morocco, Tunis, and Tripoli.[22] They also backed Washington's "carrot and stick" approach toward

[20] In addition to roll call votes on the Jay Treaty of 1794, this measure includes Republican-sponsored proposals to upset Anglo-American trade patterns (e.g., James Madison's efforts in 1789 to impose discriminatory tonnage rates on British goods). These roll call votes were coded as votes against appeasing London.

[21] The classification of members of Congress as Federalist or Republican is based on Martis (1989).

[22] Although the Barbary pirates began seizing American merchantmen as early as 1785, the issue took on new urgency with the outbreak of war in Europe. Traditionally, the British Navy limited the Barbary pirates' access to the Atlantic. However, as part of its efforts

the British-backed Indian insurgency in the trans-Appalachian West.[23] In both cases, Washington's actions posed little risk of antagonizing London, while promising considerable benefit to core Federalist constituencies: merchants, shipbuilders, and land speculators (Sprout and Sprout, 1944, 28–38; Bell, 1973, 68–94, 151–53; D. V. Jones, 1982; Millett and Maslowski, 1984, 95).

By contrast, most Republicans opposed federal efforts to combat piracy on the high seas and to pacify the western frontier. In part, this reflected Republican fears about a strong central government, especially after Washington opted for military force to put down the Whiskey Rebellion in 1794.[24] Republicans were keen on gaining control of Indian lands, but they strongly preferred using local militia for this purpose, fearing the development of a permanent federal army. Moreover, Republicans argued with considerable justification that Washington's policies benefited Federalist interests at the expense of Republican constituencies.[25] As already noted, one reason Republican opposition to the Jay Treaty was so vehement is that many of its provisions hurt southern districts and states (Fry, 2002).

---

to discourage U.S. trading with France, London gave the Barbary states a more or less free hand to prey on U.S. merchant vessels. In response, Washington asked Congress in 1794 to fund the construction of six frigates to "compel peace" (Bauer, 1965, 29). In the end, only three of the ships authorized by Congress were built because Washington was able to successfully negotiate a treaty with Algiers. Votes for naval construction are coded as votes to deter Barbary piracy.

[23] After achieving independence, the United States attempted to assert total sovereignty over territory acquired from Britain but inhabited by Indians. This "right-of-conquest" strategy during the Confederation period proved too difficult to implement against the Indians and had the effect of driving the Native Americans into the waiting arms of Britain (and Spain). Native American resistance proved so effective that the federal government was forced to reverse itself and during Washington's tenure adopt a "dual policy" (Millett and Maslowski, 1984, 92), relying as much on diplomacy and negotiation as on military force. Federalist support for the army was contingent on this diplomatic track. Federalists believed that aggressive American frontiersman, not the Indians, were the primary source of frontier violence. They also viewed diplomacy as a more cost-effective means to ultimately acquiring Indians lands and promoting land speculation. Thus, votes for military spending and treaty negotiation with the Indians are coded as support for *federal* efforts to pacify and stabilize the frontier.

[24] The Whiskey Rebellion was a popular uprising against the excise tax imposed by Washington to help pay off the national debt. The rebellion began in 1791 and culminated in 1794 when Washington invoked martial law to summon local militias to put down the protest. It was the first time the federal government had used military power. Washington's actions were viewed with alarm in southern and western districts.

[25] This was obvious in the case of the navy, but spending on the army also benefited Federalists because Alexander Hamilton, Washington's secretary of the treasury, had skillfully linked military spending to the Federalist-backed protective tariff (Clarfield, 1975).

In the 1790s U.S. foreign policy was viewed in zero-sum terms: policies benefiting one faction were resisted by the other. To be sure, there were occasions when Washington's actions won grudging Republican support. This was especially true on matters involving the frontier, settlement, and land. Treaties with foreign powers or Indian nations that opened the frontier to white settlement were popular among the yeoman farmers who were the Republicans' core constituency (D. V. Jones, 1982, 162). The political advantages of making Mississippi Valley lands available to settlers were not lost on Washington, as he skillfully demonstrated in the case of Pinckney's Treaty with Spain.[26] Under this agreement, Spain gave the United States free navigation of the Mississippi River and a port of deposit at New Orleans. In an effort to short-circuit public anger over appeasement of Britain through the Jay Treaty, Washington's Federalist backers planted rumors that the British and Spanish treaties "must fall or stand together" (Sharp, 1993, 131). Western voters and their elected representatives, eager for new lands and a southwestern water outlet for their goods, were outflanked by the president's maneuver. They were unwilling to oppose the Jay Treaty.

Washington's deepening commitment to Hamilton and to the Federalist's program for economic development had far-reaching geopolitical implications (Elkins and McKitrick, 1993). Most importantly, it meant that Washington could not afford to do anything that might provoke Britain's ire. In the 1790s, England took the lion's share of U.S. exports, and British manufactures accounted for roughly 90 percent of all U.S. imports (Ferling, 2009, 311).[27] Jefferson and Madison claimed that France could make up the difference if Britain decided to use trade to punish the United States, but Washington was rightly skeptical of these arguments. Trade with France was but a fraction of U.S. trade with Britain. Moreover, the Royal Navy controlled the sea lanes that U.S. shippers relied upon, and the British did not hesitate to interdict American vessels when suspicions of contraband were aroused. For better or worse, America's economic fortunes depended on British commerce and, ultimately, its political tolerance. In geopolitical terms, this meant

---

[26] When Madrid saw how warmly John Jay was treated in London, it worried that an Anglo-American alliance was in the offing, which would put its holdings in the New World at the mercy of land-hungry Americans. In an effort to neutralize the United States and preempt even bigger territorial losses, Madrid offered to negotiate free navigation of the Mississippi and a port of deposit at New Orleans. The result was the Treaty of San Lorenzo of 1795. Americans named the treaty after Thomas Pinckney, who negotiated the treaty for the United States.

[27] Washington also rejected another Republican idea that involved substituting direct taxation for the duties collected on British imports. The burden of this tax would have fallen on his Federalist supporters.

keeping Paris at arm's length and avoiding actions, however popular they might be domestically, that would fuel suspicions in London about American intentions.[28]

Washington was alert to the strategic implications of America's dependency on Britain. As he observed with remarkable prescience, the United States would not be in a position to risk war with the Britain for at least a generation or, as he put it, "for about twenty years" (Ellis, 2004, 227).[29] Yet even if Washington had preferred a more assertive response to British power to deflect Republican criticism of his economic policies, he would have had to overcome the opposition of his own Federalist supporters. As table 3.1 indicates, Federalists in Congress favored some increases in military spending, but they put strict limits on such investments, believing America's interests lay with London and that the federal debt was already too high. The only military expenditures aimed at Britain that the Federalists would sanction were those for defensive coastal fortifications.

Washington's relationship with the Federalists was complex. Jefferson claimed that the tail was wagging the dog—that Washington was doing the Federalists' bidding. Washington did depend on Federalist support and especially on Hamilton's keen advice. But the president was quick to reject Federalist ideas when they did not serve his strategic interests. Washington's stinging rebuff of Hamilton's call for a "defensive treaty of alliance" with Britain is a case in point. Hamilton floated the proposal months before war broke out in Europe, seeing it as a way to force Spain to open the Mississippi to American commerce and pressure France to sever its alliance with the U.S. Yet Washington judged closer ties to London premature and unnecessary.[30] The situation in Europe was still too fluid. Of course, Washington did eventually move closer to England. But domestic politics was not the decisive factor. The decisive factor was France's declaration of war on Britain, which in a single stroke threatened to eviscerate what little security the United States enjoyed (along with Washington's domestic agenda, which depended on British support).

In the end, Washington's political challenge was figuring out what would suffice to mollify London. Historian James Thomas Flexner (1974) described Washington's solution as "passive acceptance" of Britain's demands concerning U.S. policy toward France. If Washington wanted to call that "neutrality," London could live with that. Appeasing Britain angered France. Paris protested what it considered the "equivalent of an inti-

---

[28] This was one reason that Washington rejected Jefferson's proposed "grand bargain" with Spain to secure the Mississippi for the United States.

[29] The U.S. was pitted against Britain in the War of 1812.

[30] According to Jefferson's notes, Washington told Hamilton that his "remedy would be worse than the disease" (Harper, 2004, 105). Washington worried that alliance with Britain would antagonize France and Jefferson's followers at home.

mate alliance with our cruelest enemy" (Bowman, 1974, 39). Even worse from Washington's perspective was that the Jay Treaty inflamed France's Republican supporters in the United States. A torrent of invective was hurled at Washington for signing the treaty. Republicans attacked the president for "superciliousness and arrogance," calling him a "usurper with dark schemes of ambition" and a "tyrannical monster" who acted with all "the insolence of an Emperor of Rome" (Ferling, 2009, 344). Washington understood that the political damage to his own position would have been even greater if he had severed America's ties with France outright, and formally allied with Britain. Eager to minimize his domestic political losses, Washington shrewdly avoided this overt betrayal of France and conceded only what was necessary to placate London.

Washington thus did not appease Britain blithely, as Churchillian accounts that depict appeasement as an irrational mistake would imply. Nor did he do so to minimize the number of America's foreign enemies, as the realist "triage model" of appeasement would propose as an explanation for this strategic choice. George Washington turned to appeasement because he needed security on the cheap. This strategy was designed to resolve his political and geopolitical predicament. Other cost-saving strategies on which Washington might have relied, such as buckpassing or isolationism, were impractical or counterproductive, or both. The international system of the 1790s that pitted France against Britain was bipolar; there was no other state to which Washington could safely buckpass. Meanwhile, the United States was too integrated into the world economy, and Washington's domestic agenda too dependent on British forbearance, to countenance a strategy of isolation and withdrawal.

Abraham Lincoln, Britain, and the Confederacy

Some sixty-five years later, Abraham Lincoln faced similar cross-pressures and trade-offs. Security was scarce, and Lincoln's fragile domestic coalition was at risk of imploding under the weight of the Civil War. He also opted for a strategy of appeasement of foreign powers, with Britain first among them.

International relations scholars generally have little to say about Lincoln's approach to geopolitics and the threat of foreign intervention during the U.S. Civil War.[31] Realists treat the war as an "internal affair." *Innenpolitik* scholars ignore it altogether. Yet, as Lincoln himself quickly came to understand, domestic and foreign affairs were inseparable. This was not simply because Lincoln, in order to win the war against the

---

[31] See, however, Layne (1994) and Owen (2000).

South, had to prevent Britain from allying with the Confederacy. The linkages between domestic and foreign affairs also shaped Lincoln's options in maneuvering to keep Britain out of the war. He was particularly constrained by his need to keep his domestic wartime coalition intact. While tensions inside the Union cannot be easily modeled as a guns-versus-butter conflict, the domestic conflict *was* about how far Lincoln should go in increasing the powers of the federal government and in using those powers to restructure American society by destroying the institution of slavery.

The southern secession and the resulting Civil War left the United States more vulnerable to foreign meddling than at any time since the Napoleonic Wars. London and the other European capitals were on an American "death watch" (Bourne, 1967; Little, 2007). Shortly after the outbreak of the war, the *Economist* asserted that "every one knows and admits that the secession is an accomplished and irrevocable fact" (H. Jones, 1999, 43).[32] Across the English Channel, *La Patrie* echoed that sentiment. "The Union is completely dissolved and in our opinion, can never be restored" (Mahin, 1999, 98). Many Europeans viewed the American crisis as an opportunity to pursue their own expansionist ends in the Western Hemisphere. Some in Britain saw a permanently divided America as a means to sandwich the United States between a newly independent pro-British Confederacy in the South and British Canada in the North (Bourne, 1967, 252–53; H. Jones, 1999, 20; Steele, 2005, 520).[33] In France, Napoleon III's "Grand Design for the Americas" envisioned the Confederacy as a "buffer state" between the United States and a French-sponsored monarchy in Mexico (Bemis, 1942).

While Lincoln could not afford to ignore either of the European great powers, British policy was his primary concern. In part, this was because

---

[32] In an early dispatch sizing up the situation in the Americas, Lord Richard Lyons, Britain's minister to the United States, wrote, "If I had the least hope of [northerners] being able to reconstruct the Union, or even of their being able to reduce the South to the condition of a tolerably contented or at all events obedient dependency, my feeling against Slavery might lead me to desire to cooperate with them. But I conceive all chance of this to be gone forever. The question now is only how long and how bloody the war will be, and how much injury it will cause both divisions of the Country" (Brauer, 1977, 459).

[33] British opinion on the geopolitical advantages of a divided America was mixed. Some, such as Richard Cobden, the British manufacturer and Radical and Liberal statesman, worried that a weakened United States would actually imperil British imperial interests by making it easier for other European powers, especially France and Russia, to make inroads in the Western Hemisphere (Reid, 2003, 48–49). Similarly, the historian D. P. Crook (1974, 374) argues that many inside the British Foreign Ministry feared that a "balkanized America could engender threats by a revanchist north against Canada, and a wave of Confederate imperialism to the south; while the hemisphere might become a cockpit of European rivalries, open to all sorts of fishing in troubled waters."

disunion in North American appeared to serve Britain's larger geopolitical interests. A weakened United States would make it easier for London to focus its diplomacy and resources in Europe at a time of political unrest on the Continent (Graebner, 1985, 259–82). As a heavy consumer of southern cotton, Britain also was the foreign power that seemed to have the most to gain from intervention, whether it took the form of a mediation offer, a call for armistice, or an outright recognition of the Confederacy.[34] France, for its part, was not powerful enough to weaken the Union war effort, at least not if it acted alone (H. Jones, 1992, 72–73; Reid, 2003, 59). Britain was the world's largest military power; it was another story altogether. The combination of British sea power and the possibility of a British front along the U.S.-Canadian border was enough to convince Lincoln that "foreign involvement in the American conflict was a mortal threat to the Union" (H. Jones, 1999, 17).[35]

From the beginning of the war in April 1861, Lincoln's principal international goal was to deprive the Confederacy of external support, and especially British support. The immediate diplomatic objective was to prevent British recognition of the Confederacy as an independent nation.[36] This priority reflected both geopolitics and party politics. Geopolitically, Lincoln feared that British recognition of the Confederacy would lead other European nations to follow suit, legitimizing southern claims to independence.[37] British recognition would strengthen the peace move-

[34] At the time, more than 80 percent of the cotton used by British textile mills came from the United States (C. Campbell, 1974, 95–96). Many southern leaders believed that British dependence on "King Cotton" would force London to recognize the Confederacy as an independent state. For a summary of southern views at the time, see Fry (2002, 75–105).

[35] The principal British threat was sea power. In the 1850s London opted to invest far greater resources in a strategy of "overwhelming naval strength," reducing its military presence in Canada. Although U.S. naval capabilities in 1861 were considerably stronger than they had been a decade earlier, the U.S. fleet was no match for the British Navy. Harold and Margaret Sprout note that "the entire (U.S.) fleet could scarcely have offered battle to a single one of the sea-going ironclad warships which were beginning to appear in European navies on the eve of the American civil war" (Sprout and Sprout, 1944, 149). At the time, British leaders shared that view. While British naval and military experts agreed that territorial conquest of the United States was "a physical impossibility," there was little doubt that Britain could greatly complicate the U.S. war effort against the Confederacy by attacking American shipping, blockading and harassing northern coastal cities, and possibly invading Maine (Bourne, 1967, 241). Whether this would have forced Lincoln to the negotiating table with the South or prevented a retaliatory U.S. attack on Canada was less certain to British officials. For a discussion of British strategy and planning toward the United States during the period, see Bourne (1967, 206–47).

[36] Early on London and Paris issued proclamations of neutrality, which recognized the Confederacy as a belligerent though not as an independent nation.

[37] British *military* intervention on behalf of the South was a more remote possibility, but as subsequent events would make clear to Lincoln, he could not discount this possibility altogether.

ment in the North (McPherson, 1988, 353). Even more ominously for Lincoln, it could produce a domestic domino effect, leading pro-Union slave states, such as Kentucky and Maryland, and possibly western states, such as Ohio, Indiana, and Illinois, to secede from the Union (Weber, 2006, 12; Herring, 2008, 239). This would destroy Lincoln's domestic political base.

To avoid provoking Britain into a diplomatic move that would have fateful consequences for the United States, Lincoln pursued a strategy of moderation and conciliation in dealing with London (Mahin, 1999; Brauer, 2002; E. Cohen, 2002).[38] This was not the only option on the table at the time. Some members of Lincoln's own cabinet objected to the argument that moderation and patience were the best tools to keep London on the sidelines. William H. Seward, Lincoln's secretary of state, was much more willing to engage in brinksmanship. Seward believed in the war's early days that a "foreign enemy" could help forestall additional Union defections to the Confederacy and might even lead states that had seceded to rally around the Stars and Stripes.[39] Lincoln worried that such threats would have the opposite effect, especially if Britain responded militarily, as he feared it would. In the end, Lincoln's strategy of appeasement of Britain defined U.S. grand strategy during the Civil War.[40]

The basic logic was evident within a week of the Confederates' firing on Fort Sumter in April 1861. Lincoln responded by issuing a proclamation announcing his intention to blockade the ports of the South, from

---

[38] The main exceptions were the so-called mediation crisis after the Union loss at Second Bull Run in August 1862 and the dispute over the Confederate raider, the *Alabama*, which was built in England and took a heavy toll on American commercial shipping. With respect to mediation, Lincoln rejected a British (and French) offer to mediate a peace settlement between the Union and Confederacy. On the *Alabama*, Lincoln protested apparent British violations of neutrality, though even here, the president resisted pressure from Congress to retaliate against London by commissioning privateers to operate against British blockade runners (Rawley, 1980, 102; Symonds, 2008, 220–23).

[39] Seward first advanced his idea of a "foreign war panacea" in a memo to Lincoln in April 1861. Seward recommended provoking a war with Britain and seizing the British provinces in Canada. Lincoln ignored Seward's recommendation. As part of his strategy to bring the South back into the Union fold, Seward also favored a more lenient, conciliatory policy toward the Confederacy than Lincoln did (Rawley, 1980, 12).

[40] While Lincoln left the day-to-day management of foreign affairs to Seward, on matters of great import, which by definition included British interests, the president exercised direct control over foreign policy. Historians once thought that Seward was the driving force behind U.S. foreign policy during the Civil War. More recent treatments suggest that Lincoln was the decisive policy maker on foreign policy as well as domestic policy. British statesmen at the time apparently shared this view, viewing Seward "as a man of words rather than action, full of bluster and empty threats" (Reid, 2003, 47). For a comparison of Lincoln and Seward, see Crichlow (2005).

South Carolina to the Rio Grande.[41] In doing so, Lincoln ignored the advice of his own secretary of the navy, Gideon Welles, who recommended the more draconian move of using an executive or legislative edict to close the ports of the Confederacy (Anderson, 1977). Under international law, a blockade would allow Britain, as a nonbelligerent nation, to continue trading with the South. London had signaled that it could tolerate a blockade but that it would oppose efforts to close the ports. Recognizing that closure of the ports could draw the United States into war with Britain, Lincoln chose the less risky path, even at the expense of possibly (probably) prolonging the war against the South. As he told his cabinet, "We [can] not afford to have two wars on our hands at once" (Anderson, 1977, 190).[42]

While the blockade was less risky than closing Confederate ports, the threat of a wider war remained. Indeed, the most dangerous international episode of the war occurred in November 1861, when an American ship intercepted the British mail packet *Trent* and unlawfully removed two Confederate diplomats bound for London and Paris. The American action provoked a firestorm of criticism in Britain, triggering what one military historian calls "Lincoln's Cuban missile crisis" (Symonds, 2008, 94). London demanded that the United States apologize and release the diplomats and then turned up the heat by strengthening its military presence in Canada and the Atlantic. Though Lincoln did not issue a formal apology, he did accommodate London's demands when it became clear that Britain was prepared to go to war over the incident.[43] Although Lincoln worried that capitulating to London would be viewed as a sign of political weakness in the North as well as the South, these concerns were outweighed by his fear of a wider, two-front war involving Britain (Rawley, 1989, 87; Donald, 1996, 322–23).

Chastened by *Trent* experience, Lincoln was even quicker to appease London in the 1863 controversy sparked by the U.S. seizure of the British steamer *Peterhoff*[44] and in 1864 in responding to Confederate attacks

[41] Shortly thereafter, Lincoln extended the blockade to the newly seceded states of Virginia and North Carolina.

[42] Lincoln's blockade was not without shortcomings. For one thing, it allowed Britain and other nations to grant the Confederacy belligerent status, a possible first step toward national recognition.

[43] Lincoln's unilateral concession also came on the heels of a British decision to embargo all shipments of saltpeter, the principal ingredient of gunpowder, to the United States until the crisis was resolved. At the time, British India was the Union's main source of saltpeter (McPherson, 1988, 390).

[44] Ostensibly bound for the Mexican port of Matamoros, the *Peterhoff* was carrying contraband for the Confederacy. The British reaction was swift and unyielding. Declaring the vessel "neutral," the British press denounced the seizure as a deliberate provocation "to exasperate England and bring about war" (Symonds, 2008, 230). Meanwhile, the Brit-

against Union territory that were launched from across the border in (British) Canada.[45] In each of these cases, Lincoln sought to placate London, making unilateral concessions in hopes of reducing the chances of a wider war.[46] Even when public antipathy toward London was aroused, as it was during the *Trent* affair, the president held his fire. He resisted the political temptation to use the foreign crisis and anti-British sentiment to deflect mounting public criticism over the Union's repeated failures on the battlefield and his handling of the war at home. Such scapegoating tactics might temporarily silence domestic critics, but Lincoln feared that they would also strengthen the hand of "war hawks" in Britain who agitated for an alliance between London and the Confederate capital of Richmond, Virginia.

Lincoln thought that appeasement would allow him time to win over British opinion to the Union's cause.[47] For this, Lincoln relied on active public diplomacy. The most celebrated example is the Emancipation Proc-

---

ish Foreign Office dug in, insisting that the *Peterhoff*'s mailbags, which likely would have revealed the ship's true purpose, to be delivered unopened. Lincoln did not concede the principle of the mailbags' inviolability, but he nevertheless "chose conciliation over confrontation" (Symonds, 2008, 234). Lincoln instructed his secretary of the navy not to open the mailbags, and the crisis ended. Charles Sumner, the chairman of the Senate Foreign Relations Committee and a Lincoln confidant, had no doubts about why. Lincoln, Sumner said, was "horrified" about the risk of war with London (Symonds, 2008, 234). Lincoln apparently also worried that, short of war, any affront to Lord Palmerston's liberal government in 1863 ran the risk of tipping the electoral balance in Britain toward a more hostile Tory government (Mahin, 1999, 185–96).

[45] The most explosive of these incidents was "St. Alban's raid." It came on the heels of an effort by belligerent lawmakers in Congress to scrap the 1817 Rush-Bagot Pact, which had helped keep the peace along the Great Lakes since the War of 1812 by limiting the number and weight of naval vessels the United States and England could deploy in the Great Lakes. In autumn 1864, a small group of Confederate soldiers who had secretly assembled in Canada slipped across the border and attacked the town of St. Albans, Vermont. Lincoln and Seward responded quickly by ordering U.S. forces not to cross into Canadian territory, a move that could have widened the war by opening a front on the U.S.-Canada border and drawing in Britain (Winks, 1998, 295–336).

[46] This was also true on the question of Union privateering. In March 1863 Congress authorized Union privateers, granting to Lincoln the power to issue letters of marque. Under this action, private armed vessels could be used to slow Confederate blockade running and, ideally, run down Confederate commerce raiders, such as the *Alabama* and *Florida*, that were destroying Northern commerce. Seward backed the measure. So did the commercial centers of the Northeast (Sprout and Sprout, 1944, 162–63). However, "Lincoln decided that there was little to be gained, and much to lose, by instituting a program of Union privateering. Whatever benefit the threat of privateers might have on British behavior, there was simply too much risk. He was determined to fight only one war at a time" (Symonds, 2008, 223).

[47] Appeasing London also made it easier for British officials, worried more about geopolitical developments in Europe (e.g., the Polish insurrection of 1863, Prussia's war against Denmark in 1864), to concentrate more of their efforts on the continent (Reid, 2003, 49).

lamation, which shifted coalitional alignments not only at home but also abroad. In the early 1860s, antislavery sentiment was a potent political force in England (Crook, 1974; Jenkins, 1980; H. Jones, 1992). It constituted a source of cross-pressure on British leaders, who were inclined to give a favorable hearing to pro-Confederacy British commercial interests. The foreign target on this occasion was the British political establishment. Lincoln saw British opinion as a means to tip the balance of power away from the war hawks and toward "moderates" who opposed southern slavery. Similar considerations influenced Lincoln's support for joint Anglo-American efforts to end the African slave trade (the Lyons-Seward Treaty of April 1862) and U.S. recognition of black governments in Haiti and Liberia in June 1862 (Brauer, 1977; Rawley, 1980; H. Jones, 1999).

A purely realist theory of appeasement, which would suggest that appeasing Britain was about buying time to deal with other foreign powers, does not hold in this case. France was the only other foreign power that Lincoln had to worry about, and Lincoln pursued appeasement with France as well (Graebner, 1959, 89–91; Donald, 1995, 412–16).[48] Appeasing England and France served more immediate and important *domestic* goals, namely, putting down a secessionist rebellion and avoiding an international crisis that would strengthen those in the North favoring peace at any price, including permanent division of the United States. The need to hold together his domestic political coalition gave Lincoln compelling reasons for resisting brinksmanship and the diversionary war tactics that *Innenpolitik* theory would predict and for keeping Britain placated on the sidelines.

Having won the presidency in 1860 with only 40 percent of the popular vote, Lincoln had no secure lock on this office (McKitrick, 1967; Foner, 1970; Holt, 1992). Once hostilities broke out, Lincoln's Republican supporters quickly divided over the war's purposes—some favored emancipation of the slaves; others favored merely reuniting with the wayward southern states. Lincoln sought the support of northern Democrats, but they too were divided over how to restore the Union and over what sort of Union to strive for. On the Democratic side, the key question was whether to rely on force or negotiation. "War Democrats" backed the war and a restored Union that allowed slavery. "Peace Democrats" (or Copperheads) strongly opposed the war, and favored a negotiated end to the conflict that could effectively concede autonomy to the South. British recognition of the Confederacy was certain to exacerbate these divisions. This alone was likely to have led conservative border states like Kentucky and Missouri to defect to the Confederacy, fueling calls by Peace Demo-

---

[48] On the question of French intervention in Mexico in 1862, Lincoln favored a policy of neutrality (Graebner, 1959, 89–91; Rawley, 1980, 166–67; Mahin, 1999, 106–21, 218–38).

crats for European mediation, an end to the blockade, and acceptance of southern autonomy.[49]

British recognition of the South, along with other moves that could lengthen or raise the cost of the war, also threatened to fuel the spreading discontent in the West, which Lincoln ominously referred to as "the fire in the rear" (Donald, 1995, 416–21). In dealing with western states like Ohio, Indiana, and Illinois, Lincoln was trying to retain the support of a non-slave-holding part of the country whose conscripts were essential to the war's successful prosecution. Western votes were also critical to his ability to win a national election. Dissent in the region was so pronounced that many political observers at the time expected that the Western states "would secede from the Union if the South were successful in its effort to break away" (Weber, 2006, 12).

The *timing* of the Emancipation Proclamation was determined largely by Lincoln's attempts to manage his fissiparous domestic coalition.[50] In the first two years of the war, Lincoln was pressured away from emancipation by elements within his own coalition for whom this was not a priority (or who were opposed to it). However, Lincoln's core Republican backers in the Northeast pressed strongly for this, and Lincoln's decision to issue the Emancipation Proclamation allowed the president to provide a rationale for the war that bucked-up their support (Williams, 1969, 3–19). He timed the Emancipation Proclamation to follow a decisive Union victory on the battlefield, carefully exempting the slave-holding border states. Although Lincoln paid a price among his moderate supporters, this turn in the war helped him abroad, for it hamstrung British war hawks at a critical moment and helped raise British abolitionists to their full strength in support of the Union.[51] Lincoln believed that those moderate voters in the West and border states would come to see emancipation in their interest "if not immediately, soon" (McPherson, 1988, 557). Lincoln thus timed the Emancipation Proclamation to achieve max-

[49] Early in the war, Robert E. Lee's efforts to rack up quick military victories against Union forces were aimed at securing British (and French) recognition. Lee believed that British recognition would strengthen the northern peace movement, tipping the North's 1862 midterm elections in the Confederacy's favor. On Lee's political objectives and the northern peace movement, see Weber (2006, 61–62).

[50] Strategic considerations also influenced the timing of the proclamation. Slaves were crucial to the Confederate war effort, performing critical support functions for the rebel army and manning southern factories. Black soldiers were also critical in boosting the Union's war-fighting capability. On Emancipation's strategic advantages, see Millet and Maslowski (1984, 194–202) and McPherson (1988, 563–67).

[51] The Emancipation Proclamation consisted of the two executive orders issued by Lincoln. The first was issued on September 22, 1862, in the immediate aftermath of the Battle of Antietam, where Union forces turned back a Confederate invasion of Maryland. The second order was issued on January 1, 1863.

imum political advantage both at home and in maintaining support for the Union effort in Britain. Had Lincoln's own party been more united, and the Union racked up battlefield victories sooner, he could have declared Emancipation much earlier, and thus probably expended less time and political capital trying to appease British war hawks.[52]

Appeasement of Britain enabled Lincoln to reconcile conflicting international and domestic goals.[53] It was a means to gain time to secure Union victories on the battlefield and constrict if not completely cut off vital supplies to the South; a way to strengthen the hands of moderate British voices opposed to the slave-trading Confederacy; and a critical element in Lincoln's efforts to hold together a tenuous domestic wartime coalition that was vital to the success of his presidency and to the preservation of the Union itself. As table 3.2 indicates, Republicans in Congress strongly supported Lincoln's efforts to appease Europe, blockade the Confederacy, and mobilize manpower for the war effort.[54] Indeed, Republican support for appeasement (narrowly) exceeded support to mount an offensive military campaign on the ground by mobilizing manpower and the accompanying naval blockade.[55]

Other grand strategies that Lincoln might have adopted did not offer the strategic advantages of appeasement. Allying with the pro-Union Russia would offer little strategic leverage, given Britain's command of the seas. It would have only antagonized Britain, especially after the Pol-

---

[52] Henry Adams, the son and secretary of the Union minister in London, Charles Francis Adams, observed at the time, "The Emancipation Proclamation has done more for us than all our former victories and all our diplomacy" (Mahin, 1999, 139). Adams was engaging in hyperbole, for Emancipation did not end the battle for British opinion. Still, diplomatic historians consider Lincoln's edict a turning point in the effort to keep Britain (and France) on the sidelines.

[53] Fiscal constraints also help to account for Lincoln's logic of appeasement. The war's huge economic costs did nothing to ease Lincoln's foreign policy problems. Goldin and Lewis (1975; 1978) put the total direct costs (government expenditure, physical destruction, and loss of human capital) of the Union's war against the Confederacy at roughly $150 per capita—roughly equal to one year's income. The federal government imposed higher tariffs, excise taxes, and the first ever income tax in U.S. history. It also adopted inflationary policies, issuing $250 million worth of "Greenbacks" (currency not backed by gold) and Treasury notes to borrow funds from the public. Inflation was reflected in the consumer price index: it rose from 100 at the war's start to 175 by the end of 1865. Over the course of the war, the federal debt grew from $65 million to $2.7 billion (Ransom, 2001, 12–14).

[54] Appease Europeans includes votes to extend recognition to Haiti and Liberia, emancipate slaves in the Confederacy and Union, and support Lincoln's policy of neutrality toward the crisis in Mexico. These roll call votes were coded as votes to prevent British and European recognition of the Confederacy and reduce the risk of a wider international conflict.

[55] Votes in favor of naval construction were coded as votes for Lincoln's strategy of blockade. Votes for military appropriations were coded as votes for Lincoln's strategy of military "exhaustion" and "annihilation" on the ground (Millett and Maslowski, 1984, 161).

TABLE 3.2.
Republican and Democratic support for Abraham Lincoln's foreign policies, 1861–1865

	Appease Europeans		Naval Blockade		Mobilize Manpower	
	Party support	Party cohesion	Party support	Party cohesion	Party support	Party cohesion
Republicans	85%	70%	68%	46%	82%	70%
Democrats[a]	12%	93%	40%	45%	32%	71%

[a] Democrats include "War Democrats" and "Peace Democrats."

Roll call voting in the U.S. House of Representatives from the 37th and 38th Congresses. Number of roll call votes: appease Europeans (18); naval blockade (12); mobilize manpower (32).

ish insurrection against Russia in 1863 raised the specter of war between London and Moscow (Reid, 2003, 49).[56] Meanwhile, London's rapid military build-up in Canada in response to the *Trent* affair underscored the limitations of the kind of confrontational stance that Seward had advocated early on.[57] Confrontation might have produced a temporary boost in Lincoln's popularity and in support for the Union war effort, but it risked British retaliation and intervention on the side of the Confederacy.

Lincoln understood that British "neutrality" toward the American conflict would suffice to serve his government's strategic needs. The United States and the Great Britain had thus traded places since the 1790s. Then, London had required U.S. neutrality to achieve its primary objective, which was to deny revolutionary France an important ally and thus thwart its drive for European hegemony. Now, America's goal was to deny the Confederacy a strategic alliance that would have been a complete game changer on the North American continent.

FRANKLIN ROOSEVELT, HITLER, AND APPEASEMENT, 1936–1939

Washington and Lincoln each maintained a steady commitment to appeasing British power. By contrast, Franklin Roosevelt's appeasement of Hitler's Germany was short-lived, starting in late 1936 and lasting roughly two years. It peaked around the time of Chamberlain's September 1938

[56] For a contrasting view of the geopolitical possibilities of a Russian-American alliance, see Herring (2008, 244–47).

[57] London continued to deploy most of the troops it had sent to Canada as a result the *Trent* seizure long after the crisis subsided (Bourne, 1967, 252).

Munich Conference, which conceded both territory and political advantage to Hitler. By March 1939 the shortcomings of this approach had become too obvious to risk appeasing Germany any longer. Yet during this critical two-year juncture in Germany's rise to power, appeasement ran "like a *leitmotif*" through U.S. grand strategy (Marks, 1985, 982). This was clearest in Roosevelt's consideration of a peace initiative known as the Welles Plan. Yet it was also evident in a series of back-channel diplomatic missions authorized by Roosevelt that sought to address long-standing German grievances, split the emerging Berlin-Rome-Tokyo axis, and more generally reduce the risk of war. By 1939 Roosevelt shifts to buckpassing, still trying to deal with the crisis in Europe without investing the United States wholly in the task of stopping Hitler. I argue that all of these efforts were aimed at reducing American strategic exposure at a price that would not compromise Roosevelt's commitment to domestic recovery from the Depression.

Roosevelt's approach to international matters changed substantially over the course of his presidency in response to the deterioration of the geostrategic environment.[58] During his first term, he took few foreign policy initiatives. Only one sentence of his 1933 inaugural address was devoted to foreign policy. In large part, this is explained by the gravity of the Great Depression and the intense battles over the New Deal programs that Roosevelt had proposed to rebuild the economy and restore public confidence. Yet it also reflected international circumstances. Roosevelt entered office at a time when security was plentiful (Braeman, 1982, 369; Heinrichs, 1988, 6–10; Farnham, 1997, 8–9; Reynolds, 2001, 36). American security was not significantly threatened by events that were unfolding in Europe or Asia. This happy state of affairs did not last. While the economic crisis continued, the international situation worsened.

As early as 1936, Roosevelt considered the rise of Nazi Germany a serious threat to American interests (Dallek, 1979, 102; Farnham, 1997, 7). Like many of his advisers, FDR initially defined that threat in economic as opposed to military terms (MacDonald, 1981, 1–15; Hearden,

---

[58] Historians disagree about Roosevelt's approach toward Germany during the 1930s (Trachtenberg, 2006, 80–88). Some (e.g., Divine, 1962) view the period as a more or less unbroken chain of isolationism and neutrality toward the European crisis. Others (e.g., A. Offner, 1969) characterize Roosevelt's behavior throughout the period as one of appeasement. Most analysts, however, view Roosevelt's approach to Germany as dynamic and shifting, changing in response to changing international and domestic circumstances. They divide, explicitly or implicitly, Roosevelt's behavior into overlapping phases. I follow this basic approach to Roosevelt's foreign policy, drawing heavily on Dallek (1979), MacDonald, (1981), and Reynolds (2001), among others. Whatever sympathy Roosevelt had for isolationism in his first term (1933–36), he devoted much of his second term (1937–40), the focus here, to actively trying to diffuse and then, contain German power, albeit using largely inexpensive diplomatic strategies that fall under the heading of scenario III in figure 2.2.

1987, 88–122; Ninkovich, 1999, 122). According to this view, America's prosperity could not be guaranteed in a world in which the United States was cut off from international trade and in which Europe remained the single most important overseas market for American producers (Trubowitz, 1998, 108). The United States was too dependent on foreign trade to view with indifference the division of Europe into closed trading blocs.

To many, the future of America as well as that of Europe hinged on the outcome of a struggle in Germany over how to promote economic growth (MacDonald, 1981, 5). Hitler's advisers were divided between a group made up of party extremists (or "war men") and one of party moderates. The extremists urged Hitler to pursue policies of autarky, militarization, and foreign expansion. The moderates, mostly from industry, the Army, and the Foreign Office, lobbied for freer capital markets, fewer trade restrictions, and diplomatic efforts to revise the unpopular Versailles Treaty.

Roosevelt was keenly aware of the geopolitical implications of this power struggle inside Germany (MacDonald, 1981, 14). An autarkic Germany would deprive the world access to Germany's internal market. Stagnation of trade in Europe would place tremendous economic pressure on Britain and France, two countries that were key in any strategy to check German power. This would leave Germany's smaller neighbors in Mittleuropa even more isolated and vulnerable to Nazi "salami tactics" and economic coercion. These worries were only heightened by Germany's remilitarization of the Rhineland in March 1936 and Hitler's decision later that year to sign "defensive" security pacts with Fascist Italy and imperial Japan. If Germany's political moderates lost their battle to reintegrate Germany into the international economy, the United States would suffer not only economically but also geopolitically as Hitler built spheres of influence in Europe and beyond.

FDR understood that a system of closed trading blocs would also create domestic political problems (Trubowitz, 1998, 118–37).[59] Southern planters and Wall Street bankers, core Democratic constituencies, depended on access to foreign markets. Roosevelt had reason to worry that if international markets dried up, he would have to resort to levels of regulation of the national economy that none but the most devout New Dealers thought advisable. Those worries deepened in the fall of 1937, in Roosevelt's second term, when the national economy worsened unexpectedly, triggering one of the steepest economic descents in U.S. history (Kindleberger, 1973, 272). Unemployment jumped from 7.7 million in

---

[59] On Roosevelt's thinking about Germany's domestic politics and its sensitivity to economic developments, see also Casey (2001, 6–8).

1937 to 10.4 million in 1938 (Weatherford, 2002, 240). Rates of jobless-ness were even higher in leading industries like autos and steel.

The "Roosevelt recession" of 1937 and 1938 gave Republicans plenty of political ammunition to use to attack the New Deal (Patterson, 1967, 210–49). The downturn also lent an air of urgency to the case for the low-cost foreign policy solution of appeasing Hitler (Dallek, 1979, 153, 158–59).[60] Roosevelt needed to reduce the drift toward economic closure in Europe and to do so in a way that neither jeopardized liberal New Deal reformers' continued support for the reforms or for FDR himself nor provided a rallying point for the budding alliance between laissez faire Republicans and conservative Democrats.[61] The president's politi-cal calculus was complicated by public attitudes toward the situation in Europe. In 1936, 95 percent of all Americans wanted Roosevelt to stay out of any conflict in Europe (Casey, 2001, 23).

Isolationism was a powerful political current in the United States throughout the 1930s.[62] It found expression in Congress in a series of neutrality laws designed to limit the president's ability to pick sides in foreign military conflicts in Europe and beyond. The first of these laws was enacted in August 1935, shortly after Mussolini's Italy attacked Ethiopia. It prohibited the export of arms and munitions to warring nations. In February 1936 isolationists went a step further: in addition to extending the arms embargo, they prohibited Americans from issu-ing loans to belligerents. An even more comprehensive law was adopted the next year—the so-called permanent Neutrality Act of 1937. Passed in the midst of the Spanish Civil War between the German-backed Na-tionalist rebellion led by General Francisco Franco and the democratic government supported by the Soviet Union, the 1937 law extended the main features of the earlier laws to foreign *civil* wars. More importantly, it prohibited American merchant ships from carrying arms or munitions to belligerents.

[60] If Roosevelt considered using the Nazi threat to deflect Republican attacks (and there is no evidence that he did), then he did not entertain such thoughts for long.

[61] New Dealers did not object to increased military spending per se. Federal outlays for the navy and army could help the economy and strengthen civilian planners' authority and control. As Roosevelt came to appreciate, defense spending could also be used to weaken the alliance between the Republicans and southern Democrats. By 1937 Republicans could count on southern Democratic support when it came to blocking New Deal measures that threatened southern autonomy. But southern lawmakers were among the most vigorous proponents of expanded defense spending, preferring it to more intrusive social spending. On defense spending and the New Deal and southern attitudes toward military prepared-ness, see Ehrhart (1975, 21–27, 223–26) and Trubowitz (1998, 126–45).

[62] There is a substantial literature on isolationism during the 1930s. See, for example, Jonas (1966); W. Cole (1983); Trubowitz (1998, 145–64); and Doenecke (2000); Casey (2001, 22–25).

These laws had real bite. They made it virtually impossible for Roosevelt to make the kinds of external balancing commitments that might deter German aggression (Stein, 1993, 101–2). Though frustrated by Congress's actions, Roosevelt felt he had little choice but to sign each of the neutrality bills into law. The issue was not simply that Roosevelt was reluctant to get too far ahead of public opinion. The problem was that isolationist sentiment ran strong in the progressive wing of the Democratic Party, and Roosevelt's New Deal priorities in Congress depended on its support. Indeed, "many isolationists believed that any marked interest in foreign affairs by the President was virtually a betrayal of progressivism" (Burns, 1956, 263). Progressive lawmakers used their powerful positions in Congress to draw public attention to these guns-versus-butter trade-offs. Needing the support of progressives to pass his New Deal legislation, Roosevelt sought to avoid a test of strength with Congress on neutrality matters.

FDR's strategic options were thus highly constrained by both geopolitical and domestic realities. Americans on the left wing and right wing of the domestic political spectrum favored strategies of disengagement or isolationism, but for Roosevelt these were unviable, strategically and politically.[63] Turning a blind eye to Europe would only encourage economic nationalism on the continent while threatening Roosevelt's core Democratic constituencies in the Northeast and South. Balancing against German power was a better strategy for Roosevelt, at least geopolitically. As the situation in Europe worsened, Roosevelt did move in this direction (Reynolds, 2001; Trachtenberg, 2006; Schuessler, 2010). Spending on national defense increased, but Roosevelt remained reluctant to put the country on a war mobilization footing, or to tie U.S. interests to Britain or France, because of the cost he would have to pay domestically (Burns, 1956, 383–84; Dallek, 1979, 223–27; Stein, 1993, 112; Reynolds, 2001, 69–101).[64] Before Pearl Harbor, the president was able to secure congressional backing only for improved national defense by selling it as part of a narrower, less costly, and less risky hemispheric defensive program

---

[63] Arguably, the path of least resistance for Roosevelt in 1937 was the strategy of disengagement or isolationism favored by progressives within his own party. Internationalist constituencies would have certainly objected, and that was one consideration. Geopolitics was another. Passively tolerating Nazi Germany would only encourage economic nationalism and Nazi intimidation on the Continent; FDR ignored Hitler at his peril. Roosevelt had to weigh the risks of discounting the German threat against the benefits of catering to isolationist sentiment within his party.

[64] Indeed, measured in relative terms, the U.S. military weakened during Roosevelt's first two terms. According to Marks, in 1939, the U.S. Army ranked nineteenth in the world, putting it behind Portugal and just ahead of Bulgaria. The U.S. ranked forty-fifth when measured by percentage of its population under arms (Marks, 1988, 112).

(Ehrhart, 1975, 209; Millett and Maslowski, 1984, 388–89). During the 1930s, because of domestic political constraints, actively balancing against the Nazi threat was never seriously in the cards (Ehrhart, 1975).

In 1937 Roosevelt thus saw little alternative to trying to placate Nazi Germany, although he himself expressed mixed opinions about the prospects of such a strategy (Freidel, 1990, 259). The clearest expression of the appeasement strategy toward Germany was the Welles Plan developed by Sumner Welles, a close adviser of Roosevelt's and the number two man (undersecretary of state) in the State Department.[65] It came on the heels of Roosevelt's quarantine speech (October 1937), in which the president sought to educate the American public about the nature of the security challenge facing the country and seemed to raise the possibility of collective action against nations that threatened the status quo (Dallek, 1979, 149–57; Brands, 2008, 484).[66] Welles's scheme, however, doubled down on appeasement. It was laid out to Roosevelt in October 1937 and gained immediate traction as a possible course of action.

At its core, Welles Plan would offer Germany an opportunity to revise the terms of the Versailles Treaty. In so doing, it sought to achieve two goals simultaneously: first, to weaken the position of German hard-liners who gained domestic political traction by exploiting the German public's resentment over the terms of Versailles and, second, to break up the emerging grouping of "dissatisfied" powers (Germany, Italy, and Japan), which, as Roosevelt suggested in his quarantine speech, refused to accept the existing international system. The Welles Plan called for a world conference under American auspices, which would establish new rules of international conduct, discuss arms limitation, and consider methods for promoting economic security and stability. By offering Germany an opportunity to revise Versailles and to improve its economy, it would be possible, Welles argued, to split the dissatisfied powers and politically isolate and weaken Italy and Japan.

Roosevelt initially endorsed the Welles Plan. He had domestic reasons as well as international reasons for doing so. By November 1937

[65] An earlier 1937 effort spearheaded by Secretary of State Cordell Hull also envisaged summoning a conference. Under the Hull plan, the United States and Britain would make economic concessions to Germany in return for a German pledge to abandon autarky and armaments. The plan foundered. Britain objected to Hull's efforts to link political, economic, and disarmament questions. Germany refused to abandon autarky before Britain and others powers met its demands for economic redress (MacDonald, 1981, 9–10, 28–31). A second effort by Roosevelt, which called for military cutbacks by both Britain and Germany, ran up against British opposition and was abandoned as well.

[66] According to Marks, in an effort to appease German sensibilities at the time about the speech, Roosevelt made it clear, in private, to Germany's ambassador to the United States, that the president's implied threat of collective action did not apply to Germany (Marks, 1985, 973).

the economy appeared to be in free fall. Many Americans believed that "it was 1929 all over again" (Burns, 1956, 319). Roosevelt knew that he would not have the means to satisfy the expectations that his quarantine speech had aroused at home (Dallek, 1979, 153; Brands, 2008, 484). Domestically, for Roosevelt the plan "satisfied his desire to take some dramatic initiative in world affairs while remaining firmly rooted in a policy of peace and neutrality which, it was assumed, the American public would support" (MacDonald, 1981, 41). In fact, Roosevelt considered launching the American initiative on November 11—Armistice Day—to maximize its effect on domestic as well as international opinion.[67] Roosevelt sent Welles as his envoy to Britain in an attempt to get British agreement to moving forward in a joint Anglo-American effort. Diplomatically, FDR probed the Germans' receptiveness to a series of economic concessions and accommodations that could be formalized in the negotiation process proposed by Wells. Yet Roosevelt encountered resistance on both the international front and the domestic front. Secretary of State Hull, especially, opposed the idea (Dallek, 1979, 149). As the weeks passed, the president continued to cajole and pressure Britain and Germany.

The prospects for mobilizing broad consensus around the Welles Plan dimmed, however, as the geostrategic ground shifted. Germany, Italy, and Japan's announcement of the Tripartite Alliance in November 1937, the sinking of the USS *Panay* on the Yangtze River by Japanese warplanes in December, and, perhaps most importantly, Britain's decision to initiate bilateral efforts to appease Germany (and Italy) prevented Roosevelt from getting the backing he needed to launch the Welles Plan. A final round of efforts to move the plan forward was launched again in early 1938. Roosevelt had not abandoned all hope for engineering an international peace conference that could resolve some of Germany's needs and grievances at the negotiating table.[68] At the same time, Roosevelt backed Britain's Chamberlain as he took the lead in appeasing Germany.[69]

---

[67] Frustrated by the disappointing reaction to his October speech, Roosevelt hoped that a dramatic meeting of diplomatic representatives at the White House on Armistice Day would wake up the public to the international challenge the nation faced (Burns, 1956, 352–53).

[68] All together, the White House postponed the Welles Plan five times, the last time in March 1938.

[69] While giving Britain its lead, Roosevelt continued to look for ways to assuage Germany privately, involving back-channel missions by Welles, Norman Davis (the president's roving envoy), and James Mooney (General Motors' vice-president). The Mooney mission offered a number of concessions to Germany, including an acknowledgment of Germany's right to colonies in Africa and economic concessions in the form of tariff relief and a "free gift" of American gold. The mission was scuttled when plans of Mooney's concessions were leaked to the press. The White House denied any involvement in Mooney's mission (Marks,

Like his predecessors Washington and Lincoln, Roosevelt needed security on the cheap. Appeasing Germany proved to be only a temporary fix, but this does not mean that the cross-pressures Roosevelt had to manage from 1936 to 1940 were any less real. As historian C. A. MacDonald 1981, 182) puts it, "The President was caught between the desire to play a larger part in world affairs and the necessity of preserving his political position at home." Indeed, once Chamberlain's efforts failed and Hitler's annexation of Czechoslovakia made appeasement unsustainable domestically, Roosevelt quietly abandoned it in favor of another cost-saving strategy: passing the buck to Britain and France. Starting with his January 1939 State of the Union address, Roosevelt stressed the importance of aiding Britain, France, and others. After the Nazi invasion of Poland that September, the White House launched a major campaign to convince Congress to repeal the arms embargo. The best way to avoid American involvement, Roosevelt argued, was to help the Allies fight Germany.

This was buckpassing. Recognizing that appeasement had failed, Roosevelt looked for ways to aid Britain and France. Roosevelt called Congress into special session to reconsider the neutrality question. After four weeks of fierce debate, Congress repealed the arms embargo. Roosevelt's victory proved to be a turning point, and the White House gradually wrenched greater control over foreign policy from Congress. Steps were taken, sometimes in secret, to shore up Britain's defenses and ratchet up the pressure on Germany. "Cash and carry," "destroyers for bases," and "lend-lease" were the most prominent initiatives. The United States became the "arsenal of democracy," and Britain became America's first line of defense.

From a strategic point of view, Roosevelt hoped that the closer he tied American security to that of Britain, the more likely Germany was to be deterred from further expansion and aggression, and the better positioned the United States would be militarily if and when deterrence failed. As David Reynolds (2001, 43) argues convincingly, Roosevelt's worries about the possibility of the failure of deterrence deepened over the course of 1938 and 1939 as a result of a technological development that seemed to give the advantage to the offense: German airpower. Roosevelt's perceptions of the geostrategic situation were shifting: he was increasingly concerned about the possibility that Hitler would be able to convert airpower into control over Europe, North Africa, and the Middle East and, worse, over the southern portion of the Western Hemisphere (Haglund, 1984; Desch, 1993). Whether these concerns were overblown matters less in explaining U.S. strategy than Roosevelt's growing perception, shared

---

1985, 977–78). See also Craig (1985, 181–84) for other efforts to sound out Hitler and see whether he might be dissuaded diplomatically.

by many around him, that Germany had gained a decisive edge in air-power and that if it were not deterred in Europe, it would eventually convert that edge into influence and control in the Western Hemisphere.[70]

Buckpassing also became more viable politically as Democratic voters grew more anxious about developments in Europe (Berinsky, 2009, 88–89). This shift in public opinion made it easier for Roosevelt to solidify Democratic support in Congress for greater involvement in the European crisis. Ironically, so did the New Deal's failure to deliver on its guarantee of economic prosperity. Many liberal northern Democrats came to see increased military spending as a second-best solution for priming the pump (Trubowitz, 1998, 124–25). Southern Democrats were even more enthusiastic about Roosevelt's increasing emphasis on military preparedness. Military spending was less socially disruptive than redistributive New Deal programs, making it especially appealing to the conservative white southerners (Fry, 2002, 210–12).

This easing of guns-versus-butter trade-offs in the Democratic Party did not make Roosevelt any less subject to the force of external events. But as table 3.3 suggests, it did make it easier for the president to use those events to move Democratic lawmakers his way.[71] Roosevelt's efforts to support Britain, expand the navy, and strengthen the army received solid Democratic backing. This was a far cry from partisan alignments over foreign policy in Roosevelt's first term, when Democrats were just as apt as Republicans to favor neutrality and balk at bigger military

[70] As Reynolds (2001, 178–79) points out, airpower became an "obsession" for Roosevelt. "He believed that the bomber had made America's oceanic barriers obsolescent and had invalidated the concept of a secure Western Hemisphere." Reynolds notes that it also increased the strategic value of real estate (in West Africa, the Caribbean, and, most importantly, the British Isles) that formerly was not so important to the defense of the United States. Reynolds summarizes the logic of the argument: American security depended on British naval dominance; if London fell to German air power, Britain's navy would be neutralized and Germany would be in a position to penetrate Latin America, establish military bases in the region, and ultimately threaten the United States. There was a lot of "ifs" in this scenario, but with the outbreak of war in September 1939, Roosevelt judged it to be a very real one and the costs associated with ignoring it too serious to ignore. Moreover, Roosevelt was not alone in worring about the vulnerability of the Western Hemisphere to Nazi penetration. A detailed and comprehensive study commissioned by the General Staff concluded that "violation of the Monroe Doctrine by European power is not beyond the realm of possibility" (Ehrhart, 1975, 189). For a more sanguine retrospective assessment of the geopolitical situation facing the United States in the hemisphere, see Art (2005).

[71] In addition to roll call votes on lifting the arms embargo, the measures to aid Britain include votes to revise the cash-and-carry system. These votes were coded as votes to aid Britain. Roll call votes to increase spending on the Navy were coded as votes for naval build-up. The preparedness measure includes votes to produce military aircraft and build military bases, to train pilots, to modernize ground forces, to order National Guard and retired army personnel into active service, and to establish a peacetime military draft. Votes for each were coded as votes for preparedness.

TABLE 3.3.
Democratic and Republican support for Franklin Roosevelt's foreign policies,
1937–1941

	Aid Britain		Naval Build-up		Preparedness	
	Party support	*Party cohesion*	*Party support*	*Party cohesion*	*Party support*	*Party cohesion*
Democrats	86%	71%	72%	59%	88%	77%
Republicans	6%	87%	59%	72%	47%	65%

Roll call voting in the U.S. House of Representatives from the 75th and 76th Congresses.
Number of roll call votes: aid Britain (8); naval buildup (12); preparedness (15).

budgets. As late as 1936, more than 85 percent of lawmakers from both
parties voted in favor of neutrality. By 1939, when Roosevelt pressed
Congress to repeal the arms embargo, 88 percent of Democrats backed
him. Only 12 percent of Republicans favored repeal.[72] On foreign policy
matters, politics in Roosevelt's second term was markedly more partisan
than in the first four years.

As Roosevelt shifted from appeasement to buckpassing, it also became
easier for the White House to put Republicans on the political defensive.[73] This was especially true on military rearmament, where many Republicans, looking for political cover, voted with the president. Roosevelt
could play political hardball. During the debate to lift the embargo on
weapons sales to Britain and France, he warned Republicans that they
would be blamed for any failure of foresight to meet the nation's security
needs should war come. "They made a bet," Roosevelt said at a press
conference in August 1939, referring to the Republicans' prediction that
war would not come to Europe. "But if they are not right and we have
another serious international crisis, they have tied my hands, and I have
practically no power to make an American effort to prevent such a war

[72] On the 1936 extension of the 1935 Neutrality Act, 89 percent of Republicans voted
for the extension. Ninety-six percent of Democrats voted in favor. Calculations by author
based on data at Voteview.com.

[73] Roosevelt adopted a two-pronged approach toward Republicans. On the one hand,
he raised the political stakes by shifting the onus of failure to them should war come to
the United States. On the other hand, Roosevelt looked for ways to win over moderate
Republicans to provide some measure of bipartisanship. In the campaign to repeal the arms
embargo, Roosevelt enlisted the support of prominent Republicans like Alfred "Alf" Land-
on and Frank Knox, the 1936 Republican presidential and vice-presidential candidates,
and Henry Stimson, Herbert Hoover's secretary of state. Roosevelt also made Republicans
stakeholders in his foreign policy by appointing Stimson and Knox as secretary of war and
secretary of the navy, and working closely with Wendell Willkie, the Republican candidate
he defeated in the 1940 election, to combat isolationism.

from breaking out. Now that is a pretty serious responsibility" (Brands, 2008, 522).

Roosevelt thus did not move abruptly from domestic policy to foreign policy—from "Dr. New Deal" to "Dr. Win-the-War." James MacGregor Burns (1956, 383) points out that "there was never a sharp turning point when Roosevelt's absorption with domestic matters left off and his concern for foreign affairs began." Even when mobilization did come, Roosevelt was careful to place control over the process "largely in his own hands where he could assure against a breakdown or cancellation of New Deal achievements" (Dallek, 1979, 224). Roosevelt often over-ruled his military chiefs and their business allies when mobilization plans threatened to infringe on the New Deal's social gains. Throughout his presidency, Roosevelt balanced competing geopolitical and domestic de-mands—the need to respond to fast-moving events abroad and economic and political pressures at home. He recognized that any fundamental re-orientation of U.S. grand strategy would, at a minimum, require solid Democratic backing. "It is a terrible thing," Roosevelt told speechwriter Sam Rosenman, "to look over your shoulder when you are trying to lead, and to find no one there" (Brands, 2008, 484).

One measure of the gradual shift in political sentiment in favor of a deepening involvement in the European crisis was increased support for defense spending in Congress. Overall, spending on national defense went from less than 7 percent of federal spending in 1934 to more than 13 percent in 1939, more than 17 percent in 1940, and almost 50 percent in 1941 (Stein, 1993, 109). More striking still were the effects. Even be-fore the United States entered the war at the end of 1941, it had acquired a military production capacity that exceeded that of Germany and Japan combined. By 1939 it was already outproducing Germany and Japan in military aircraft, and had reestablished its edge in naval strength over Japan. Meanwhile, American war plans had begun to change. Blueprints were developed for a two-ocean war, and by the spring of 1939 U.S. mili-tary planners were giving priority to the Atlantic (Stoler, 2000, 23–40; Trachtenberg, 2006, 117–21). If America had to fight, it was going to take the war to the enemy. And in 1941, when Japan attacked Pearl Har-bor, buckpassing gave way to active "offshore balancing" (Mearsheimer, 2001, 237, 252–57) and defensive war against Hitler.

Appeasement Reconsidered

What are the implications for our understanding of why leaders try to appease their foes? The first and perhaps most obvious point is that Washington, Lincoln, and Roosevelt did not engage in the kind of naive thinking that critics of appeasement typically attribute to appeasers. Each displayed a clear-eyed understanding of the international circumstances he confronted.[74] As this chapter shows, each viewed appeasement as a "second-best" strategy: the strategy that offered the best hope of reconciling the needs of security with the demands of domestic politics.

Appeasement is often equated with passivity, yet this analysis shows that this view is too simplistic. Appeasement was a defensive attempt to mollify a potential aggressor. It was also a component of active diplomatic strategies by which Washington, Lincoln, and Roosevelt sought to shape and influence domestic political dynamics inside the target state. In part, each viewed appeasement as a means to tip the domestic balance of power *inside* the adversary state toward leaders and groups whose policy preferences were most favorable (or least hostile) to American interests. Clearly, Washington and Lincoln were more successful in influencing British opinion than Roosevelt was in supporting the "moderates" in Hitler's Germany. One explanation for this difference is that Britain's democratic political system was more open and vulnerable to American pressure and persuasion than Hitler's Germany. Washington and Lincoln were also more successful in their resort to appeasement strategies than Roosevelt, perhaps partly because the first two were using appeasement to mollify an established power, whereas Roosevelt was seeking to check a rising power engaged in an attempt to revise the structure of the international system.

Strictly *Innenpolitik* explanations cannot account for Washington's, Lincoln's, or Roosevelt's diplomacy of appeasement. Their domestic circumstances were ripe for the kind of diversionary war machinations that *Innenpolitik* predicts. Each president could have tried to use expansionist rhetoric and policies to deflect popular attention from domestic setbacks and hardships.[75] None did. In the cases of Washington and Lincoln, cabinet members floated such options—Jefferson in Washington's case, Seward in Lincoln's—and were rebuffed. Whatever short-term domestic relief diversionary war tactics might afford, Washington and Lincoln feared that such gambits would only make a difficult international situ-

---

[74] Roosevelt did not labor under deep illusions about Hitler's intentions. As MacDonald (1981) makes clear, Roosevelt was careful to hedge against failure, preferring to let Britain's Chamberlain take the lead in trying to mollify Germany's grievances. Roosevelt had other cost-saving strategies (i.e., buckpassing) available to him should appeasement prove ineffective.

[75] A domestic explanation that focuses only on distributional gains also comes up short. In each case, economic interests were divided over how best to respond to the foreign threat. This is especially clear in the cases of Washington and Roosevelt. Yet it can also be seen in Lincoln's case, where proslavery border states did not see eye to eye with commercially oriented northern states on the naval blockade and recognition of Haiti and Liberia, to say nothing of Emancipation.

ation worse. Washington and Lincoln focused more on what saber rattling and foreign scapegoating might cost them geopolitically than what it might buy them domestically.

The analysis here also suggests that realist scholars who argue that appeasement sometimes works to mollify one foe to allow the defender to concentrate on another enemy are often right. Lincoln's case shows that this argument can hold when one of those enemies is internal. The limitation of realism is that it cannot explain why appeasement is selected over other seemingly rational (or apparently *more rational*) defensive strategies. The contribution of the present analysis is to explain these apparent "anomalies" by showing that strategic choices are not made in a domestic political vacuum. The realities of party politics gave Washington and Lincoln powerful incentives to conciliate Britain and also gave Roosevelt reason to do the same toward Germany. Similarly, domestic political constraints precluded or greatly raised the costs of other strategic options. These should be understood as deliberate, calculated responses to international *and* domestic incentives. What differentiates appeasers (satisficers) from balancers or expansionists are the parameters of choice—the combination of international and domestic incentives that shape strategic choice. As I show in the next chapter, when those incentives change, so too does the type of strategy leaders prefer.

CHAPTER FOUR

When States Expand

WHY DO STATES SEEK TO EXPAND their political influence abroad? Realists of various persuasions argue that the explanation lies in the international system and the uncertainty its anarchical structure creates for statesmen. As a state's power (meaning its material resources) relative to that of other nations increases, so will its desire to extend its political influence and control internationally—to do what it can, militarily, economically, and diplomatically to enhance its security in an uncertain world (Krasner, 1978; Gilpin, 1981; Zakaria, 1998). Robert Gilpin (1981, 94) calls this the "realist law of uneven growth" and argues that it is the central dynamic of international politics. In order to increase their own security, growing states will actively seek to change their international environment in ways that will offer them greater political, economic, and territorial control. In the realist model, expansionism has little to do with leaders' own political ambitions, or with the interests of their partisans. Leaders expand abroad because they can and when they can, not when it pays *domestically* for them to do so.

THEORIES OF EXPANSIONISM

In this chapter, I argue that foreign ambition cannot be easily divorced from leaders' political self-interest. Expansionist foreign policies aim at extending a nation's geopolitical reach and political control beyond its borders. These efforts can take the classic form of imperial conquest and subjugation of foreign peoples, but there are also other, less formal methods of expansion. Leaders can create protectorates, annex contiguous territories, build military bases, or establish spheres of influence. I argue that leaders are mostly likely to pursue such expansionist goals when they enjoy geopolitical slack *and* when expansionism pays domestically. I show that increased military power does give leaders greater flexibility or latitude in deciding where and how to use that power. However, whether leaders actually try to convert the state's power advantage into international influence depends greatly on their domestic priorities, the interests of their core supporters, and their party's clout in national politics.

I develop this argument by comparing and contrasting the foreign policies of three U.S. presidents: James Monroe, William McKinley, and George W. Bush. All three defined the country's security interests broadly, expanded greatly the nation's military and diplomatic capabilities, and seized opportunities to extend the country's geopolitical reach. They did so, I argue, because there was little strategic danger, and considerable partisan advantage, in pursuing these ambitious foreign policy agendas. Monroe, McKinley, and Bush held office when national security was relatively plentiful. There was minimal risk of strategic encirclement or foreign coercion. In matters of grand strategy, the leaders discussed in this chapter had a free hand abroad. The key question for them was whether to capitalize on their geopolitical advantage.

I show that in each case, strategic choice turned largely on domestic politics. Each of these presidents represented core constituencies that stood to gain, either economically or politically or both, from overseas expansion. A foreign policy that put a premium on extending American power allowed Monroe, McKinley, and Bush to strengthen their party's hold on power. Monroe and McKinley were more successful in this than Bush. There are two reasons for this. First, Bush's foreign policies met with greater international resistance. Second, Bush had less latitude domestically. In contrast to Monroe and McKinley, whose parties dominated national politics, Bush's Republican Party competed on equal footing with the Democrats. The success of an expansionist push obviously does not depend on domestic politics alone, however; it also depends on how other nations respond.

This argument departs from strictly *Innenpolitik* explanations of expansionism. *Innenpolitikers* recognize that expansionism can serve leaders' political self-interest. They attribute the expansionist drive to the dominance of powerful outwardly oriented economic interests, the influence of atavistic militaries and ideological groups, or to the palliative effects of expansion (and even war) on the "public mind" during times of domestic instability and unrest. *Innenpolitik* explanations suffer from two shortcomings, however. First, they ignore or downplay the ways in which geopolitical constraints (i.e., whether security is plentiful or scarce) affect leaders' willingness to countenance expansion. Second, they are insufficiently attentive to the fact that leaders preside over domestic coalitions that may include both pro- and antiexpansionist elements. The leader's coalition may thus have a mixed or ambivalent stake in expansionism, and the leader may find himself or herself better served politically by minimizing foreign commitments and cutting military expenditures. Leaders thus behave in ways that a narrow analytic focus on proexpansion may not predict: even when security is abundant and they are egged on by imperialistic supporters, they may pursue strategies of retrenchment.

In the cases of Monroe, McKinley, and Bush, expansionism was not the only strategy available to the president. When leaders have geopolitical slack, they have the luxury of choice, and in each of these cases, the party out of power (in Monroe's case, factions within his party) urged a less ambitious and less expensive foreign policy. Geopolitically, there would have been little risk in accommodating them. Yet, as these cases illustrate, whether leaders opt for expansionism depends greatly on their domestic priorities, on how much their parties benefit from investing in military power and territorial expansion, and on their party's relative power in the domestic arena. Here, I focus on presidents who stood to gain, electorally and otherwise, from foreign ambition. In the next chapter, I take up presidents who eschewed foreign expansion in the absence of such a compelling partisan incentive to expand.

James Monroe, Republican Factionalism, and the Monroe Doctrine

After the end of the Napoleonic Wars and the War of 1812, and for much of the nineteenth century, U.S. presidents were largely unconstrained by external forces and pressures. The United States was surrounded by two vast oceans and weak neighbors, and effectively protected by a British Royal Navy (at least after the Treaty of Ghent of 1814) that was intent on keeping other European powers out of the Western Hemisphere. Presidents generally had a great deal of geopolitical slack. The historian C. Vann Woodward famously referred to it as "free security." Although presidents could not ignore world politics, they were largely free of the geopolitical constraints that the power struggle between Britain and France had imposed on American leaders in the nation's first decades. For some, this reprieve from the pressures of European power politics was a welcome opportunity to attend to domestic priorities. For others, it was an invitation to expand.

No presidency better exemplifies the expansionism of the era than James Monroe's. On Monroe's watch (1817–25), the United States secured the long-desired prize of Florida, established a "window on the Pacific" by wresting the Pacific Northwest from Spain, and, most famously, "fenced in" the Western Hemisphere as America's sphere of influence.[1] The flexing of national muscle that began with the de facto military conquest of

---

[1] "Fenced in" is historian Richard Van Alstyne's (1960) phrase.

Florida in the Seminole War of 1817 culminated in the promulgation of the Monroe Doctrine in 1823. By defining American interests in hemispheric or regional terms, as opposed to strictly continental terms, the Monroe Doctrine transformed America's definition of its security needs (Gaddis, 2004). It was accompanied by a significant expansion of U.S. naval power and the beginning of what one naval historian has called "the golden age of American 'gunboat diplomacy'" (Hagan, 1991, 92).[2] "American foreign policy," writes another about Monroe's era, "became more offensive than defensive, more aggressive than passive, more self-righteous than studiously impartial" (Stuart, 1982, 160).

The nation also rebuilt and expanded its military defenses after the War of 1812 (Barness, 1966; Millett and Maslowski, 1984). Monroe's war planners devised more flexible and professionalized systems to rapidly mobilize manpower in wartime. A vast military build-up enhanced the nation's capacity to protect its rapidly growing commercial interests in Latin America and beyond (Whitaker, 1964; Long, 1984; Hagan, 1991; Weeks, 1992). The president deployed permanent naval squadrons in major international trouble spots—the West Indies and Caribbean, the east and west coasts of South America, and the Mediterranean. Even the Panic of 1819, which prompted calls for "military retrenchment" in Congress, did not lead Monroe to reconsider his geopolitical ambitions and priorities. Military expenditure dwarfed all other outlays, reversing the normal peacetime pattern (Katznelson, 2002, 91–94). It would be many years before another president would preside over a peacetime military build-up of similar scale or expense.

Why did Monroe invest so heavily in expansionism? Certainly, part of the answer is because he could do so without fear of foreign retaliation. As presidential scholar Stephen Skowronek (1997, 86) notes, "Monroe was the first president to take office free of preoccupations with the survival of the Republic." While this had more to do with Napoleon's defeat in the Old World and the weakening of Spain's position in the New World than with material change in America's own power, the net effect was decisive: America was less geopolitically vulnerable when Monroe took office in March 1817 than it had been before the War of 1812 (W. Cole, 1968, 128; Stuart, 1982, 150; Pelz, 1991, 58–59; Cunningham, 1996, 23; Herring, 2008, 134–35). The British had been fought to a standstill in the Americas and were preoccupied with revolutionary unrest on the European continent. They were ready to sit down and negotiate their differences with the

---

[2] Strictly speaking, the build-up began under James Madison with the Naval Expansion Act of 1816. Monroe, Madison's secretary of war in 1814–15, was the architect of the build-up and continued it as president.

United States over trade matters, the Canadian boundary, and American claims to the mouth of the Columbia River in the Pacific Northwest.

The focus of Monroe's strategic manipulations was Spain. The Napoleonic Wars (1799–1815) had severely weakened Spain's grip on its colonies in the New World. Napoleon's removal of the Bourbon dynasty from the Spanish throne in 1808 had precipitated a political crisis, sparking rebellion in South America. Venezuela and Río de la Plata (Argentina) moved to break free of Spanish control. Chile, Mexico, Colombia, and others followed suit. Years of international conflict and civil war left Madrid too weak to reestablish control over its former dominions in South America, and too vulnerable to resist U.S. pressure for territorial concessions in North America.

Deftly combining diplomacy and force, Monroe and his brilliant secretary of state, John Quincy Adams, successfully isolated Spain from Britain and the other European powers and bullied Madrid into submission. Britain's hand was weakened even further. The payoff was the Transcontinental Treaty of 1819 (Adams-Onís Treaty), which gave the United States possession of Florida and the Pacific Northwest. On the critical question of whether to recognize the newly independent South American states, Monroe favored a "cautious policy—one that expressed sympathy for revolutionists but maintained a position of neutrality" (Cunningham, 1966, 149). The temptation to press America's strategic advantage was tempered by worries that Spain's allies in Europe that made up the Holy Alliance, Russia, Austria, and Prussia, might feel compelled to balance against the United States by restoring Madrid's authority in its former colonies. A policy of "impartial neutrality," Monroe argued, would give "to the colonies [in South America] all of the advantages of a recognition, without any of its perils" (Hart, 2005, 97–98).

In the post-Napoleonic era, the only potential threats to American interests were piracy, smuggling, and instability in Latin America. Of these, only the prospect of "state failure" in the Western Hemisphere was a matter of any geopolitical import (Stuart, 1982, 158; Gaddis, 2004, 17–18; Herring, 2008, 144–46). Both Washington and London feared that the Holy Alliance of Russia, Austria, and Prussia might intervene in Latin America to take advantage of crises in the colonies and to protect their interests. Britain went so far as to propose an Anglo-American alliance to guarantee the Western Hemisphere's security.[3] Those fears quickly

---

[3] In August 1823 the British foreign secretary, George Canning, privately proposed that London and Washington form an alliance to guarantee the security of the newly independent states of Latin America from outside (European) interference, including any attempt by Spain to regain what it had lost or to transfer sovereignty to any other power. The proposal was the subject of a great deal of deliberation in Washington, and a number of those advising Monroe argued in favor of alliance (see below).

passed, and Britain withdrew its offer of alliance, but not before Monroe fully aired the issue and London's offer with his cabinet and with his fellow Virginians, Thomas Jefferson and James Madison. Jefferson and Madison favored the essentially conservative option of alliance, ironically, because both had viewed Britain's geostrategic machinations with great suspicion in the past. John Quincy Adams was dead set against any such arrangement with England. He saw little need for allies and worried about a possible entrapment that could constrain the expansionist ambitions of the United States in the future.[4] In the end, Monroe sided with his secretary of state. At Adams's urging, the president used the occasion of his seventh State of the Union address to claim Latin America and the Western Hemisphere as a U.S. "sphere of influence."

The Monroe Doctrine was the capstone of Monroe's expansionist grand strategy. Claiming the America's to be of "free and independent condition," the Monroe Doctrine declared further colonization "by any European powers" to be unacceptable in the Western Hemisphere. Any attempt by a European power to intervene in the Western Hemisphere would henceforth be considered "dangerous" to the "peace and safety" of the United States—as a threat to the nation's vital interests that would not be tolerated. At the same time, Monroe assured Europe that the United States had no intention of intervening in the ongoing Greek struggle for independence from Turkey.[5] Monroe thus pledged reciprocity: nonintervention in the European sphere of influence in return for no European meddling in America's new sphere of influence. The Monroe Doctrine's three basic principles—noncolonization, nonintervention, and noninterference—added up to "the doctrine of two spheres" (Perkins, 1955, 373).

In declaring the Western Hemisphere "hands off" to Europe's great powers, Monroe was careful to grandfather-in existing British claims in the region. This was an implicit acknowledgment that the geopolitical slack America enjoyed was contingent on British forbearance and on London's concern with international matters closer to home. In addition, Monroe stipulated that he had no intention of tying America's security to the fortunes of the "democracy movements" sweeping Latin America or

---

[4] Adams worried that the purpose behind the British offer was really to get Washington to publicly renounce further acquisitions of territory, most notably Cuba and Texas.

[5] These principles had first been made clear in the spring of 1821. Fighting broke out between Greeks and Turks when the former rebelled to gain independence. The Greek resistance movement modeled its declaration of independence on that of the United States and petitioned European capitals and Washington for formal recognition. A vocal minority in the United States urged Monroe to extend financial and even military aid to the Greek rebels. Monroe expressed his sympathy with the Greek's cause but steered clear of the imbroglio, recognizing that any argument for American involvement on behalf of "freedom" and "democracy" could easily be used against the United States in Latin America.

of involving the United States in European power politics.[6] Many South American revolutionaries had mistakenly interpreted the Monroe Doctrine as an offer of Pan-American solidarity and alliance. Monroe was more cautious than they realized. Although he was ready to recognize the South American independence movements (and had begun doing so in 1822), he had no intention of rejecting London's offer of an "entangling" alliance only to align with America's weak, unstable neighbors to the South.

Monroe's proclamation was bold, but it was not reckless. There was little chance of challenge from any European power, and Monroe and Adams were well aware of this (May, 1975, 65–131). The deterrent to European challenge was not American power per se. What mattered in European capitals were British power and interests, and London was just as opposed to European interference in the Western Hemisphere as Washington was.[7] This is why London had proposed an Anglo-American alliance in the first place, despite all of its doubts and worries about the United States. Secretary of State Adams recognized that geopolitically such a formal alliance was unnecessary; London would tacitly support Monroe's efforts to exclude any European power that did not already have a presence in the Americas.[8] Adams recognized that the United States "had nothing to gain by allying with Great Britain and nothing to fear if it did not" (Weeks, 1992, 180).

Monroe's grand strategy was every bit as consistent with his political self-interest as it was with the nation's newfound geopolitical position. As Ernest May put it in his classic account of the Monroe Doctrine, Monroe's expansive view of America's national interest was in keeping with his desire "to leave the presidency without being followed by recrimination and to be succeeded by someone who would not repudiate his policies" (May, 1975, 255). May recognized that Monroe was playing defense domestically. Monroe was the last of the Virginia Dynasty to hold the presidency. As the heir to the legacy of Jefferson and Madison, Monroe enjoyed a reservoir of public goodwill. But the collapse of the Federalist Party during the War of 1812 and the concomitant "rise of

[6] In this respect, the Monroe Doctrine simply restated one of the key principles (noninvolvement in European affairs) Washington had laid out in his Farewell Address.

[7] According to historian Paul Schroeder (1994b, 635), European capitals were more relieved than anything else by the Monroe Doctrine. The Monroe Doctrine "really suited European wishes, applying to Latin America the principles of mutual non-aggrandizement and renunciation of force which Europe was practicing at home and which helped prevent European competition throughout these years [1815–23] from getting out of hand."

[8] Duncan Campbell (2007, 124) observes that, "for all the suspicion, hostility, and accompanying rhetoric, in this instance (the Monroe Doctrine) Britain and the United Sates had colluded rather than collided."

the new West" (Turner, 1906) exposed deep fissures in the ranks of the ruling Republican Party, and left Monroe vulnerable to ambitious rivals seeking popularity by opposing his presidential programs. For Monroe, expansionism was a means to keep his political rivals at bay and to tamp down factional pressures that threatened to destroy the Republican regime. These pressures were incarnated in Speaker of the House Henry Clay of Kentucky in the West and Senator William Crawford of Georgia and Representative John C. Calhoun of South Carolina in the South. All had their eyes on the presidency, and each commanded a loyal following. As the leader of the "New West," Clay posed the most immediate threat to Monroe's leadership.

Before the War of 1812, fear of the Federalists had been the main source of Republican unity. Solidarity against a common domestic enemy had enabled Thomas Jefferson and James Madison to sustain domestic support for unpopular measures, including Jefferson's 1807 embargo on U.S. trade with Europe during the Napoleonic Wars, and to smooth over differences between Republicans in the South and West. The collapse of the Federalist Party left Republicans without a ready means to reconcile internal party differences (Hockett, 1933, 482–83; Binkley, 1947, 98; McCormick, 1966, 27; Silbey, 1984, 3). The Republicans' challenge was complicated by the economic rise of the West, which was the most important political development of the era, second only to the end of the war with Britain (Turner, 1906, 67). Spectacular growth in the West translated into greater political clout in Congress, sparking a political insurgency that would eventually destroy the Republican alliance between planters and merchants that had dominated American politics since Thomas Jefferson's triumph over John Adams in the presidential election of 1800. While Monroe won the 1816 election against Federalist Rufus King handily, securing the Republican nomination proved difficult.[9] Support for the so-called Virginia–New York alliance was weakening, especially in the West.

Henry Clay was the first national politician to try to harness the West's economic and political potential. Adapting Adam Smith's theory of free trade, Clay advanced a strategy designed to make the nation less dependent on Europe (Hockett, 1917, 89). Clay called it the "American System," but in reality his system of protective tariffs, internal improvements (building canals and roads), and a stronger central bank was biased in

---

[9] Monroe won the November election of 1816 by a landslide. The real battle was inside the Republican Party between Monroe supporters and those backing William Crawford. The Republican congressional caucus, the mechanism Republicans had used since 1800 to select its national ticket, met in March 1816 to nominate a presidential candidate. Monroe barely won, with 65 votes to 54 for Crawford. On the influence of the Virginia–New York alliance in the 1816 election, see Remini (1973).

favor of farmers and factory workers (Hockett, 1933, 478–79). Clay and his many Western followers viewed the protective tariff as means to win over the new dynamic industrial sectors in New York and Pennsylvania and to create stable markets in the United States to dispose of surplus western foodstuffs. Instead of relying on London and other European capitals for markets and credit, the United States would develop a huge home market to meet the growing needs of both the farmer and the factory worker.[10]

The policies that promised prosperity for Western farmers and the Middle-Atlantic manufacturers threatened hardship for southern planters and New England merchants. Tariffs against British imports meant higher prices without compensation for southern and New England consumers, while raising the risk of British economic retaliation. Southern and New England interests considered "internal improvements" such as the Erie Canal (New York governor DeWitt Clinton's "Big Ditch") and the westward extension of the Cumberland road to St. Louis, Missouri, equally harmful. Opposition to the building of new transportation infrastructure to link the West to the Mid-Atlantic was especially strong in Congress, where the South's Old Republicans viewed efforts to connect the West and the Northeast as little more than a tax on southern income—a redistributive scheme that was of little value to planters along the South Atlantic seaboard already close to East Coast markets. To orthodox Republicans, Clay's scheme was anything but an *American* System.

Monroe aligned squarely with Republican orthodoxy (Skowronek, 1997, 102). Like Clay, he claimed to speak for all sections. In truth, Monroe represented the old seaboard South: the South Atlantic states of Maryland, Virginia, the Carolinas, and Georgia (Hockett, 1917, 117). Yet even here, in what once formed the core of Jefferson's electoral coalition, Monroe had to avoid locking horns with the region's favorite sons, Calhoun in South Carolina and Crawford in Georgia. Preserving the old order would be no easy task. In an earlier era, Jefferson and Madison had been able to use the political threat represented by the Federalists to keep potential internal challengers off balance, and to foster Republican unity. Monroe did not have this option. Writing to James Madison, Monroe revealed a keen appreciation of this dilemma: "Where there is an open

---

[10] Clay recognized that Western interests were still too weak to succeed at the national level without political allies. By appealing to the interests of burgeoning industries in New York and Pennsylvania, Clay hoped to win over a decisive number of the states' lawmakers. It was a plausible strategy. Jefferson's alliance between planters and merchants had appealed to New York as a commercial hub. One reason Monroe experienced trouble is that as vast as New York's commerce was, by 1815, "the real interest of the section [New York] was bound up with developing resources of the interior of the nation" (Turner, 1906, 50).

contest with a foreign enemy, or with an internal party, in which you are supported by just principles, the course of action is plain, and you have something to cheer and animate you to action, but we are now blessed with peace, and the success of the late war has overwhelmed the Federal party, so that there is no division of that kind to rally any persons together in support of the administration" (Ammon, 1990, 507–8).

To safeguard the Old Republican order, Monroe had to find new allies to compensate for defections in New York and Pennsylvania in the Middle Atlantic and South Carolina and Georgia in the Old South. Ironically, the key to this effort was securing the support of New England's merchants, traders, and creditors who were once the Republicans' bête noire (W. Cole, 1968, 118–19, 137). Because New England still held a significant share of seats in Congress, the region's backing was now indispensable to Monroe's political survival.[11] Building on his political base in Virginia and elsewhere in the Old South, Monroe sought to cultivate support in New England and among commercially oriented interests in the Middle Atlantic. Monroe was every bit Clay's equal as a political strategist. With the Federalists humiliated and badly weakened by their opposition to the war with Britain, Republican strength in the traditionally Federalist stronghold had surged (Livermore, 1962).[12] New England was ripe for the taking.

Precisely such political considerations influenced Monroe's surprising choice of John Quincy Adams of Massachusetts as secretary of state. The significance of Monroe's choice was not lost on the region's commercial interests, especially because many saw Henry Clay as the odds-on favorite for the post—then considered to be the stepping-stone to the presidency (Ammon, 1990, 361). Monroe's decision to meet with Rufus King, the leader of the vanquished Federalist Party and the head of the New York mercantile establishment, had the same political effect. Monroe "extended forgiveness" to the Federalists for their wartime mistakes and, by meeting with King, signaled his desire to work with New York's *commercial* interests (Weeks, 1992, 48). Most famous of all was Monroe's "national reconciliation" tour up the Atlantic seaboard in the summer of 1817—the first such tour made by an incumbent president since George Washington's

---

[11] In 1817 New England accounted for roughly 22 percent of the seats in Congress. By comparison, the Middle Atlantic region held 31 percent of the seats; the Old South, 33 percent; and the New South 14 percent. Calculations based on congressional data at Voteview. com. Regional classifications are from Hockett (1933).

[12] In 1814 the Federalists controlled 74 percent of New England's seats in Congress. By the time Monroe was inaugurated in 1817, the tables had turned. The Republicans now held 54 percent of the region's congressional seats. Calculations based on congressional data at Voteview.com.

in 1789.[13] Billed as an inspection of the nation's military fortifications, Monroe's real purpose was to garner support in the Northeast. His gambit had the desired political effect. One Boston newspaper announced the start of an "Era of Good Feelings" (Dangerfield, 1952, 95).

Political symbolism and cabinet appointments were not enough to win and sustain New England's support or to keep Monroe's political rivals in the West in check. Monroe had to advance policies that would appeal to the *interests* of New England as well as to those of the South. As Skowronek (1997, 98) argues, Monroe quickly surmised that given his international and domestic constraints and opportunities, it would be easier to "play the rainmaker"—build and sustain a winning coalition—in foreign policy than in domestic policy. It is no accident that historians remember Monroe mostly for his foreign policy activism and achievements.

As it turned out, Spain's hapless situation in North America created opportunities that were tailor-made for coalition building. Ever since Jefferson had secured the Louisiana Purchase (1803), Republicans in the South had rallied to the cause of continental expansion (Horsman, 1989). With Adams in charge of negotiations with Madrid, Monroe also had reason to expect New England to fall into line. The president was not disappointed. In fact, elected officials from every region and both parties of the country backed Monroe's Transcontinental Treaty, even if some of his erstwhile Republican rivals, like Henry Clay, argued that Secretary Adams should have driven a harder bargain over Texas.[14] On other important foreign policy issues—the debate over recognition of the new South American states, naval expansion, and coastal defense—national consensus was not possible because the interests of New England and the South diverged from those of the West. Monroe avoided initiatives in areas that would have generated resistance and thus opened the door to his Republican rivals.

As Monroe anticipated, New England's support for him and his foreign policies was decisive politically. Tables 4.1 and 4.2 summarize party and regional support for Monroe's foreign policies. Thanks to New England votes, the Federalists evidenced much stronger support for Monroe's policies than the regionally divided Republicans did. On the critical question of support for South America revolutionaries, Federalists applauded Monroe's go-slow approach, putting off recognition until after the conclusion of negotiations with Spain over Florida and the Pacific

---

[13] Monroe made a similar tour of the South and West two years later.

[14] Under the treaty, Monroe ceded claim to Texas. For a discussion of the politics surrounding this decision, see Weeks (1992, 166–68).

TABLE 4.1.
Republican and Federalist support for James Monroe's foreign policies, 1817–1825

	Isolate Spain		Protect Commerce		Fortifications	
	Party support	Party cohesion	Party support	Party cohesion	Party support	Party cohesion
Republicans	51%	39%	61%	25%	57%	43%
Federalists	90%	80%	78%	57%	70%	38%

Roll call voting in the U.S. House of Representatives from the 15th through 18th Congress. Number of roll call votes: isolate Spain (16); protect commerce (4); fortifications (13).

Northwest (Weeks, 1992, 88–91).[15] The vote reflects the fact that like the cotton-exporting South (whose elected representatives also generally backed Monroe's policies aimed at isolating Spain), New England's prosperity depended primarily on expanding transatlantic trade (Turner, 1906, 29). Many East Coast merchants looked eagerly upon South America's markets, but the promise of profits there had to be weighed against the risk that recognition would compel Europe to intervene. Withholding recognition from the South American regimes was the price to pay for protecting established currents of transatlantic commerce.

By contrast, support for recognition of the new South American regimes was strongest in the West. Unlike New England and the South, the West derived little benefit from transatlantic trade. Merchants of the Ohio and Mississippi valleys looked southward and viewed diplomatic recognition as a first step in opening up the South American market.[16] So did the representatives they sent to Washington. Henry Clay, Monroe's most vocal critic in Congress, led the charge. Using his position as Speaker of the House, Clay attacked the president's authority to decide when and

[15] Votes against South American recognition are coded as efforts to isolate Spain. This is because recognition would have caused the European powers to rally around Spain. Clay's legislative maneuvering on behalf of recognition thus directly challenged Monroe's diplomacy designed to isolate Madrid from its European allies, win Spanish concessions at the negotiating table, and minimize the risk of European intervention on behalf of the Spanish monarchy. In addition to roll call votes on South America, this category includes votes on Monroe's use of force on Amelia Island, on upholding existing Spanish-American treaties regarding expatriation, and on an attempt by Clay to usurp presidential prerogative by having Congress send a minister to Argentina. I drew on Nielsen (1968) to code many of these votes.

[16] Westerners also saw closer ties to South America as a means to gaining access to an alternative source of gold and silver to reduce the region's dependence on eastern banks (Weeks, 1992, 94).

TABLE 4.2.
Regional support for James Monroe's foreign policies, 1817–1825

	Isolate Spain	Protect Commerce	Fortifications
New England	74%	76%	56%
Mid-Atlantic	57%	63%	63%
Old South	60%	64%	59%
New West	40%	47%	49%

Roll call voting in the U.S. House of Representatives from the 15th through 18th Congress.
Number of roll call votes: isolate Spain (16); protect commerce (4); fortifications (13).

where to recognize South America's revolutionaries. Clay viewed the issue of opening up South America as complementing his pro-Western agenda for economic development.

Western opposition to Monroe's foreign policies is the key to explaining the comparatively higher levels of support that Monroe received from Federalists than from his fellow Republicans. When the same votes are used to measure regional support for Monroe's foreign policies, the logic of Monroe's strategy is revealed. As table 4.2 indicates, Monroe's grand strategy appealed to every region *except* the West.[17] Support was strongest in New England, but support in the Old South and the Middle Atlantic was enough to ensure that Monroe never lost a critical foreign policy vote. Only when support in the South and New England wavered (as it sometimes did over military fortification and military mobilization) did Monroe's Republican rivals enjoy any success. Yet even on these issues, Monroe usually prevailed (Skeen, 1972; C. Smith, 1976).[18] Traditional Republican fears about how a large peacetime military might be used domestically had not disappeared, but they had eased considerably now that the Federalist Party was a shadow of its former self. The president had his way with Congress in foreign affairs. This was not the case in domestic affairs, where Monroe's Republican rivals often blocked his policies.

[17] Members of Congress in table 4.2 are classified by region. New England includes Connecticut, Maine, Massachusetts, New Hampshire, Rhode Island, and Vermont. The Middle Atlantic includes Delaware, New Jersey, New York, and Pennsylvania. The Old South includes Maryland, Georgia, North Carolina, South Carolina, and Virginia. The New West includes Alabama, Illinois, Indiana, Kentucky, Louisiana, Mississippi, Missouri, Ohio, and Tennessee. Regional classifications are based on Hockett (1933).

[18] Clay was more successful on the tariff question, which northeasterners favored but southerners opposed. See Strahan et al. (2000).

For Monroe, a strategy of expansionism was a win-win situation. There was little political risk of foreign retaliation or of losing domestically. Southern Republicans, who had long favored territorial expansion and benefited from commercial expansion, had little incentive to coalesce against Monroe's efforts to extend the nation's geopolitical reach and promote foreign trade.[19] Western Republicans favored a more aggressive approach toward Latin American recognition, but they could not muster sufficient support outside the West to force Monroe to shift strategy. For their part, Federalists had little incentive to oppose Monroe's grand strategy: the president's foreign policy agenda advanced the interests of New England's commercial shipping interests as much as those of the southern planters. Expansionism did not restore the flagging Jeffersonian alliance; rather, it allowed Monroe to hold on to power and pass it on to his successor, Adams, at a time when traditional domestic policy tools no longer sufficed to build a nationally dominant political coalition. For the first time in the nation's history, international and domestic politics aligned decisively in favor of expansionism: the opportunity to project American power coincided with domestic coalition-building incentives to do so.

William McKinley, Cuba, and the Threat of Domestic Populism

During William McKinley's tenure (1897–1901), the United States brandished an assertive, outward-looking foreign policy, geared to opening new markets in Latin America and East Asia. Few presidents' actions have had a more far-reaching impact on the direction of U.S. foreign policy than McKinley's. Though it is now commonplace among historians to say so, many of McKinley's contemporaries also saw things in exactly this way. While critical of McKinley's expansionist policies, Woodrow Wilson nevertheless acknowledged McKinley's influence on the country's foreign policy. In the fifteenth edition of *Congressional Government*, Wilson observed that "no president, except Lincoln," had exercised as much influence on foreign affairs since the nation's earliest years (W. Wilson, 1900, preface).

What makes McKinley intriguing is that he was a reluctant expansionist. Indeed, historians have struggled to explain McKinley's outward ambition. How could a president as eager to avoid war as McKinley clearly was in his dealings with Spain over Cuba, so suddenly shift course, intervening in the Philippines, annexing Hawaii, and seizing Cuba, Puerto Rico, Guam, and the Wake Islands? Early analysts tried to square the

---

[19] On Republican attitudes toward territorial expansion, see Horsman (1989).

circle by arguing that McKinley was a passive president who was stampeded into expansion by a yellow press and a xenophobic public (e.g., Pratt, 1936; May 1961). Subsequent scholarship has revealed a more nimble, strategic, and savvy commander in chief, one closer to Woodrow Wilson's view of the president as a confident, proactive, hands-on statesman (e.g., Trask, 1981; Gould, 1982; J. Offner, 1992). In this view, McKinley took office in March 1897 believing that the Cuban problem could be best handled diplomatically—a judgment based on his reading of geopolitical circumstance and domestic constraint. Yet by the spring of 1898, these international and domestic realities had changed enough to make expansionism far more palatable, and even useful, politically, for McKinley.

Because McKinley's grand strategy was defined by his decision to go to war with Spain over Cuba, the analysis here focuses largely on the Spanish-American War and the events that led up to it.

The origins of the war date back to 1868, when Cuban nationalists rebelled against Spanish colonial rule.[20] The rebellion lasted until 1878, when Spain managed to buy a temporary peace by promising colonial reforms. Most of those reforms never materialized, and in 1895 a new rebellion against Spanish rule broke out on the island. Larger and better led, the Cuban insurgency of 1895–98 devastated the island's economy. Spain responded by sending more than 200,000 troops to Cuba. In an effort to isolate the rebels from the local population, Madrid also moved hundreds of thousands of Cuban peasants from their homes to cities and towns controlled by Spanish troops, even though few preparations had been made to accommodate the huge influx of people into urban areas. Madrid's "reconcentration" strategy worsened the economic situation and triggered a humanitarian crisis.

By early 1897 word of the disaster in Cuba had spread in the United States. Domestic pressure mounted to protect U.S. business investments and relieve the human suffering. At first, Republicans criticized the Cleveland administration for tolerating Spanish attacks on American property and to Madrid's abuse of the Cuban people. When McKinley assumed the presidency in 1897, Democrats were quick to take up the cause of Cuban independence, seeing it as a possible means to divide Republicans and, more importantly, to smooth over a split within the Democratic Party that had surfaced in the 1896 presidential campaign over the silver question.

McKinley's initial judgment was that diplomacy would be sufficient to wrest Cuba from Spain. It was based on two critical assumptions. First, McKinley believed that given time and an opportunity to bow out grace-

---

[20] For a good concise history of the war, see J. Offner (2004).

fully, a strategically overextended Spain would make the necessary concessions to the United States by granting Cuba its freedom (Gould, 1982, 30; Pérez, 1998, 11–12).[21] Thus, Spain would relinquish Cuba peacefully.[22] Second, should war come and the United States fail to defeat Spanish forces quickly, McKinley believed that European capitals would intercede on Spain's behalf, demanding a cease-fire and arbitration. This raised the risks and costs of adventurism to the United States, and to McKinley personally. Gradually, however, McKinley came to see that he had underestimated Spanish intransigence and overestimated European solidarity, and thus the Europeans' ability to intervene effectively on Spain's behalf.[23] As tensions between Washington and Madrid rose, support softened in Europe for Spain's cause, especially in London.

As a practical matter, Britain was the only nation that McKinley had to worry about, other than Spain itself. Were London to favor international arbitration of the Cuban crisis, France, Germany, or Austria-Hungary would have found it easier to intervene diplomatically on Spain's behalf.[24] However, by the late 1890s British leaders were looking to improve relations with the United States and reduce Britain's strategic presence and costs in the Americas (Neale, 1966; Kennedy, 1981, 23–24; Rock, 2000, 25–47). A series of confrontations over Brazil, Nicaragua, and Venezuela during Cleveland's presidency had made it clear to British officials as early as 1896, long before the Spanish-American War, that they could no

[21] McKinley's opposition to Spanish claims of sovereignty in Cuba did not mean that he automatically favored Cuban independence and self-rule. Indeed, McKinley threatened to veto any congressional resolution recognizing Cuban independence. On this point, see Pérez (1998, 12–15).

[22] McKinley's initial reluctance to use military force against Spain is sometimes mistakenly construed as support for the status quo in the Caribbean and elsewhere. From the very start of his administration, McKinley sought to get Spain to give up Cuba. The only question was how and when. A similar preoccupation with means and timing shaped McKinley's approach to the question of Hawaii. Just as he favored the rebel cause in Cuba, McKinley favored Hawaiian annexation—a Republican objective since Benjamin Harrison's administration. However, here too McKinley found it prudent politically to wait for a propitious moment to consummate annexation. See Gould (1982, 12–13, 25, 30, 136).

[23] There is some question of whether Spain would have made the necessary concessions on Cuba if the Spanish prime minister, Antonio Cánovas del Castillo, had not been assassinated in August 1897 (J. Offner, 1992, 53).

[24] The possibility of foreign retaliation over Cuba was never great, but whatever chance there was, it quickly receded in the face of Spanish intransigence over Cuba. London's behavior was crucial for McKinley, because, in the absence of British calls for arbitration, any demands issued by France, Russia, Germany, or Austria-Hungary could be fended off without much difficulty. Indeed, European capitals had to balance support for Spain against the possibility that diplomatic action against the United States in the Caribbean would strengthen Anglo-American relations, giving London a freer hand in dealing with Europe (J. Offner, 1992, 59).

longer stand in the path of America's advance in the hemisphere (Neale, 1966, 214; Bourne, 1967, 340; LaFeber, 1993, 125).[25] British efforts to improve relations met with a positive response from the new president, who saw advantage in improved Anglo-American relations. By the time the crisis with Spain erupted into war, Britain "was conspicuously friendly to the United States" (Bailey, 1942, 511).

As concerns about European retaliation waned, Republican demands for war waxed. When McKinley first entered office in March 1897, the powerful business elites on whom he depended worried that war with Spain would mean trade disruptions, increased volatility on Wall Street, and possibly a currency crisis (C. Campbell, 1974, 247–48; LaFeber, 1993, 141–42; Kirshner, 2007, 44–51; Narizny, 2007, 94). The United States was still laboring under the weight of a depression that had begun during Grover Cleveland's administration. Yet the economy showed signs of improvement in the summer and fall of 1897. As it became increasingly evident that London was firmly on America's side in the dispute with Spain, business opposition to the use of military force to "free" Cuba began to evaporate (Phillips, 2003, 91; Narizny, 2007, 94–95). Enthusiasm for the money to be made began to mount. By the spring of 1898, Republican leaders in Congress who had largely supported McKinley's diplomatic track on Cuba were telling the White House that they could no longer hold back a rising tide of Republican support for military action.

With the 1898 midterm elections approaching, many Republican lawmakers feared a Democratic sweep or, worse, the return of "Bryanism."

---

[25] In 1893 British interests, fearful of growing U.S.-Brazilian commercial ties, quietly backed a rebellion by the Brazilian navy against the Brazilian government. When the Brazilian navy imposed a blockade of the harbor of Rio de Janeiro to bring the government down, Washington ordered U.S. warships to accompany American merchant ships, forcing the rebels to relent and ending the revolt. A second confrontation occurred the next year in Central America. The new Nicaraguan regime of General José Santos Zelaya attempted to take control of a British protectorate on the Atlantic that many envisioned as the entrance for a Nicaraguan isthmian canal. London threatened to retaliate with military force, posing a dilemma for the Cleveland administration. On one hand, British action would have violated the Monroe Doctrine. On the other hand, General Zelaya's action threatened U.S. business interests, which operated freely in the British protectorate. Seeking to protect America's sphere of influence while avoiding a war, Cleveland promised to protect British interests while pressuring the Nicaraguan government to accept U.S. authority in the protectorate, thus supplanting London. The third confrontation arose over disputed territory between British Guiana and Venezuela. Though greatly overblown, the Venezuela crisis of 1895 did concern important interests—control over commerce into South America and the inviolability of the Monroe Doctrine. Claiming that the Monroe Doctrine gave the United States the right to intervene in the dispute between Britain and Venezuela, Cleveland pressured London and Caracas to resolve the issue through arbitration. In all three cases, London gave way to Washington's demands. For a good summary of the episodes and their implications for Anglo-American relations, see LaFeber (1993, 121–26).

Although McKinley had defeated William Jennings Bryan handily in the 1896 election, his victory was hard-won, and Republican strategists believed that the outcome was due in large part to Bryan's political inexperience. For two decades Republicans and Democrats had competed on virtually equal footing in national elections, where voter turnout rates were often as high as 89 percent. Party identification rates ran nearly as high. As a result, national elections were won or lost at the margin (H. Wayne Morgan, 1963; Burnham, 1970; Kleppner, 1979; James 2000). Voters who did not align squarely with either major party regularly determined the outcome. This meant that Republicans spent a good deal of time worrying about Bryanism. The populist resentment that Bryan had tapped remained a potent force in many Republican districts, where the cry of "free silver and free Cuba" could be heard (J. Offner, 1992, 153).[26] If the Cuban issue was allowed to fester, Republicans feared that Democrats would retake Congress and perhaps even the White House in 1900. Already, gubernatorial elections in the fall of 1897 had gone against the GOP.

Geopolitical opportunity and the pressure of party politics combined to produce McKinley's turn to expansionism. Once McKinley committed to war with Spain, Republican control of Congress made war momentum easy to sustain. The U.S. Navy made quick work of Spanish squadrons in Manila. When news of Admiral Dewey's victory in the Philippines arrived from Hong Kong, the president's political stock soared domestically. John Hay, the U.S. ambassador to Britain and soon-to-be secretary of state, upon learning of Spain's defeat, told his fellow Republicans Theodore Roosevelt and Henry Cabot Lodge that things are moving "our way." "I do not see a ghost of a chance of Bryanism in the next few years" (Logevall, 2002, 99).

With military success following military success, public opinion discounted the government's blunders (e.g., the army's mismanagement of health conditions in the Philippines that led to the loss of 2,500 troops from disease). And as domestic support for McKinley's leadership increased, the Republicans invested ever more heavily in this winning political formula. Military spending on the navy and army spiked, and new initiatives to expand America's presence overseas easily gained domestic political traction. The naval build-up meant jobs for northern workers, which in turn meant votes for Republican politicians. While most of the money for shipbuilding went to safe Republican districts, the expansionist grand strategy generated other benefits that were more widely distributed.

---

[26] Bryan called for the free and unlimited coinage of silver bullion at the ratio of 16 to 1 to gold, roughly twice the market value. As an inflationary measure, free silver was especially attractive to debt-ridden farmers.

Military spending was one of the means the Republicans used to recycle the government's budgetary surpluses through the domestic economy and keep the protective tariff that so favored their partisan interests. The huge budgetary surpluses that the federal government ran year in and year out were generated by the high tariff that Republicans slapped on imported manufactured goods. The tariff was the main source of national revenue during the Gilded Age (accounting on average for 50 percent of total federal revenue) (Trubowitz, 1998, 85). It paid handsome political dividends for the Republican Party.[27] It not only protected manufacturing interests and workers in the Northeast, who were closely aligned with the Republican Party, but also produced huge revenues that Republicans "targeted at segments of the population that were otherwise hostile to Republican tariff policy—for example, workers and consumers in the North as well as farmers in the West" (Pollock, 2009, 235). Expansionism generated military spending that turned customs duties into political capital that was spent to counter the powerful and seductive appeal of populism in the West (Trubowitz, 1999, 119–20).

Given the huge political dividends Republicans reaped from expansionism, it is not surprising that Democrats opposed it vociferously. Bipartisanship during the 1890s was rare—in foreign policy as well as domestic policy. Whatever misgivings Republicans voiced in party caucuses about McKinley's handling of the Cuban situation, on the House floor the Republicans were a model of party unity. As table 4.3 indicates, Republican support for creating a more modern, professional army was rock solid.[28] Republican support for naval build-up was softer, but even here it averaged nearly 70 percent, 40 percent greater than Democratic support.

Democrats lined up solidly against McKinley's expansionism. Democratic constituencies, mostly southern, agrarian, and export-oriented, saw little advantage in war, imperialism (in Cuba or elsewhere), or naval build-up. Recent experience with the 1890 "Force Bill"—a move to give federal courts power to supervise elections in congressional districts—made Democrats apprehensive about policies that would increase the coercive power of the federal government (Trubowitz, 1998, 48–51, 70–75). What assurances were there that a larger, more professionalized military needed to suppress political resistance in foreign lands would not someday be used to coerce citizens at home? Opposing expansion certainly helped Democrats in their districts, but as long as the Republicans

---

[27] Democrats in Congress, especially those hailing from the export-oriented, cotton-producing South, opposed high tariffs but rarely succeeded in rolling them back.

[28] Votes on U.S. policy toward Cuba were coded on the basis of Gould's (1982) account of McKinley's foreign policy preferences. Votes in favor of naval spending and military modernization were coded as support for McKinley's foreign policies. See Millet and Maslowski (1984, 269–74) and Trubowitz (1998, 37–52).

TABLE 4.3.
Republican and Democratic support for William McKinley's foreign policies,
1897–1901

	Secure Cuba		Naval Build-up		Modernize Army	
	Party support	Party cohesion	Party support	Party cohesion	Party support	Party cohesion
Republicans	97%	92%	68%	54%	94%	88%
Democrats	16%	89%	26%	65%	19%	74%

Roll call voting in the U.S. House of Representatives from the 55th and 56th Congresses.
Number of roll call votes: secure Cuba (19); naval buildup (10); modernize army (13).

retained control of Congress, Democratic opposition posed little threat to McKinley's approach to matters of war and peace.

The pace and direction of McKinley's expansionism were shaped by calculations of geopolitical slack. Even after Spain was defeated, the president recognized that there were geographic limits to how far the Republicans could reliably project U.S. power. In Latin America, American power was dominant. The new entente with London gave McKinley a more or less free hand in the region.[29] But the United States did not enjoy the same latitude in East Asia (Zakaria, 1998, 162–63). There, France, Germany, Britain, and Japan stood too strong to allow McKinley to commit to more than lofty principles, such as those expressed in Secretary of State John Hay's famous Open Door notes.[30] Hay privately acknowledged to McKinley that the United States could do little to enforce adherence to those principles in Asia: "The inherent weakness of our position is this: we do not want to rob China ourselves, and our public opinion will not permit us to interfere, with an army, to prevent others from robbing her. Besides, we have no army. The talk in the papers about 'our preeminent moral position giving us the authority to dictate to the world' is mere flap-doodle" (LaFeber, 1993, 175).[31]

---

[29] To be sure, McKinley was careful not to push London any farther than necessary to achieve his geopolitical or partisan ends. In 1900, for example, McKinley muted American criticism of Britain's war against the Boers in South Africa (1899–1901), by squelching a pro-Boer plank in the 1900 Republican platform (H. Wayne Morgan, 1963, 225, 350–51).

[30] The Open Door notes asked all of the great powers with interests in China to preserve the Middle Kingdom's territorial and political integrity.

[31] Hay was also aware that domestic support "in certain quarters of the 'Senate and people'" for decisive American action in East Asia was quite limited. This was especially true if Washington was seen as cooperating actively with London (Neale, 1966, 201).

Where the risks of strategic failure were relatively low, as they proved to be in Latin America, McKinley had little to fear and much to gain domestically from embracing expansionism, and doing so on his own political timetable. By contrast, in Asia, where McKinley had substantially less room for maneuver, he defined American interests more narrowly, even when powerful Republican interests lobbied for more assertive action to block European and Japanese ambition.[32] The case underscores the fact that geopolitical slack varies not only over time but also cross-sectionally—that is, from one region of the world to another. This proves to be key in explaining George W. Bush's response to the attacks of September 11.

George W. Bush, September 11, and the Promise of Party Realignment

George W. Bush's presidency will be forever associated with the September 11 attacks and the Iraq War. In many realist accounts, the war on terrorism and Bush's war in Iraq are viewed as part of a larger grand strategy aimed at "locking in" America's strategic advantages in an era of unipolarity and U.S. primacy. From this perspective, Bush's forceful and unilateral projection of U.S. power had little if anything to do with domestic politics. Realists argue that Bush's expansive foreign policy is better understood as a logical, if poorly conceived and executed, effort to capitalize on America's unrivaled position in the international system (see, e.g., Jervis, 2003, 2009; Layne, 2006). Disproportionate international power gave Bush a strong incentive to deepen America's influence in the Middle East, a resource-rich region of the world of vital geopolitical significance.

I explain why a strictly realist reading of the determinants of Bush's grand strategy is inadequate, and how my theory of executive choice can improve our understanding of why Bush pursued an expansionist grand strategy. My purpose is not to show that realists are wrong about Bush. Indeed, because of the unipolar structure of world politics, Bush did have a freer hand internationally than his Cold War era predecessors did. However, unipolarity alone cannot explain Bush's grand strategy. Bill Clinton was also president during America's "unipolar moment," but he did not engage in offensive war or "big stick" diplomacy (see chapter 5 for an analysis of Clinton's grand strategy). Moreover, George Bush him-

---

[32] This did not preclude using military force when American lives and property were at risk. In early 1900, McKinley responded, along with the European powers and Japan, to the Boxer Rebellion in China by sending five thousand troops to protect property and restore order. On the episode, see Herring (2008, 331–35).

self did not arrive in Washington bent on projecting U.S. power militarily. Like McKinley, Bush entered office preoccupied with domestic matters. He did not change course, I argue, until it became politically advantageous to do so.

During the Cold War, the central strategic question facing presidents was how to balance against Soviet power. With the collapse of the Soviet empire, the key question became how to capitalize on the increased security that unipolarity afforded. Republicans and Democrats disagreed sharply on the answer (Trubowitz, 1993; Kupchan and Trubowitz, 2007). Democrats generally viewed the "unipolar moment" as an opportunity to retrench geopolitically and to devote more attention and federal resources to economic and social problems that they contended were neglected during the Cold War, especially during and after the Reagan years. By contrast, most Republicans considered the unipolar moment as an opportunity for America to press its geopolitical advantage in critical regions such as East Asia and the Persian Gulf, to provide an added measure of security by building up U.S. defenses, and to check Democratic designs for spending the so-called peace dividend. Worried about the redistributive consequences of the Democrats' social agenda, Republicans favored combining hefty tax cuts with continued investment in Pentagon spending.[33]

---

[33] Much of the post–Cold War struggle over foreign policy originated in uneven patterns of growth that that gave rise to the new sectionalism that political analysts referred to as the struggle between "Red America" and "Blue America" (Black and Black, 2007). Higher tax rates, labor costs, and energy prices in the Northeast made it harder for elected officials from Blue states to find common ground on foreign and domestic policy with Red state officials who had competing economic concerns. So did the uneven effects of globalization (Trubowitz, 1998, 196–219; Kupchan and Trubowitz, 2007). The outsourcing of American jobs hit the aging industrial centers of the Northeast especially hard. Well-paying, unionized jobs in manufacturing were the first to be lost as production lines were moved abroad and cheap imports arrived from low-wage economies. The Northeast moved to the forefront of efforts to reign in America's commitment to free trade. Free trade's most reliable advocates came from the South and, especially, the Mountain West: ironically, the one part of the country that had consistently opposed Roosevelt's efforts to liberalize trade in the 1930s. The South and the West also provided the surest support for foreign policies that put a premium on military power.

Changes in the economic and political geography of military spending and production made it harder for politicians from different parts of the country to find common ground on national security policy in the post–Cold War years (Trubowitz, 1998, 219–32). Since the 1970s, Pentagon spending on military procurement and research and development benefited the South and West at the expense of the Northeast, contributing to the decline of the manufacturing sector in the North. In addition, southern and western states that make up the so-called gunbelt have consistently received a larger share of the resources spent on military bases and personnel. Seen in this light, the fights between Republicans and Democrats over national security in the 1990s were battles in a larger political struggle for control of the national political economy.

In the 1990s, the Democrats held the upper hand because foreign policies that put a premium on military power were a difficult sell domestically. In the aftermath of the Cold War, security appeared plentiful to most voters (Lindsay, 2000). This is why George Bush had such strong incentives to focus his 2000 presidential campaign on domestic issues. Running as a "compassionate conservative," Bush hoped to blunt the Democrats' electoral advantage on domestic issues such as education and health care (Skowronek, 2008, 117–49). On foreign policy matters, Bush was careful to qualify and hedge his national security agenda (Leffler, 2004, 24–25; Dueck, 2006, 148–52; Chollet and Goldgeier, 2008, 294–310).[34] Even after he assumed the presidency, he sought to harmonize core Republican interests with mainstream public opinion and especially with the preferences of moderate, independent voters who put a premium on domestic concerns (Price and Coleman, 2004).[35] Such political hedging was no longer necessary after September 11, 2001. National security issues—terrorism, weapons of mass destruction, and Saddam Hussein's Iraq—now dominated opinion polls.

I argue that the September 11 attacks resolved the tension that existed between what America's international position made possible geopolitically and what domestic opinion would allow the militarist wing of the Republican Party to get away with. With the collapse of the Twin Towers, Republican preferences for a heavy investment in national security, out of public favor since the fall of the Berlin Wall, were suddenly in sync with mainstream domestic sentiment. Having appointed so many hard-line Republicans to top national security posts, Bush was well positioned to implement a more aggressive agenda.[36] Uncertainty in Democratic ranks about how best to respond also made Bush's slim majority in Congress less of an impediment than it would otherwise have been.[37] By thrusting

[34] During the campaign, the only national security issues that Bush discussed in any depth were military preparedness and national missile defense. He pledged to modernize the nation's military capabilities and to deploy a missile defense system, but he was vague about costs and timetables. See Mann (2004, 255–56).

[35] In his inaugural address, Bush devoted only a few sentences to foreign policy and national security and in his first address to Congress a few weeks later, identified education his "top priority" (Wirls, 2010, 94–95).

[36] Though Bush appointed moderate Colin Powell as secretary of state, he relied more heavily on Vice President Dick Cheney and Secretary of Defense Donald Rumsfeld. Cheney and Rumsfeld strongly favored investing in military power and were skeptical of substituting multilateral diplomacy for the exercise of raw U.S. power. Neoconservative Republicans who espoused the use of U.S. power to achieve ideological (e.g., "democracy promotion") as well as geopolitical ends aligned easily with Cheney and Rumsfeld's brand of assertive nationalism. On Bush's foreign policy team, see Mann (2004).

[37] At the start of the 107th Congress (2001–2), Republicans held a 221 to 211 majority in the House over Democrats. (When Congress convened in January 2001, there were 2

Bush into an unassailable leadership position, the September 11 attacks initially put Democrats on the defensive (Krebs and Lobasz, 2007; Skowronek, 2008, 139).

As realists rightly point out, the terrorist attacks did not undermine America's position as a hegemonic power. Rather, the attacks centered all attention on the seriousness of a relatively new and hard-to-measure source of international threat, and dramatically shifted the terms of public debate over national priorities. George W. Bush veered sharply toward military power. Secretary of Defense Donald Rumsfeld's promise of a "revolution" in the country's war-fighting capabilities suddenly seemed achievable. The Pentagon's budget soared.[38] The defense budget grew at an average of nearly 7 percent a year (Wirls, 2010, 134–35). Military spending increased from the post–World War II low of 16.1 percent of the federal budget in 1999 to 21 percent by 2008. Spending on uniformed military personnel (excluding *supplemental* spending to wage the Iraq and Afghanistan wars) increased 40 percent over per capita spending levels for 2000 (Wirls, 2010, 136).[39]

Bush also gave multilateral cooperation and international institution building short shrift (Ikenberry, 2003; Martin, 2004; Skidmore, 2005, 223; Dueck, 2006, 152). Soon after entering office, Bush renounced the Kyoto Protocol, International Criminal Court, and Antiballistic Missile Treaty. He declined offers of NATO involvement in the war against the Taliban in Afghanistan and then went to war in Iraq without United Nations authorization and with only a handful of allies. Through much of his first term, Bush and his top advisers were openly dismissive of international institutions and multilateralism. The main exception was in the area of trade policy, where Bush made renewing fast-track authority

---

independents and 1 vacancy.) In the Senate, the party balance was even closer: 50 Republicans to 50 Democrats. In June 2001 Senator Jim Jeffords of Vermont, a moderate Republican, declared himself an independent and announced that he would vote with the Democrats, giving the Democrats a one-vote majority in the Senate. The 2002 midterm elections gave Republicans a majority in both chambers, which they held until the Democrats gained control of the House and Senate after the 2006 elections.

[38] In FY 2000, the U.S. defense budget was just over $300 billion. By FY 2008, it had risen to just over $500 billion (Wirls, 2010, 135). (These figures do not include supplemental appropriations for the Afghanistan and Iraq wars.)

[39] The substantial federal surplus that the Congressional Budget Office (CBO) was projecting for the next decade only made it easier to win public and congressional support for such a heavy investment in military power. The $282 billion surplus the CBO was projecting for 2001 was expected to swell to $5.6 trillion over the next decade (CBO, 2001). While most of that surplus would ultimately be eaten up by the huge tax cuts that Bush and Republicans rammed through Congress, it seemed to many Americans at the time that it would be possible to have both guns and butter (Wirls, 2010, 97).

a priority.[40] Bush used that authority in 2001 to help launch the Doha Development Round of multilateral negotiations under the auspices of the World Trade Organization (WTO). When the Doha negotiations stalemated over differences between advanced industrial and emerging nations, the Bush administration modified its strategy, negotiating various regional and bilateral agreements with countries in Central and South America, the Middle East, Southeast Asia, and the Asia-Pacific region (Mastanduno, 2005). Bush used these accords to reward countries (e.g., Australia) that actively contributed to the administration's war on terrorism.

None of this was an easy sell domestically. An initial surge in bipartisan unity behind the Bush administration's war on terrorism followed the attacks on the World Trade Center and the Pentagon (Trubowitz and Mellow, 2005; Busby and Monten, 2008). This subsided quickly, however. It gave way to partisan debate over how to deal with Saddam Hussein's Iraq. Should UN inspectors be given more time to determine whether the Iraqi leader was developing a nuclear capability? Could American objectives in Iraq continue to be met by relying on a strategy of containment? Should the United States act only in concert with its NATO allies? These debates revealed strong and continuing partisan disagreement over the proper scope of ambition and new investment in national security (A. Abramowitz and Saunders, 2005; Jacobson, 2007; Shapiro and Block-Elkon, 2007; Beinhart, 2008; Berinsky, 2009, 100–111). So did Bush's efforts to ramp up the defense budget and, especially, to increase spending on national ballistic missile defense. Bush's efforts to promote liberalized trade under the guise of fighting terrorism also divided Congress along sharp partisan lines. As table 4.4 indicates, Republicans and Democrats were miles apart on the Iraq War, missile defense, and trade promotion.[41]

Post-9/11 domestic political calculations had a decisive effect on American grand strategy. For Bush there were reputational dangers in underplaying the risks of another attack on American soil (Mueller, 2005). There were also potential electoral rewards in highlighting those risks.

---

[40] In 1998 Democrats in Congress voted against President's Clinton's request to renew fast-track authority to negotiate trade agreements.

[41] In addition to the initial vote authorizing the use of military force against Iraq, this table is based on votes on emergency supplemental appropriations for the wars in Iraq (and Afghanistan) and the reconstruction of Iraq. The Bush administration's efforts to expedite deployment of a national missile defense system were coded as votes for missile defense. Votes to cut Bush's proposed budget increases were coded as votes against missile defense. Votes on Bush's free trade agreements with Chile (2003), Singapore (2003), Australia (2004), Bahrain (2005), Oman (2006), Peru (2007), Colombia (2008), and the 2005 Dominican Republic–Central America Free Trade Agreement (CAFTA) were coded as votes for trade promotion. This category also includes the 2001 and 2002 votes giving Bush trade promotion authority.

Table 4.4.
Republican and Democratic support for George W. Bush's foreign policies,
2001–2009

	Iraq War		Missile Defense		Trade Promotion	
	Party support	Party cohesion	Party support	Party cohesion	Party support	Party cohesion
Republicans	97%	93%	64%	88%	93%	86%
Democrats	36%	71%	39%	45%	34%	58%

Roll call voting in the U.S. House of Representatives from the 107th through 110th Congress. Number of roll call votes: Iraq war (15); missile defense (9); trade promotion (15).

Moderate Democrats were especially vulnerable to Republican charges of "weakness" on national defense. This helps explain the lower cohesion scores for Democrats in table 4.4.[42] Bush had political incentive to emphasize foreign threats *and* to make national security a tool of partisan warfare. Any doubts about whether the White House would do both were erased in January 2002 when Karl Rove, Bush's chief political strategist, vowed at a Republican luncheon in Austin, Texas, to make the "war on terrorism" an issue in the upcoming congressional elections (Judis, 2007). As Rove explained to his Republican colleagues, "We can go to the country on this issue because they trust the Republican Party to do a better job of protecting and strengthening America's military might and thereby protecting America. Americans trust the Republicans to do a better job of keeping our communities and our families safe."

National security was a tool of partisan warfare, especially at election time (Kupchan and Trubowitz, 2007, 26; Snyder, Shapiro, and Bloch-Elkon, 2009).[43] In the 2002 campaign, the White House used national security to drive up Republican turnout in key districts and states and to deflect public anxiety about a weak economy (Drew, 2003; Lemann, 2003; Judis, 2007). In the 2004 presidential election, Bush focused his campaign on the threat of terrorism, charging that the country would

[42] In the case of trade promotion, free-trade-oriented Democrats from western states were the ones most vulnerable to Bush's policies.

[43] Bush used national security to consolidate his political base as much as to peel off voters who might otherwise vote Democratic on election day (Judis, 2007). In 2002 the White House used the war on terrorism to offset Democratic advantages over the economy (then in recession) and the Enron corruption scandal and to win over independents and Democrats in upscale suburbs. In 2004 Republicans emphasized the war on terrorism, partly to offset growing disenchantment with the war in Iraq and to strengthen the party's hold on prosperous "exurbs" and poorer rural areas, especially in the South.

"invite disaster" if the Democrats were to win (Alberts, 2004). Vice President Richard Cheney pursued the same critique of the opposition, warning, "If we make the wrong choice [of candidates], then the danger is that we'll get hit again" (Silva, 2006). The rhetoric continued in the 2006 midterm elections, with Bush insinuating that a Democratic victory means "The terrorists win and America loses " (Abramowitz, 2006). Republican gains in the 2002 congressional elections and Bush's reelection as president two years later were widely interpreted as proof that an expansive grand strategy paid rich political dividends for Republicans on election day (Langer and Cohen, 2005; Edsall, 2006; Judis, 2007).

In the end, Bush was unable to convert these electoral victories into lasting support for his expansionist grand strategy. One reason was the grinding frustrations of his war in Iraq and the inconclusiveness of U.S. action in Afghanistan. Even in an era of unipolarity, translating power into effective policy was not assured in the face of local resistance. International opposition to the Iraq war and to Bush's foreign policy more generally was costly diplomatically, even if it did not lead other states to actively balance against U.S. power (Katzenstein and Keohane, 2007). There were also limits to how widely the Bush administration could apply its corollary doctrine of "preventive war." Iraq was only one of three "Axis of Evil" nations that Bush identified for possible "regime change." Iran and North Korea were the others. Attacking either raised the risk of an even larger, more costly conflict.

The problem was not only that Bush suffered from a legitimacy deficit—though the court-imposed determination of the electoral-college vote in 2000 did complicate the task of governing before the September 11 attacks. The larger problem concerned the *domestic* balance of power. In the United States, political power at the start of the new millennium was evenly divided between the two parties. Popular images of "Red America" and "Blue America" and a "50–50 Nation" (Barone, 2001; Brownstein, 2007; Mellow, 2008) captured this essential division and the problems it posed for governing in the foreign policy arena, as well as in the domestic policy arena. Unlike Monroe or McKinley, Bush did not enter the White House with an electoral mandate or sizable House and Senate majorities.

The September 11 attacks gave Bush a measure of political legitimacy that the 2000 election had denied him (Skowronek, 2008, 139). However, the attacks did not offer enough of a political buffer to protect his foreign policy agenda from Democratic broadsides once public support for the war in Iraq had dissipated.[44] Ironically, debate over the wisdom

---

[44] Bush's grand strategy combined with tax cuts helped produce a huge federal deficit. Between 2000 and 2007, the national debt increased from about $5.6 trillion to about $9 trillion (Wirls, 2010, 135). The deficit made it easier for Democrats on Capitol Hill to play

of launching the war reinforced the partisan divisions that had been inflamed by Bush's disputed election in 2000 and contributed to the political standoff at the national level between the two parties (Jacobson,
2007). Neither party could gain a decisive edge.

Bush's election in 2004 proved to be the high high-water mark of his
presidency. Two years later, the President suffered a stinging rebuke at
the polls. Democrats, campaigning against the Iraq War, gained control
of Congress. The Republicans appeared to have lost their long-standing
edge with voters on matters of national security (Goble and Holm, 2009).

EXPANSIONISM: NECESSITY OR CHOICE?

Realists are not wrong to stress the importance of relative power or geopolitical balances in explaining expansionism. Increased military power
relative to that of rivals did mean greater freedom of choice in making
grand strategy for Monroe, McKinley, and Bush. Moreover, each of these
presidents expanded the U.S. reach internationally, much as realists predict: by taking on weak, vulnerable states. When confronted by a supe-
rior power or a great power that possessed local superiority in a region
of interest, each president was careful to trim America's geopolitical sails.
In the 1820s, Monroe was quick to avoid issues like the Greek rebellion that risked entanglement in European power politics. In the 1890s,
McKinley was careful not to seriously commit U.S. power in East Asia,
where European powers and a rising Japan held sway. In dealing with
a possible nuclear threat posed by North Korea, Bush adopted a less
confrontational approach than he did toward Saddam Hussein's Iraq,
implicitly acknowledging China's interests and clout in Asia.

A state's relative power in the international arena can tell us a great
deal about where and how leaders expand. By itself, however, this variable cannot tell us *when* leaders will seek to project power and influence abroad. As the analysis in this chapter makes clear, whether leaders
choose to exploit their state's power advantages depends critically on
their domestic political circumstances: whether expansionism conflicts
with their domestic priorities, whether their supporters will benefit from
expansionism, and whether their party is strong enough to carry the day
against domestic opponents. Monroe, McKinley, and Bush all led parties
that gained from military spending, territorial expansion, and the spoils
of war, albeit to varying degrees. In different ways, expansionism worked
to the party's electoral advantage. In Monroe's case, it was a means to

---

on public doubts about Bush's competence. These were reinforced by the evident failures of
command in the war in Iraq.

outflank a western insurgency within the Republican Party. In McKinley's case, it was a means to preempt a Democratic takeover of Congress. And in Bush's case, expansionism was a political wedge to divide the Democratic Party and win over some of its voters and elected representatives.

Each of these cases also reveal the limits of a purely *Innenpolitik* explanation of grand strategy. This is perhaps clearest in McKinley's case, where expansionism was driven more by fears of losing power to Populism than by pressure from commercial and financial interests lobbying for increased foreign markets and investment opportunities. In all three cases, presidents used foreign policy to consolidate their party's power as *Innenpolitik* would predict. However, they did so by playing on latent divisions within the opposing party or, in the case of Monroe, by playing factions within his own party against one another, rather than by rallying the public at large. This was politics of "divide and rule," not the consensus-building politics of diversionary war theory. The fact that all three leaders held office at a time when fiscal constraints were loose reminds us that leaders' willingness to invest in expansionist foreign policy depends on how much political resistance to increased military spending they can anticipate. Unlike Washington, Lincoln, and Roosevelt, who faced high resource mobilization hurdles, Monroe, McKinley, and Bush (in the immediate wake of 9/11) had little to fear internationally *or* domestically from investing in the build-up of military power.

The analysis also suggests that party strength is a better predictor of expansionism than state capacity. Some realists (e.g., Zakaria, 1998) argue that centralized states are more likely to expand than institutionally divided states that lack the institutional capacity to mobilize resources. However, the institutional fragmentation of the American state did not prevent Monroe, McKinley, or Bush from pursuing expansionism. Nor did the increase in state capacity that accrued over time with the development of the imperial presidency (Schlesinger, 1973) and "national security state" (Koh, 1990) guarantee foreign policy success. Party dominance was the decisive factor. Monroe and McKinley enjoyed party domination over the national government, and they found it easier to sustain domestic support for expansionism than did Bush, whose party's grip on power was weaker. As I show in the next chapter, when leaders have too little domestic power, they are inclined to avoid ambitious and costly grand strategies, even when international opportunity beckons.

CHAPTER FIVE

Why States Underreach

MANY REALISTS ARGUE that as a state's power increases, so will its international ambitions. Often this is true, although, as chapter 4 on expansionism explains, a realist explanation that considers only geopolitical factors is incomplete. This limitation of realism is also evident in the fact that states' ambitions often do not keep pace with their power. States in this situation are characterized by what might be called "strategic underextension." They punch *below* their weight in international politics. Instead of exploiting their relative power advantages, leaders of these states do the opposite, by scaling back (or not making) foreign commitments and slashing (or forgoing) military spending. International opportunities to extend the nation's geopolitical reach are ignored, and domestic priorities and concerns remain front and center. For realists, this phenomenon poses a dilemma. On the one hand, it occurs too often to simply discount it as an "exception that proves the rule." On the other hand, to account for strategic underextension by introducing auxiliary, ad hoc domestic-level assumptions and arguments, as realists tend to do, weakens realism's explanatory power.[1]

Strategic underextension also poses problems for *Innenpolitik* explanations of grand strategy. Perhaps most obviously, the phenomenon does not lend itself easily to foreign policy theories that attach inordinate weight to the expansionist drives of economic interests, military services, or other domestic pressure groups. In the cases of strategic underreach that are considered here, these "imperialist interests" do not hold sway. Moreover, leaders often choose strategies such as retrenchment and disengagement that are difficult to reconcile with diversionary war theories. Instead of looking for ways to move foreign policy to the "front burner" to distract their publics from domestic troubles, these leaders do all they can to keep foreign policy on the "back burner" so that they can concentrate on the home front. Why should leaders who would appear to have so much to gain domestically from foreign expansionism, and so little to lose internationally, retrench?

---

[1] To account for underextension, realists usually emphasize domestic factors such as poor leadership (Kindleberger, 1973), strategic misperception (Friedberg, 1988), or weak institutions (Zakaria, 1998). For a critique of this methodological move, and what issues it raises for realism's explanatory power as a theory of statecraft, see Legro and Moravcsik (1999).

STRATEGIES OF RESTRAINT

In this chapter, I argue that our theory of how executives choose grand strategy offers a more parsimonious explanation for strategic underextension. I show that leaders are most likely to underreach when they have geopolitical slack but see little partisan advantage in expansionism. Under this combination of international and domestic incentives, leaders have little to fear geopolitically and much to gain domestically from pursuing a strategy of restraint—that is, from limiting or scaling back strategic commitments and capabilities. I develop this argument through an analysis of the foreign policies of Martin Van Buren, Herbert Hoover, and Bill Clinton. Despite their different circumstances, I argue that Van Buren, Hoover, and Clinton faced strikingly similar structural incentives. In each case, security was relatively abundant and opportunities to expand the nation's interests were plentiful. Yet all three had to contend with powerful constituencies in their own parties that opposed foreign expansionism and saw greater advantage in investing in domestic priorities and policies.

Van Buren and Hoover behaved as the theory predicts. In addition to cutting military spending, each resisted opportunities to project U.S. power. Van Buren declined opportunities to acquire territory on the North American continent; Hoover held back when faced with the chance to exert U.S. influence in Europe, Asia, and especially Latin America. Contra realism, each did the minimum in the foreign policy domain by keeping commitments in check and, where possible, relying on cheaper economic and diplomatic means. Contra *Innenpolitik*, Van Buren and Hoover resisted the temptation to manipulate foreign crises for domestic gain. Instead of using foreign policy to deflect popular anger over the economy, Van Buren and Hoover considered foreign policy an area for belt-tightening.

The theory of the determinants of grand strategy that is advanced here is only partially successful in accounting for U.S. grand strategy under Clinton. Clinton made many of the strategic adjustments I expect: during his first term in office, the pace of military spending slowed, reliance on cheaper economic tools increased, and costly, risky foreign interventions were avoided.[2] However, under Clinton many of the strategic policies that characterized U.S. foreign policy during the Cold War continued. Little effort was made to scale back America's far-reaching international commitments. Indeed, on Clinton's watch, NATO's geopolitical reach expanded and America's commitment to international free trade deepened.

---

[2] Clinton showed some willingness to use military force in Haiti, Bosnia, and Kosovo, but only within very narrow limits.

The chapter takes up the Van Buren, Hoover, and Clinton's presidencies in chronological order. I conclude by considering why grand strategy under Clinton conforms less well to the model's predictions than grand strategy under Van Buren and Hoover, and what this tells us about foreign policy choice. Among other things, I argue that the partial anomaly of Clinton highlights the importance of resource availability in explaining strategic underreach. Van Buren and Hoover held office during two of the worst economic depressions in U.S. history; resources were scarce. Clinton's fiscal circumstances were happier. He presided at a time of rapid economic growth and federal budget surpluses. This made it less imperative for Clinton to generate savings through strategic retrenchment and thus easier, politically, to resist pressure within his party to do so.

JACKSONIAN FISSURES AND MARTIN VAN BUREN'S STRATEGIC ADJUSTMENT

Little of consequence in foreign affairs occurred during Martin Van Buren's four years in office (1837–41). There were no ambitious foreign adventures, no strategic military breakthroughs, and no diplomatic fiascos to speak of. In contrast to his predecessor, Andrew Jackson, Van Buren made no effort to expand the nation's territorial reach. Military spending, which increased on Jackson's watch, fell on Van Buren's. In fact, Van Buren actively blocked efforts by Congress to modernize the navy and nationalize state militias. Van Buren also rarely used military force. The one exception was the Indian campaign known as the Second Seminole War—a war that Jackson began but could not finish.[3] Yet even here, Van Buren refused to expand the scope or size of Jackson's military commitment. As the strategist Harold Sprout (1944, 113) observed many years ago, Van Buren pursued "a policy of retrenchment."

Van Buren is best remembered for his amazing party-building skills as Andrew Jackson's political lieutenant in the 1820s. Yet the "Little Magician," as he was widely known, was also savvy in the ways of international power politics. As Andrew Jackson's secretary of state, he demonstrated a firm grasp of his diplomatic portfolio and an uncanny ability to resolve the thorny international disputes that Jackson precipitated from time to time (Herring, 2008, 164). This means that as president, Van Buren's reluctance to commit time, resources, and political capital to foreign policy thus did not stem from any lack of foreign policy experience. As

---

[3] It proved to be the army's most costly and lengthy Indian War. Van Buren's successor, John Tyler, actually completed the military campaign against an alliance of five thousand Seminole Indians and roughly one thousand African Americans, many runaway slaves.

I show here, the explanation for Van Buren's strategy of retrenchment lies in the configuration of international and domestic circumstances that marked his presidency.

From 1837–1841, the United States faced no geopolitical challenger. Britain, the only European power in a position to actively project power on the North American continent, was preoccupied with developments in Europe (Bourne, 1967, 76–78; Carroll, 2001, 197). Liberal democratic movements had emerged in Portugal, Spain, Belgium, Italy, and Greece. Under Whig leadership, London abandoned its traditional policy of supporting autocratic powers against popular unrest in favor of a more proactive and assertive foreign policy to aid the democratic insurgencies (Ziegler, 2003, 29–54; Haas, 2005, 98–102). North America was a secondary or tertiary concern; London was content with the status quo.[4] Britain's one cause for concern in North America was the political rebellion that broke out in Canada and spilled over the border with New York in the fall of 1837. In theory, an American president might have tried to exploit the situation in hopes of gaining territory or pandering to war hawks, but the British Foreign Office, led by Viscount Palmerston, expressed confidence that Van Buren would do all he could to keep the peace (M. Wilson, 1984, 161; Carroll, 2001, 206).

At the time, Palmerston might have been criticized for premature judgment. Van Buren surely had incentives to exploit a foreign policy crisis with Canada in order to strengthen his domestic position. Shortly after Van Buren took office, the U.S. economy collapsed. A speculative boom during the waning years of Jackson's presidency led the Bank of England to impose strict limits on credit to firms doing business in the United States (H. Watson, 1990). The credit crunch forced many British importers to cut purchases of cotton—then America's leading export. As British demand for cotton fell, so did prices, causing a panic in commercial circles in the United States. With mercantile houses from New York to New Orleans teetering on the edge of bankruptcy, the crisis spread to the banks and then to firms and their workers. Prices plummeted. Businesses shuttered. The ranks of the unemployed swelled.

The economic crash quickly became a political disaster as well (D. Cole, 1984; Widmer, 2005; Wilentz, 2005). Van Buren's political opponents, the Whigs, blamed the economic disaster on "Martin Van Ruin" and Jacksonian-Jeffersonian economic policies that had left the country too vulnerable to the vicissitudes of the world economy. As the economic crisis deepened, the Whigs grew stronger. Even more worrisome for Van Buren were the intensifying sectional tensions within his party.

---

[4] Indeed, much of London's attention during Van Buren's term was absorbed by a series of crises in Afghanistan, Egypt, and China (Bourne, 1967, 76).

With Jackson at the head of the party, Democrats had usually been able to finesse their North-South differences. But the alliance was fragile, and Van Buren, for all his political talent, did not have Jackson's political standing.

Nor did Van Buren have the tools necessary to turn the economy around. In part, this was the Democrats' own doing. Many historians believe that Jackson's destruction of the Bank of the United States had eliminated one possible instrument of fiscal control.[5] Van Buren convened a special "Panic" session of Congress to take steps to alleviate the economic crisis—the first time Congress had been called into special session to deal with a nonmilitary crisis—but the Democrats were divided over what should be done. Some favored measures to promote the use of "hard money" (gold and silver) in transactions with the federal government. Others wanted Van Buren to support paper money and to actively support the private, regionally based banks that held the depreciating paper currency. What no one urging was a major infusion of federal dollars into the economy. While the Democrats did not favor spending on butter, they were also opposed to investing in guns. Their overall agenda was to reduce the role of government in the economy and to let "free market forces" mete out their harsh judgment. The Whigs, by contrast, favored more government activism to bail out the banks and to support individual debtors caught in the economic crisis—through new bankruptcy laws, for example.

As if the economic depression did not make governing difficult enough, party politics compounded matters (Silbey, 2002). Van Buren won the presidency in 1836 by an uncomfortably close margin, benefiting from the fact that the Whigs could not agree on a single national candidate (Curtis, 1970, 49–50).[6] His electoral vulnerabilities were especially apparent in the South, where his 1836 vote tallies ran well behind the votes that Jackson had racked up in 1828 and again in 1832 (Holt, 1992). Though Van Buren actively courted the southern vote by openly supporting such measures as the so-called Gag Rule, southern Democrats did not trust the former senator from New York (Curtis, 1970, 152).[7] Having worked so hard to win the support of southern Democrats, Van Buren ironically could not take the North for granted either. Many northerners thought Van Buren was too solicitous of southern opinion. Hoping

---

[5] See, for example, Temin (1969), M. Wilson (1984), and Wilentz (2005).

[6] Van Buren faced challenges, of varying strength, from four Whig candidates in the 1836 election: William Henry Harrison, Hugh Lawson White, Daniel Webster, and Willie Person Mangum.

[7] In 1836 the House passed the Pinckney Resolutions, which included a rule that automatically "tabled" all petitions for the abolition of slavery, preventing them from being read or discussed.

to prevent either wing of the party from bolting to another candidate in 1840, Van Buren labored to keep foreign policy questions that had potentially explosive sectional implications off the national agenda. The annexation of Texas and response to the Canadian rebellion were two such issues. Van Buren's handling of these issues exemplifies his administration's strategy of foreign policy restraint.

In the mid-1830s, a majority of Americans favored adding Texas to the Union (Silbey, 2005). Given Van Buren's precarious political situation, one might have expected him to use this international issue to buck up his domestic standing. However, Van Buren realized that the sectional fallout from efforts in that direction could destroy his presidency (M. Wilson, 1984, 151–53). The Texas Constitution sanctioned slavery, which made it anathema in the North. Hoping to finesse the issue, Van Buren turned down Texas's offer of annexation, but in a transparent effort to appease southerners, he pressured Mexico to accept international arbitration of the many outstanding U.S. claims against it (Curtis, 1970, 152–69).[8] In doing so, Van Buren rejected the advice of close political advisers who privately urged him to start a war with Mexico over Texas, believing it would take Americans' minds off their economic woes while posing little risk of military failure (M. Wilson, 1984, 100). Van Buren feared military action to annex Texas would have precisely the opposite effect by blowing his fragile domestic political coalition apart. "Eager for reelection, Van Buren warily turned aside Texas proposals for annexation" (Herring, 2008, 194).

These same political sensibilities shaped Van Buren's response to the more serious crisis stemming from the Mackenzie-Papineau insurrection in Canada (Carroll, 2001). Issues of landownership and religious freedom sparked a rebellion in Canada in the summer of 1837. British forces quickly crushed the rebellion, but many of the rebels fled for safety across the border into the United States. There they found sympathy and support among American "patriot militia" who backed the Canadians' fight for freedom. In December 1837 tensions flared when British units crossed the border into New York to intercept a small steamship transporting supplies to the Canadian rebels, killing one American in the raid and prompting retaliatory strikes by patriot militia groups across the border. Van Buren reacted quickly, issuing two strong proclamations of neutrality, calling upon the militias of New York and Vermont to enforce the proclamations, and sending General Winfield Scott to the Niagara

---

[8] As historian Donald Cole (1984, 321) observes, to keep the Democrats united "Van Buren decided to sweep the Mexican claims and Texan annexation under the rug." See also Curtis (1970, 169). Southerners, eager to fold Texas into the Union, took a dim view of Mexico's claims on Texas.

frontier as a mediator. The president also sent a personal note to Palmerston, delivered by his own son, assuring the foreign minister of America's peaceful intentions. The crisis quickly subsided.

Exploiting Canada's internal conflict might have bolstered Van Buren's public image in the short term. Supporting the patriot militia would surely have appealed to Americans along the border who sympathized with the Canadian cause or saw the crisis as an opportunity for annexation. There were many in the North who viewed the acquisition of Canada as a possible sectional counterweight to the probable annexation of Texas (D. Campbell, 2007, 129). "Annexation fever" ran high along the northern border (J. Smith, 1945, 115). However, Van Buren understood that the price of intervening in Canadian politics would be increased sectional animosity within the Democratic Party. Worse, the patriot militias' freelancing along the border could trigger a long, drawn out war with Britain, a war that the United States could ill afford, especially given that over half of the U.S. Army was bogged down fighting an Indian and slave insurgency in Florida (Carroll, 2001, 204). Having few tools at his disposal, Van Buren looked for ways to stabilize the frontier and prevent inadvertent war.

A second crisis with London that occurred during the winter of 1838–39, this one along the Aroostook River between Maine and New Brunswick, raised many of the same strategic issues. For years Maine and New Brunswick had claimed these timber- and soil-rich lands. In January 1839 John Fairfield, the governor of Maine and an old Jacksonian, moved unilaterally to deploy some three hundred militia to the region with the expressed purpose of driving out Canadian timber "trespassers." Tensions escalated. Van Buren, again fearing that local initiative might lead to war with Britain, quickly intervened to find a peaceful solution. Condemning the Canadian trespassers, the president reprimanded Fairfield for moving unilaterally and called on Maine to withdraw its militia from the Aroostook. Many in Maine condemned the president for inaction and passivity. But with the bulk of the army's forces tied down in Florida, Van Buren could not have moved more forcefully against the Canadians along the Aroostook, even if he had desired to do so.[9] Moreover, few southern Democrats were willing to support a military build-up on the northern frontier, seeing no advantage in a war with London. Foreign interventionism would have also required a military build-up that ran straight against the Democrats' credo of small government and free markets.

The anti-expansionist thrust of Van Buren's foreign policy was reflected in his military priorities. When Van Buren entered office, the army was

---

[9] As one of Van Buren's biographers, Major Wilson (1984, 188), notes, "Van Buren's commitment to peace with Britain in 1839 was thus reinforced by the realization that the nation was simply unprepared for war."

weak, disorganized, and plagued by frequent desertions (R. Watson, 1948). The nation's fortifications were in disrepair and undermanned. Along the Canadian frontier, many had been abandoned (Prucha, 1969). Jackson's efforts to expand the army and the fortification system had met with congressional resistance. The situation worsened under Van Buren, in part because he was less able or willing to invest federal resources in the army. Initially in favor of a proposal by his secretary of war, Joel Poinsett, to create an "active" and "movable" military, Van Buren beat a hasty political retreat when members of his own party challenged Poinsett's proposal on constitutional grounds (M. Wilson, 1984, 189). Spending on the army during Van Buren's presidency fell by roughly half, dropping from $20 million in 1837 to less than $10 million in 1840 (M. Wilson, 1984, 189; Katznelson, 2002, 93).

Naval spending also declined, though less precipitously because of congressional intervention to increase the size of the navy.[10] Indeed, Van Buren displayed little interest in the navy throughout his presidency, seeing little reason to exploit the strategic advantages that technological advances in steam power promised (Sprout and Sprout, 1944, 113; J. Schroeder, 1985, 37–55; Hagan, 1991, 106–7). The president also rejected domestic pressures to create a "home squadron" to protect America's shores, seeing little need for such a force at a time of relative quiet on the international front. Van Buren was content to rely on the navy's narrower peacetime mission to protect American commerce against piracy. Van Buren's most notable achievement was the navy's expedition to explore the South Pacific and the coast of Antarctica.

Van Buren's strategy of retrenchment was shaped by domestic as well as international considerations. Opportunities to promote foreign expansionism presented themselves, most notably in the case of Texas. Yet Van Buren did not respond the way *Realpolitik* or *Innenpolitik* might predict. His Democratic Party was too fragile and too committed to laissez faire to exploit those opportunities for geopolitical gain or domestic profit. The Little Magician realized that he could pursue a policy of retrenchment in foreign affairs at little political risk. Table 5.1 indicates that for the most part, Van Buren was right. Policies of neutrality, naval retrenchment, and military reform were guaranteed to invite Whig resistance, especially from northern and western Whigs.[11] But Van Buren could afford

---

[10] Standing at $5.7 million in 1837, the navy's budget was cut by about $1 million over the next two years, before rising again in 1840 (M. Wilson, 1984, 178). Congress did authorize construction of three steam warships in 1839, but the initiative came from Congress, not Van Buren's administration.

[11] Neutrality refers to votes on how to respond to the Niagara and Maine frontier crises. Votes consistent with Van Buren's preferences are coded as votes for neutrality. Naval retrenchment includes votes on naval appropriations, the development of steam engine vessels, and naval expeditions. Votes against increased spending on the navy are coded as votes

TABLE 5.1.
Democratic and Whig support for Martin Van Buren's foreign policies,
1837–1841

	Neutrality		Naval Retrenchment		Downsizing Army	
	Party support	Party cohesion	Party support	Party cohesion	Party support	Party cohesion
Democrats	80%	54%	73%	63%	75%	59%
Whigs	56%	49%	24%	65%	33%	59%

Roll call voting in the U.S. House of Representatives from the 25th and 26th Congresses.
Number of roll call votes: neutrality (5); naval retrenchment (15); downsizing army (15).

to write them off. Most Democrats would line up behind foreign policies that did not involve greater federal intervention in the economy; they did not spend much time worrying about leaving the country strategically exposed or about a foreign policy blunder that would leave the party vulnerable to second-guessing. At a time when resources were scarce, and the country's economic crisis seemed to get worse with each passing month, London showed little inclination to exploit America's internal difficulties. Van Buren's strategy of retrenchment was politically safe. Although the policy of strategic retrenchment offered few political upsides, for Van Buren, the decisive fact is that it posed little downside risk. In this respect, Van Buren's situation was comparable to that of Herbert Hoover many years later.

HERBERT HOOVER, REPUBLICAN SECTARIANISM, AND STRATEGIC RETRENCHMENT

Few presidents have been judged as harshly as Herbert Hoover (1929–33). Yet popular images of Hoover's "passivity," "incompetence," and ideological intransigence in the face of one of the country's worst economic depressions bear little resemblance to the facts. Far from ignoring the severity of the depression, Hoover equated tackling the domestic crisis to an all-out wartime effort. He mobilized a wide repertoire of policy responses, many of which broke with the Republican *idée fixe* of

---

for naval retrenchment. Military downsizing refers largely to efforts to limit the growth and professionalization of the army. Votes against army spending are coded as votes for downsizing.

the era— laissez faire (Skowronek, 1997). Hoover's foreign policy was less innovative than his domestic policy, but he was just as pragmatic and nonideological in defining ends and choosing appropriate means.[12] Hoover held office at a time when America faced no international threat, and the Republican Party had little appetite for expansion. In the arena of grand strategy, he responded as the theory of executive choice predicts: he pursued a strategy of retrenchment.

Hoover's presidency is a good test of my argument about how leaders choose their grand strategies. When he was inaugurated in March 1929, many expected an activist foreign policy. Few presidents had as much firsthand international experience as Hoover before entering the White House (Doenecke, 1987, 312). Few also took a more direct command of foreign affairs once in office (DeConde, 1989).[13] An ardent internationalist in the early 1920s (Lovin, 1988), Hoover distanced himself from Republican "irreconcilables" over the League of Nations and backed America's entry into the new multilateral institution. As secretary of commerce under both Warren Harding and Calvin Coolidge, Hoover had worked so tirelessly to promote U.S. foreign investment that his critics on Capitol Hill complained that he was too deferential to Wall Street and America's burgeoning multinational corporations.[14] The idealistic rhetoric about international cooperation and peace that marked Hoover's inaugural address reinforced the general perception that as president, he would pursue an active, outward-oriented foreign policy.[15]

Those hopes were dashed by Hoover's efforts to respond to the global economic crisis that began in October 1929 with the crash of the U.S. stock market. The president's commitment to internationalism weakened considerably. Instead of leveraging America's industrial power for broad international purposes, Hoover acted narrowly and defensively and substituted less-expensive economic means for military ones. He looked

---

[12] Some scholars attribute Hoover's internationalism to his Quaker faith. While there is little doubt that Hoover disliked war, he did not rule out the use of military force (DeConde, 1989, 97).

[13] Early accounts of Hoover's foreign policy stressed the role of Secretary of State Henry Stimson. Subsequent scholarship revealed Hoover to be a more his hands-on manager of foreign affairs. On changing views of Hoover, see DeConde (1989, especially 88 and 99). See also Degler (1963).

[14] Indeed, before the 1928 Republican convention, some Republicans confidently predicted that Hoover's internationalist leanings would make it impossible for the party to nominate him (Schwarz, 1970, 47).

[15] So did the 1928 election results. Hoover entered office with the political wind at his back, having scored a decisive electoral victory, with 58 percent of the popular vote and 444 electoral votes. When the 71st Congress opened in March 1929, the Republicans held a 270 to 164 majority in the House and a 56 to 39 majority in the Senate. (There was one Farmer-Labor Party member in both the House and the Senate.)

for ways to protect agriculture from foreign competition (e.g., Farm Board) and to buck up rural and farmers' support for his domestic legislation. While he still advocated U.S. outward investment, now it was mostly because Hoover saw overseas investment as the logical extension of his measures to revive the domestic economy (Rosenberg, 1982). Meanwhile, Hoover's efforts to boost U.S. direct investment in Latin America and financial support for Europe were tempered (if not contradicted outright) by his unflinching support of higher tariffs (Smoot-Hawley) on foreign goods.[16]

Hoover's retrenchment from bold internationalism was also evident in his geopolitical strategies. In Latin American, Hoover favored a lower political-military profile, relying less on the stick of military coercion and more on the carrot of economic and cultural exchange (DeConde, 1951; Joan Wilson, 1975; Gellman, 1979, 1–9). In Asia, Hoover embraced the "Open Door" policy that presidents since McKinley had favored. When Hoover suddenly found that policy tested by Japan's seizure of Manchuria (1931), he did edge away from the commitment, refusing to recognize Japanese annexation of Chinese territory, but this was hardly the strongest response open to him. It fell far short of what one might have expected from a committed internationalist (Ferrell, 1957; W. Cohen, 2000, 108–12; Narizny, 2007, 146–47).[17] To the relief of many internationalists on Wall Street, in 1931 Hoover did offer a temporary moratorium on European war debts owed to the United States, but he disappointed them by refusing to address the crucial, related problem of European war reparations (Driggs, 1958, 817; Joan Wilson, 1975, 185–86; Leffler, 1979, 234–45).[18]

---

[16] To be sure, when Hoover called Congress into special session in March 1929 to revise the tariff, he envisioned a more moderate revision than the one that lawmakers ultimately produced. Hoover also threatened to veto the bill if it did not make room for a stronger, more independent Federal Tariff Commission to set rates. However, in the final analysis, Hoover did little to prevent Congress from enacting the most infamous tariff on record; "Congress was effectively given a free hand in setting tariff rates" (Lake, 1988, 199). On Hoover's approach to the Smoot-Hawley tariff and foreign trade more generally, see Joan Wilson (1975, 175–79) and Leffler (1979, 195–202).

[17] The real purpose of nonrecognition, generally referred to as the Stimson Doctrine after Hoover's secretary of state, Henry Stimson, was to avoid coordinating policy with the League of Nations and angering nationalist critics at home.

[18] Throughout the 1920s, Republican presidents had relied on private rather than public funds to help Europe recover from the trauma and dislocations caused by World War I. Under the so-called Dawes Plan of 1924, the United States financed the German economy, which in turn financed the cycle of German war reparations and war debt repayment to France and others. In the aftermath of the U.S. stock market crash of October 1929, private American investment in Europe (and elsewhere) declined sharply, producing a liquidity crisis. Hoover felt mounting international and domestic pressure to cancel the war debts the Allied countries owed the U.S. Treasury. In the end, Hoover was only able to win congres-

Under Hoover, America's international commitments were scaled back. So were available military means. Hoover favored a policy of "economical preparedness," which meant a low-cost military establishment (John Wilson, 1974, 47).[19] To this end, he looked for ways to cut the army and navy, arguing that the country did not need a large, offensive military to guarantee its security.[20] To maximize his leverage over military spending, Hoover simplified the military budgeting process and reduced the range of strategic contingencies the military could plan against.[21] Calls for a navy strong enough to defend the nation's commercial sea lanes and to defend U.S. interests in the Philippines were turned aside in favor of a narrower, cheaper definition of strategic interests that focused on Latin America.[22]

Hoover's domestic efforts to use the budget to rein in military spending were supplemented by efforts on the diplomatic front that were aimed at the same purpose (DeConde, 1989, 103–5). Over the navy's opposition, Hoover used the London Conference of 1930 to push for tonnage limitations that would allow the United States to reduce its budget for naval construction.[23] A few years later, Hoover proposed further reductions at the Geneva Disarmament Conference, though this time he failed because the various parties at the negotiating table could not reach an agreement on limits. Having lost Republican domination of Congress in 1930, Hoover was unable to exert the effective leadership

---

sional backing for the moratorium by agreeing to a "no-cancellation" amendment sprung by Democrats, who now controlled Congress (Schwarz, 1970, 78–88).

[19] When Hoover entered office in 1929, military spending accounted for more than half of the federal budget (Holcombe, 1996, 181).

[20] Hoover experienced uneven success before the full weight of the Depression was felt. With congressional support, the army and especially the navy were able to fight off deep cuts until the Depression forced reductions.

[21] Hoover introduced the "functional or pocket budget." This new, simplified budget combined army and navy spending with veterans' benefits and the principal and interest on the national debt due to World War I expenditures, making it easier to justify reductions (Joan Wilson, 1975, 194). Hoover also ordered the General Staff to undertake a detailed survey of the army to identify places where the military programs could safely be reorganized, consolidated, or abolished to generate budget savings (John Wilson, 1974, 42). In addition, Hoover blocked efforts by technology-minded lawmakers who favored the development of the navy's new carrier-based aviation program (John Wilson, 1974, 44). See also Millett and Maslowski (1984, 373–85) and D. Cohen (1994).

[22] As one detailed account of Hoover's defense planning puts it, "By limiting his conception of preparedness to the Western Hemisphere, which was reasonably secure, he freed himself to follow the least expensive path within his restricted framework" (John Wilson, 1993, 216).

[23] Indeed, after the conference Hoover proposed major cuts in naval shipbuilding that were well below the treaty ceiling (Narizny, 2007, 147).

on disarmament that he had displayed at the London Conference (Joan Wilson, 1975, 195).[24]

Hoover's strategy of retrenchment is difficult to square with *Innenpolitik* theories of diversionary war. If ever there was a president who had an incentive to use foreign policy to divert public attention from the economy, it was Hoover. Yet Hoover consistently chose not to manipulate the foreign crises that arose during his presidency. As the diplomatic historian Alexander DeConde (1989, 115) puts it, "Within a four year period, he [Hoover] turned aside more opportunities to use American power in foreign interventions than did any of the presidents of the 20th century over a similar time span." Most of these opportunities arose in Latin America, where Hoover could project U.S. power with little fear that foreign powers would rush to the defense of Cuba, Mexico, or others. Meanwhile, Hoover disengaged militarily from Nicaragua and developed similar plans for Haiti.

Hoover's grand strategy also poses problems for realism. Indeed realist scholars have long found Hoover's actions puzzling.[25] Why, they ask, would the leader of a nation as powerful as the United States in the late 1920s refuse to provide the leadership the world so desperately needed? As historian John Braeman (1982, 369) points out, part of the problem with this question is that scholars implicitly conflate the geopolitical circumstances that Republican leaders like Hoover faced in the 1920s with those faced by Franklin Roosevelt later in the 1930s. Hoover's and Roosevelt's strategic circumstances were fundamentally different. Roosevelt had little geopolitical slack; security was scarce. Hoover, on the other hand, had considerable room for error internationally.[26] The United States faced no immediate geopolitical threat. This perception was reflected in the Joint Army-Navy Board's "Blue-Orange" strategic assessment of January 1929 (Greene, 1961, 368; E. Cohen, 1994, 441), to say nothing of the public's indifference and apathy toward international affairs (Klingberg, 1952, 248). An "overwhelming sense of security" permeated the nation's politics (Braeman, 1982, 358). Hoover echoed that judgment.[27]

---

[24] The Republicans lost badly in the 1930 midterm elections. When the new 72nd Congress met in March 1931, control of the highly polarized House fell to the Democrats (218 Democrats to 216 Republicans, with 1 Farmer-Labor Party representative). The Republicans retained a slim 48–47 majority (1 Farmer-Labor Party) in the Senate.

[25] See, for example, Osgood (1953); Ferrell (1957); and Kindleberger (1973).

[26] As Braeman (1982, 369) puts it, "Perhaps at no time in its history—before or since [the 1920s]—has the United States been more secure." For a similar assessment of the geopolitical landscape, see Leffler (1979, 363).

[27] Hoover was far more sensitive to public sentiment than is generally appreciated. Indeed, he was the first president to systematically collect opinion data in the White House and the first to rely on the use of newspaper editorials to measure public opinion about national issues (Eisenger, 2000; Rottinghaus, 2003).

TABLE 5.2.
Republican and Democratic support for Herbert Hoover's foreign policies,
1929–1933

	Trade Protection		Economical Defense		Debt Relief	
	Party support	Party cohesion	Party support	Party cohesion	Party support	Party cohesion
Republicans	88%	88%	78%	57%	90%	81%
Democrats	12%	89%	46%	37%	48%	57%

Roll call voting in the U.S. House of Representatives from the 71st and 72nd
Congresses. Number of roll call votes: tariff protection (14); economical defense (14);
debt relief (4).

In a July 1929 speech, the president declared the risk of war "lower than
at any time in more than half a century" (John Wilson, 1993, 58).

In the absence of a compelling international threat, Hoover had a
strong incentive to retrench on the geopolitical front. Even before the
bottom fell out of the economy in 1929, powerful Republican voices had
opposed internationalism. The Republican Party was internally divided
(Skowronek, 1997, 263). In the foreign policy realm, regional East-West
tensions over trade protectionism, European war debts and reparations,
and military spending were persistent themes in Republican politics
throughout the 1920s (Grassmuck, 1951). Still, as table 5.2 suggests, a
much wider gulf separated Republicans from Democrats.[28] Those divisions hardened with the onset of the Great Depression. Hoping to outflank Hoover and the Republicans, Democrats urged greater belt tighten-
ing at home and reduced involvement overseas.

Republican lawmakers generally stuck by Hoover, but often reluctantly
and only after extracting concessions from the White House to protect
themselves from Democratic attack. Hoover could not take Republican
support for granted.[29] The fact that neither western insurgent Republicans
nor the party's Eastern Old Guard really trusted Hoover (Fausold, 1985,
48; DeConde, 1989, 95) only narrowed his options. In dealing with Congress, Hoover had to rely on Republican leaders like the popular Speaker,

[28] Trade protection includes votes on Smoot-Hawley and other tariff-related legislation
that Hoover and the Republicans favored. Economical defense includes votes to reduce
army and navy budgets, to consolidate the army and navy, and to authorize funding to attend international arms control conferences, among other items. Debt relief refers to votes
on Hoover's one-year European debt moratorium as well as to an earlier effort to postpone
or settle France's war debt. Votes for trade protection, economical defense, and debt relief
are coded as votes in support of Hoover's foreign policy preferences.

[29] Hoover's relationship with the Senate was particularly bad. See Schwarz (1970, 49).

Nicholas Longworth of Ohio, to manage and smooth over differences with the Republican caucus and forge a united front against the Democrats (McKee, 1931, 136; Schwarz, 1970, 58). Although the United States was in a position to exercise power internationally, Hoover had to weigh any hoped-for advantages against the opportunities for mischief this would create for Democrats, and the havoc it would cause within Republican ranks. The result was the halfhearted internationalism, or retrenchment from internationalism, for which Hoover is rightly remembered.

BILL CLINTON, THE DEMOCRATS, AND SELECTIVE ENGAGEMENT

By any measure, the United States was the dominant international power when Bill Clinton took office in 1993. The collapse of the Soviet empire left America unrivaled militarily, economically, and politically. Militarily, the United States was spending more than the combined sum spent by all of its potential adversaries, and more than all its main allies combined. The U.S. defense budget of roughly $280 billion was well over three times the total of Russia and China together (Butfoy, 2006, 99). America's economic advantages were less clear-cut, but even here the U.S. economy was more than twice the size of that of Japan or China, its closest economic peers. Politically, the United States was the only international power with interests and reach in every part of the globe. This preponderance of power gave Bill Clinton a degree of political latitude in making foreign policy that American leaders did not experience during the long Cold War with the Soviet Union.

The domestic political significance of this favorable shift in America's geopolitical circumstances was not lost on Clinton. During the presidential campaign, Clinton promised to use the peace dividend and "focus like a laser beam on the economy" (Destler, 1998, 89). Foreign policy goals were at most an afterthought.[30] For the most part, he kept his campaign promise, devoting the lion's share of his presidency to domestic policy. Still, Clinton was less disciplined in this regard than either Van Buren or Hoover, or than my theory of the determinants of grand strategy would predict. Clinton eschewed costly international commitments, but he did not favor wholesale retrenchment.

---

[30] Shortly after winning the 1992 election, Clinton met with a group of Democratic leaders on Capitol Hill to solicit their views about the major issues and challenges ahead. When it was his turn, Lee Hamilton, the veteran Indiana congressman and head of the House Foreign Affairs Committee, emphasized international matters and the problems posed by post-Soviet Russia and China. Clinton, evidently irritated, suddenly interrupted Hamilton, "Lee, I just went through the whole campaign and no one talked about foreign policy at all, except for a few members of the press" (Halberstam, 2001,168).

As president, Clinton made many of the strategic adjustments one would expect from the leader of a Democratic Party with strong preferences for investing in butter over guns (domestic consumption over military spending). Clinton slowed the pace of Pentagon spending in his first term, resisting big-ticket Republican items such as missile defense (Schick, 2000a, 28, 39, 76).[31] He increased reliance on cheaper tools of foreign policy such as multilateral diplomacy and avoided foreign interventions that would require large, expensive deployments of U.S. troops (Cox, 1995; Walt, 2000; Butfoy, 2006; Dueck, 2006; Brzezinski, 2007; Kupchan and Trubowitz, 2007). At the same time, Clinton increased spending on social programs of particular interest to core Democratic constituencies (e.g., education) (Schick, 2000a, 76). Yet Clinton did maintain many Cold War policy orientations. He deepened America's commitment to free trade and helped expand the NATO alliance by pushing for the incorporation of former Soviet allies, doing so over the objections of many in his party.

The theory of grand strategy's determinants that is advanced here predicts that Clinton would move aggressively to downsize U.S. commitments and capabilities. This section explains why his actual grand strategy was more mixed than the theory predicts. Certainly, part of the answer is that the Cold War was barely over. The rapidity of the Soviet Union's demise after the fall of the Berlin Wall in 1989 fueled considerable uncertainty about the future of world politics. Some analysts predicted that the "triumph of the West" would usher in a relatively benign era, free of the great-power rivalries, nationalistic drives, and ideological clashes of the past (Fukuyama, 1992). Others feared that the Western alliance would fracture. In the absence of a common unifying strategic threat, economic differences between America, Europe, and Japan would intensify, making the kind of multilateral cooperation that was legend during the Cold War impossible to sustain (Thurow, 1993). Still others predicted that ancient ethnoreligious cleavages, suppressed by decades of superpower rivalry, would resurface and spark international conflict (Huntington, 1993). This means that the Clinton case cannot be coded unambiguously as one of "high geopolitical slack." Considerable uncertainty tempered the confidence born of the new unipolarity.

As a domestic coalition leader, Clinton also had an ambiguous or mixed mandate. He therefore had strong domestic incentives not to diverge too much, or too quickly, from past strategic practices. Having garnered only 43 percent of the vote in 1992, Clinton's victory was hardly a decisive mandate for cashing in on the peace dividend. Few independent analysts

---

[31] According to one estimate, inflation-adjusted defense outlays in 1998 were almost $100 billion less than a decade earlier (Schick, 2000b, 38).

interpreted his election as a rejection of core Republican principles such as free trade or a strong defense (Skowronek, 1997; Coleman, 2000, 153–54; Milkis, 2005, 395–401). Clinton himself was no ordinary New Deal or Great Society Democrat. As a former southern governor, Clinton's political interests often diverged from those of core northern Democratic constituencies, such as organized labor (Burns and Sorenson, 1999; Shoch, 2001; Klein, 2002; J. Harris, 2005). Clinton was a self-styled "New Democrat" who viewed the party's commitment to traditional liberal nostrums as a political vulnerability in the Age of Reagan. Rightly or wrongly, Clinton believed that he needed to convince moderates and independents that he represented a "third-way" between the "old, worn out policies" of the Democratic left and the Republican right.

On some highly salient issues, Clinton sought to split the difference between liberal Democrats and conservative Republicans. More frequently, he tacked between liberal and conservative positions on alternating issues—what political strategists called "triangulation" (Wills, 1996, 14). Some analysts attributed Clinton's governing style to the 1994 elections, when Republicans captured control of both houses of Congress. But Clinton's zigzagging between liberal and conservative positions began before the Democrats' midterm thrashing. Clinton was reacting to a more fundamental dilemma: governing as a Democrat in a conservative Republican era (Skowronek, 1997, 447–64). Clinton and his political advisers considered Jimmy Carter, the only Democrat to make it to the White House in the previous two decades, an object lesson in how *not* to govern at a time of Republican ascendancy. Carter had left himself vulnerable to Republican charges that he was "too liberal" and "too weak" on national security.

Some of Clinton's major domestic policy accomplishments—the deficit-reducing budget of 1993, the 1994 crime bill, and the welfare overhaul of 1996—were shaped by this political need to "play against type" (Skowronek, 1997, 455)—that is, to defy the stereotype of the old-time big-spending liberal. The same can be said of some of his major foreign policy accomplishments. In foreign economic matters, Clinton renounced protectionism and pushed for the free trade deals, NAFTA (1993), GATT (1994), APEC (1993), and granting permanent normal trade relations (PNTR) to China (2000).[32] Clinton's push for NATO

---

[32] Clinton understood that moving in this direction would anger liberal constituencies (e.g., labor, human rights groups) and, to some extent, sought to soften the blow by imposing unilateral sanctions against European and Japanese exporters accused of dumping goods in the U.S. market and using the Commerce Department to actively promote U.S. manufactured exports. Yet backing free trade created an opportunity for Clinton to demonstrate his political independence and to earn the support of fast-growing, internationally competitive high-tech and service sector industries (Shoch, 2001, 228–30). These sectors were not strongly attached to the Republican Party, and they were a huge potential source of votes and, especially, money. Liberal, redistributive Democratic programs could not win

expansion into Eastern Europe in 1997 was similar in this regard (Gold-geier, 1997, 94–95). Many liberal Democratic organizations lined up against the expansion of NATO into Poland, Hungary, and the Czech Republic, arguing that it was unnecessary geopolitically and that it need-lessly threatened Moscow's interests. For Clinton, however, just such an expansion of NATO was an opportunity to demonstrate that Democrats could be tough on national security.[33]

Insider accounts make it clear that Clinton worried about being per-ceived as a second Jimmy Carter (Halberstam, 2001). Although rhetori-cally invested in an "assertive multilateralism" that would have reduced the nation's reliance on "guns" and military power (and freed up a peace dividend for investment in the "butter" of social spending), he backed off when he encountered Republican opposition. One consequence is that Clinton, though generally supportive of multilateral diplomacy, es-pecially in foreign economic affairs, temporized when public support for a growing reliance on cost-sharing multilateral partnerships faltered in other areas (Patrick, 2002; Skidmore, 2005, 222–23).[34] Clinton turned out to be less ready to abandon the instruments of Cold War balanc-ing—military alliances, forward deployment of U.S. forces, and the direct use of military power (see chapter 6)—than his campaign promises or the changed international circumstances (end of the Cold War) would have predicted. In 1993, when eighteen U.S. soldiers died in Somalia and pub-lic backing of "humanitarian intervention" plummeted, Clinton's support for UN peacekeeping missions fell sharply. When prospects for easy Sen-ate ratification of the 1997 Kyoto Protocol on Climate Change dimmed, Clinton bowed to conservative Republican pressures, opting not to sub-mit the treaty to Congress. In 2000 Clinton signed the Rome Statute of the International Criminal Court (ICC). Yet here, too, when Republican opposition stiffened over what some saw as a surrender of sovereign pre-rogative, Clinton opted to not submit the controversial treaty for Senate ratification.[35] In short, as the level of domestic political risk for Clinton went up, the *intensity* of his support of multilateralism went down.

---

over this new class of voters and investors. What *could* help move them into the Democratic column were the promise of greater access to foreign markets and investment opportunities, and a new image of the Democrats as probusiness and forward-looking.

[33] That this appealed to ethnic voters in the suburbs surrounding big northeastern cities (e.g., Macomb County north of Detroit) who had abandoned the Democratic Party in the 1980s was an additional political bonus (Greenberg, 1996).

[34] Democrats during this period strongly favored investing in multilateral diplomacy and international institutions. By working with foreign partners and international institutions, the U.S. could defray some of the costs of international leadership (Patrick, 2002, 13).

[35] Recognizing that domestic opposition to the ICC posed a problem, Clinton had earlier begun pressing (unsuccessfully) other governments for provisions that would have given the United States effective veto power over the submission of cases to the court.

Clinton was equally sensitive to public indifference toward foreign affairs. He governed at a time when there was no clear and present threat to U.S. interests. The fiasco in Somalia erased any doubts Clinton might have entertained about this. He reminded his advisers that "Americans are basically isolationist. They understand at a basic gut level Henry Kissinger's vital-interest argument. Right now the average American doesn't see our interest threatened to the point where we should sacrifice one American life" (Chollet and Goldgeier, 2008, 82).[36]

This did not prevent Clinton from using military force, but it did lead him to rely heavily on "missile diplomacy."[37] As commander in chief, Clinton was a "half-hearted" interventionist (Dueck, 2006, 138), relying on airpower and long-range precision-guided munitions (i.e., cruise missiles) to retaliate for attacks against American overseas interests, such as the attacks against U.S. embassies in Kenya and Tanzania. Clinton relied on the same instruments to punish foreign leaders (including Iraq's Saddam Hussein and Yugoslavia's Slobodan Milosevic) for violating U.S.-backed UN security resolutions, or engaging in crimes of "ethnic cleansing."[38] At a time when the United States faced few geopolitical constraints on exercising its military power, missile diplomacy posed few *international or domestic* risks for Clinton.[39]

As table 5.3 indicates, most Democrats in Congress could support Clinton's low-risk strategy of "missile diplomacy" toward Bosnia, Iraq, and Kosovo.[40] Democrats tended to be wary of the projection of Ameri-

---

[36] Public doubts about Clinton's political authority as commander in chief only made it more essential that any use of force involve few U.S. casualties, thus reinforcing Clinton's incentives to favor missile diplomacy over ground troops.

[37] During his presidency Clinton ordered acts of war against five states or substate entities: Bosnian Serbs in 1995; Iraq in 1996 and 1998, as part of ongoing operations after the 1991 Persian Gulf War; Sudan and Afghanistan in 1998; and Yugoslavia in 1999. Yet Clinton's war-making record belies a deep, persistent reluctance, sometimes refusal, to commit troops.

[38] In 1998, for example, Clinton used missile diplomacy against Saddam Hussein for the Iraq leader's repeated violations of UN cease-fire provisions set in place after the 1991 Gulf War. In 1999 Clinton ordered the bombing of Yugoslavia in response to Serbian repression in the Yugoslav region of Kosovo. For a good discussion of these and other instances of Clinton's missile diplomacy, see Butfoy (2006).

[39] As Butfoy (2006, 106) concludes in his careful survey of Clinton's approach to the use of force, "The biggest hurdle for U.S. strategists was not enemy military capabilities, Russian objections, or the UN. Rather, it was self-deterrence. Western public opinion, as well as Congressional and Pentagon reluctance to engage, provided major constraints on the development of a comprehensive interventionist policy. This seemed to suit Clinton's preoccupation with domestic politics."

[40] Missile diplomacy includes votes on the use of U.S. military power in Bosnia, Kosovo, Iraq, Afghanistan, and the Sudan. Free trade includes roll call votes on the 1993 North American Free Trade Agreement (NAFTA), the 1993 implementation of the Uruguay

TABLE 5.3.
Democratic and Republican support for Bill Clinton's foreign policies,
1993–2001

	Missile Diplomacy		Free Trade		Missile Defense	
	Party support	Party cohesion	Party support	Party cohesion	Party support	Party cohesion
Democrats	73%	48%	64%	34%	60%	48%
Republicans	16%	70%	72%	46%	58%	86%

Roll call voting in the U.S. House of Representatives from the 103rd through 106th
Congress. Number of roll call votes: missile diplomacy (11); free trade (18); missile
defense (5).

can firepower—at least since the Vietnam War (Kupchan and Trubowitz,
2007). But they could support Clinton's brand of power projection, precisely because it was low risk and low cost. By contrast, Democratic support for Clinton's efforts to promote free trade was lower. Democratic
cohesion was also lower: Democratic lawmakers who represented high-
tech districts in California and elsewhere voted with Republicans in favor
of Clinton's move toward freer trade. On military spending, Clinton was
more in sync with his Democratic base, though even here he was careful not to align too closely with the party's most "dovish" lawmakers.
On the litmus test issue of missile defense, Clinton tried to have it both
ways (Chollet and Goldgeier, 2008, 236; Wirls, 2010, 47–51, 86–88).
He blocked Republican efforts to ratchet up missile defense spending
and commit the country to a multiyear deployment schedule. America, he
argued, had "to meet future threats at an affordable cost."[41] But he also

---

Round of the General Agreement on Tariffs and Trade (GATT), and the failed attempt to
gain fast-track trade authority in 1998. It also includes efforts by Clinton to promote trade
in sub-Saharan Africa (1998 and 2000), the Caribbean (1998 and 2000), and Vietnam
(1999 and 2000) and annual extensions of most-favored-nation trading status for China
and permanent normal trade relations (PNTR) with the People's Republic in 2000. Missile
defense includes efforts by Clinton to reduce funding as well as attempts by Republicans to
increase spending and set a deployment schedule in place. Only roll call votes where Clinton
took a position, for or against, were included in the analysis. Clinton's policy preferences
are available through the Policy Agendas Project at the University of Texas at Austin: http://
www.policyagendas.org/.

[41] Clinton reduced missile defense funding by more than 50 percent in his first term.
Republicans pressed the case for national missile defense, making it one of the planks in
their 1994 Contract with America. Two years later, Senator Bob Dole of Kansas, the party's
putative frontrunner for the presidency, proposed a Defend America Act for missile defense.
Yet these efforts amounted to little at the level of policy.

kept his distance from proposals by progressive Democrats such as Barney Frank (Massachusetts), Ron Dellums (California), and Pat Schroeder (Colorado), who urged deep cuts in missile defense.

There were thus limits to how far, and how hard, Clinton was willing to push back against Republicans on defense spending. On some issues, he looked for opportunities to appease Republicans. This is what happened on the issue of military readiness.[42] In the 1990s, Republicans managed to turn readiness into "the dominant controversy and trope surrounding military spending" (Wirls, 2010, 74). Clinton's efforts to shift federal moneys to social programs, they charged, threatened the ability of the armed forces to intervene on short notice in any number of possible "hot spots" in the Middle East and East Asia (Kagan and Kagan, 2000). Clinton was "hollowing out" the military force structure, they claimed. The Republicans' criticisms stung. As the mid-1990s economic turnaround eased the guns-versus-butter trade-off, Clinton went far in responding to Republican concerns on this front.

In his second term, the president had fiscal latitude that he had lacked in his early years in office. The tight fiscal situation of 1993 and 1994 had loosened considerably by 1998 and 1999, thanks to economic turnaround and the effects of Clinton's 1993 deficit-reducing budget. Between 1994 and 1999, federal tax revenues rose 33 percent in real terms, producing a federal surplus of $70 billion in 1998 that would balloon to $236 billion by 2000 (Wirls, 2010, 85). The large surpluses allowed Clinton to respond to Republican attacks on the readiness issue without actually forcing the Democrats to choose between guns and butter. Much of his second-term increase in military spending went to the operations and maintenance and the personnel side of the defense budget (Wirls, 2010, 82–86). At the same time, he responded to core Democratic pressures for increased domestic spending on social programs.

Leaders who preside at a time when security is abundant can afford to downplay foreign policy. Whether they do, I argue, depends on whether this strengthens their domestic coalition and their own hold on power. The Clinton case shows that this argument does not always generate unambiguous predictions, especially when there is ambiguity about how to "code" international and domestic circumstances in terms of the model. Clinton presided at a time of transition on both fronts, so it is perhaps not surprising that the case is located in the gray zones of the model. Clinton had strong partisan incentives to sharply reduce America's strategic

---

[42] In strictly political terms, readiness was "a motherhood and apple pie" issue (Wirls, 2010, 76). Everyone on Capitol Hill was for military readiness, even liberal Democrats, who had cut their political teeth during the bruising domestic battles over Pentagon spending in the Vietnam era.

commitments and capabilities and little geopolitical reason, apparently, not to do so. The model of grand-strategy determinants that is developed in this book predicts that Clinton would be an underachiever, like Van Buren and Hoover. However, Clinton presided over a fluid and novel Democratic coalition, and a time of much attention to the possibility of the emergence of a "new international threat." The net result in grand strategy was that he was ambivalent about reversing U.S. grand strategy and only partially committed to retrenchment. Contra strict realism, he did not exploit U.S. primacy to expand the nation's geopolitical footprint, but he did not shrink the country's foreign commitments or radically downsize U.S. military capabilities. As Garry Wills (1997, 44) observed, Clinton was a "foreign policy minimalist, doing as little as possible as late as possible in place after place."

THE PARADOX OF STRATEGIC "UNDEREXTENSION"

In the basic realist account of grand strategy, there is high correlation between a state's relative power and its international influence. As a state's relative capabilities increase, so will its geopolitical clout. Yet the history of world politics is littered with exceptions to this rule—states whose power outstripped their influence, and states that failed to convert their material resources into international influence. International relations scholars have traditionally focused more attention on the "anomaly" of strategic overextension, but every era also has its strategic under-achievers. In the seventeenth century, scholars agree that Holland fits this description (Brewer, 1989). Its leaders were unable or unwilling to convert their nation's great trading prowess into geopolitical influence. In the late nineteenth century, it was America whose raw power often outstripped the ambitions of its policy (Graebner, 1985; Zakaria, 1998). Today, scholars debate whether Japan, Germany, and the large, resource-rich states of Russia and Brazil deserve this unflattering appellation (e.g., Walt, 2009).

Why do states sometimes "punch below their weight?" Some scholars attribute this "failing" to cultural pathologies (Dueck, 2006). Others see weak institutions as the principal cause of underexpansion—the weaker the state, the harder it is for statesmen to exploit the nation's relative power for international gain (Zakaria, 1998). Still others claim that social fragmentation can lead statesmen to undercommit (Schweller, 2006). These explanations all assume that the source of underexpansion is *domestic*. The analysis here confirms that domestic politics does play a role, but it identifies the critical variable as party politics (or domestic coalitional politics more generally), rather than strategic culture, institutional structure, or social cohesion. Moreover, in the model developed here, international circumstances are just as important in explaining why and when leaders opt for nonexpansion. When leaders have geopolitical slack, they have little to fear internationally in pursuing a strategy of retrenchment. Whether they actually do depends on whether strategic retrenchment and other forms of nonexpansion serve their domestic political interests.

This is one lesson of the Van Buren and Hoover presidencies. In both cases, the president had geopolitical slack and, thus, little to fear internationally from focusing on domestic matters. Both Van Buren and Hoover had to contend with powerful veto constituencies within their parties who worried that foreign expansionism would harm their narrow interests. The *Innenpolitik* interests that mattered the most politically lobbied against, not for, expansionism. Having little domestic incentive to make foreign policy a priority, Van Buren and Hoover chose not to do so. This meant rejecting foreign war panaceas that they might have found more attractive under different domestic political circumstances. Van Buren and Hoover were relatively unconstrained internationally but hamstrung domestically. Strategic retrenchment was the path of least resistance. Clinton's international and domestic circumstances were comparable to Van Buren's and Hoover's: Clinton enjoyed geopolitical slack and was the leader of a political party that, in the main, opposed expansionism.[43] Given uncertainty about how long unipolarity would last, popular doubts about Clinton's suitability as commander in chief, and the attempt by "New Democrats" to craft a "centrist" grand strategy, it is not surprising that Clinton chose to soft-pedal retrenchment. The soaring federal purse and the soft budget constraint meant that Clinton was better positioned to finesse the obvious political choices between guns and butter than Van Buren and Hoover had been.

---

[43] One might plausibly point to state strength as the difference: certainly, the American state in the 1990s was stronger than the state of the 1920s, let alone the 1830s. Yet there are clear limits to this argument. Van Buren and Hoover's parties controlled the executive branch and Congress. (During Hoover's four years, the Republicans controlled the Senate for four years and the House for two.) By contrast, divided government was the norm during Clinton's presidency. (The Republicans controlled the House and Senate for six of Clinton's eight years in office.)

CHAPTER SIX

Conclusion

STATECRAFT'S TWIN ENGINES

"I CLAIM NOT TO HAVE CONTROLLED EVENTS," Abraham Lincoln wrote, "but confess plainly that events have controlled me."[1] Lincoln was hardly a passive, disinterested leader, but his admission reminds us that while leaders make grand strategy, they do not make it under circumstances of their own choosing. Leaders hold the reins of power under varying international and domestic conditions. The international environment can be security poor or security rich; the risk of foreign policy failure and political blame can be great or small. What domestic coalitions want from, and expect of, national leaders also varies greatly. Partisans may prefer guns to butter, or the reverse. How much slack leaders have internationally and how much they benefit from investing in guns as opposed to butter, goes far in predicting the grand strategy leaders will choose. Geopolitical slack and partisan preference are the twin engines of statecraft.

This conclusion summarizes the book's core argument and discusses its implications for theories of grand strategy and for U.S. foreign policy in the near future. I offer an assessment of the model that is based not so much on how well it fits with the empirical materials already presented (that is done in earlier chapters) as on its generalizability and ability to speak to the present. I begin by showing that the model can account for the well-known cases of internal balancing by the United States during the Cold War. I then discuss the book's main contribution to the study of grand strategy. The next section discusses how the basic argument can be extended to the nondemocratic regimes of Vladimir Putin's Russia and Hu Jintao's China to explain why these regimes are not actively balancing against the United States. I close by discussing the shape of things to come in U.S. grand strategy. My theory predicts that under Barack Obama, the United States will opt for strategic retrenchment, scaling back, and limiting U.S. commitments. America's geopolitical position and the policy preferences of Obama's Democratic Party explain why Obama is likely to continue to move in this direction.

---

[1] The quote is from a letter Lincoln wrote in April 1864 to Albert G. Hodges, editor of the *Frankfort (Ky.) Commonwealth* (J. Wright, 2006, 261).

AMERICAN BALANCING IN HISTORICAL PERSPECTIVE

Balancing is one of statecraft's oldest grand strategies. It is also one that America's leaders had little occasion to use, at least before World War II. Before the 1940s, the only president who could be classified clearly as a "balancer" is Woodrow Wilson (1913–21), and in Wilson's case, this was true for a two-year span (1917–18) of his presidency.[2] In the American context, the classic era of balancing was the Cold War (Mearsheimer, 2001, 323). The broad strategic principle that would guide U.S. grand strategy during the Cold War was part of U.S. strategic thinking as early as 1941, when Nicholas Spykman defined the central geopolitical goal of the United States as the preservation of a balance of power in Eurasia. The objective was to prevent any state, or coalition of states, from gaining control over the Eurasian landmass, "where alone lay the resources and population levels which, if ever amalgamated, might overwhelm American might" (Kurth, 1999, 6). What would eventually become known as the strategy of containment directed against the Soviet Union (and, for a time, China) was an axiom of U.S. planning by 1945 (Trachtenberg, 1999, 34–35).

It was the depth and durability of the commitment to containment, or internal balancing, that distinguished the country's foreign policy in this era from what had come before. All of America's Cold War presidents can be described as opting for the grand strategy that is captured in scenario I of figure 2.2. Internal balancing for all of them involved costly efforts to defend the post–World War II status quo by checking and containing Soviet power. Yet as John Lewis Gaddis (2005) points out, the Cold War consensus was not a consensus over *how much* of the state's resources to invest in national security. On this, there was variation across administrations. Harry Truman (from 1950 on), John Kennedy, and Ronald Reagan presided over large increases in U.S. military spending and constitute the starkest cases of internal balancing during the Cold War. Others, including Dwight Eisenhower, Richard Nixon, and (initially) Jimmy Carter, were internal balancers who looked for ways to dampen down arms spending.[3]

---

[2] In 1916 Wilson responds militarily to German sabotage and submarine attacks by commissioning "a navy second to none" and in 1917, by sending a substantial force of ground soldiers to France to stave off a German breakthrough and seal Germany's defeat. Having entered office with geopolitical slack and facing strong domestic pressure to invest in domestic policy (scenario IV in figure 2.2), Wilson responded to the outbreak of war in Europe initially by satisficing (neutrality) and ultimately by balancing against Germany. For a good concise account of Wilson's strategic adjustment, see Quester (2004).

[3] After initially slowing defense spending, Carter increased it sharply in 1979 in response to a series of international setbacks and mounting criticism by the Republican right.

The theory of executive choice of grand strategy that we have developed in the preceding chapters offers considerable leverage in accounting for both the similarity and the differences across the grand strategies of America's Cold War presidents. For leaders who presided over parties that strongly favored investing in "guns," geopolitical imperatives and party politics provided mutually reinforcing incentives to make heavy investments in internal balancing. In the late 1940s and early 1950s, the combination of deteriorating geopolitical conditions in Europe and East Asia and the growing support inside the Democratic Party for military Keynesianism (Fordham, 1998) gave Truman strong incentive to actively balance against Soviet power.[4] A decade later, Soviet technological breakthroughs and penetration into the Third World, and the Democratic Party's strong (if ultimately unsustainable) support for both guns *and* butter, gave Kennedy and his successor, Lyndon Johnson, every reason to double down on Soviet containment. Twenty years later, a widely held view that geopolitical events were trending against the United States, and the wholesale shift of powerful pro-defense constituencies and voting blocs to the Republican Party, led Ronald Reagan to do much the same thing (Trubowitz, 1998, 225–32). Reagan invested in expensive military strategies aimed at containing Soviet power in Europe and checking nationalist challenges to U.S. interests in the Third World (Zakaria, 1990). Truman, Kennedy, and Reagan could invest heavily in *internal* balancing against Soviet power at little political cost to themselves. Military build-up even generated domestic political advantages. What was considered good statecraft (containing Moscow) also made good party politics.

This could not be as easily said of Eisenhower, Nixon, or Carter. Each presided at a time when his party was reluctant to spend vast sums of money on military build-up (or, in the cases of Eisenhower and Nixon, on social welfare). All three cut the Pentagon's budget. For these Cold War presidents, allies were partly a substitute for arms: Eisenhower via his "New Look" network of cheaper security pacts (e.g., SEATO in Southeast Asia; CENTO in the Middle East); Nixon through his "tacit alliance" with Communist China (Mann, 2000, 56) and his American-centered system of "regional policemen" in the Middle East, sub-Saharan Africa, and Latin America; and Carter, more indirectly, through his efforts to align America's interests with the UN General Assembly.

---

[4] In the late 1940s, Truman's early post–World War II efforts to bind other nations into a new American-led international order was transformed by the rise of Soviet power and deteriorating geopolitical conditions in Europe and East Asia. Truman responded with a hybrid strategy, actively balancing against Soviet power, on the one hand, while continuing to bind Western Europe and Japan into a Pax Americana, on the other. On Truman's efforts at binding, see Ikenberry (2001, 163–214).

Throughout the Cold War, America's presidents as day-to-day reelection seekers thought as much about what geopolitics could do *to* them as they did about what it could do *for* them. The risk of strategic failure (e.g., the possibility of a technological breakthrough that would tip the nuclear balance to the Soviets, the fall of a country to communism) led them to look for ways to hedge and limit their political exposure. Because Truman's, Kennedy's, and Reagan's parties stood to benefit disproportionately from investing in guns, actively balancing against Soviet power had the virtues of being both desirable and possible. By contrast, Eisenhower, Nixon, and Carter had powerful incentive to find less expensive ways to balance against Soviet power.

GEOPOLITICS AND PARTISAN POLITICS:
MANAGING CROSS-PRESSURE

Studies of grand strategy generally give pride of place to either international or domestic variables. This book is based on the premise that this international-domestic distinction is counterproductive and unnecessary. In making grand strategy, leaders take both geopolitics and domestic politics seriously because it is in their political self-interest to do so. By going to the microfoundational level of the individual leader, it is possible to take into account both *Realpolitik*'s concern with security and power and *Innenpolitik*'s emphasis on domestic interests and coalitions. Moreover, this makes it possible to generate predictions about grand strategy that are far more nuanced, and often more valid, than either *Realpolitik* or *Innenpolitik* can generate on their own. We can incorporate core *Realpolitik* and *Innenpolitik* insights about the importance of international and domestic politics and do so in a way that is consistent with domestic political analyses of the real trade-offs and choices that leaders face in setting national priorities.

Politics and Strategy also improves our understanding of how political leaders manage conflicting geopolitical and partisan pressures. Realist theories of grand strategy offer little help in this regard because they provide no model of how party dynamics and coalition politics shape and influence foreign policy choices. Many realists recognize that domestic politics matter in foreign policy, but exactly how party politics and geopolitics interact to produce grand strategy has eluded realists' grasp.[5]

---

[5] Domestic politics can and do play a role in some versions of realism (in the form of state structure, ideology, etc.), but as a rule, realists do not highlight the independent influence that coalition (party) politics exercise on the making of grand strategy. Snyder's (1991) account of strategic overexpansion goes farthest in this direction. Among historians, Kennedy's (1981) treatment of British grand strategy is a notable exception.

These variables enter realist accounts as ad hoc factors that help explain the anomalies generated by realist theory. *Innenpolitik* theories of foreign policy suffer from the reverse problem. In drawing attention to the role of domestic interests and politics, *Innenpolitik* theories ignore or downplay the ways in which the presence or absence of international threat conditions leaders' responses to partisan demands and popular opinion. *Innenpolitikers* rightly argue that leaders respond to pressure from below, and to the demands of privileged supporters, but in international affairs leaders' ability to do so is constrained by geopolitical pressures and opportunities.

By going to the microfoundational level of the individual statesman, *Politics and Strategy* shows that it is possible to explain how political leaders forge ("choose") their grand strategies without making heroic assumptions about their statesman-like motives or, alternatively, without reducing them to the agents of powerful domestic interests. Core ideas in *Realpolitik* and *Innenpolitik* can be brought together in a parsimonious model to explain when we can expect leaders to favor ambitious and expensive grand strategies, and when they are likely to define the nation's interests more narrowly and to rely on less costly means. Indeed, this approach makes it easier to understand why some states overreach in foreign affairs while others are remembered for failing to do enough. Leaders most susceptible to strategic overcommitment are those who lead domestic coalitions that strongly prefer investing the state's resources in guns rather than butter. These leaders have powerful incentives to invest in ambitious, expensive foreign policies. They are the most susceptible to overshooting the mark, or what international relations scholars refer to as overbalancing and overexpansion. By contrast, leaders who preside over domestic coalitions that strongly prefer butter to guns are the statesmen most apt to underreach or underbalance in foreign policy. Because these leaders' coalitions favor security on the cheap, the practical realities of holding on to power make satisficing strategies and isolationism more politically attractive.

Realpolitik leads us to expect that leaders facing similar international circumstances will choose similar grand strategies. As we have seen, sometimes leaders do. However, frequently they do not. Monroe and Van Buren, for example, held office when security was plentiful; they had geopolitical slack. Yet they chose radically different strategies: Monroe favored expansionism and spheres-of-influence; Van Buren saw advantage in retrenchment. McKinley and Hoover also chose strategies that differed sharply in ambition and cost, even though both had geopolitical slack. *Relative* international power also does not account for these differences.[6]

---

[6] Neoclassical realist domestic variables such as state strength are also underdetermining. Monroe and Van Buren both held office when the American state was very much "one

The United States was on the periphery of the international system during both the Monroe and Van Buren presidencies, but these leaders did not push for the same type of grand strategy. Similarly, Hoover's America was more powerful than McKinley's, but greater economic clout did not translate into more expansive foreign policy ends or to a build-up of power projection capabilities. Hoover retrenched.

Innenpolitik also is underdetermining and like *Realpolitik*, it overpredicts expansionism. Washington, Van Buren, Lincoln, Hoover, and Roosevelt all had ample incentive to "gamble for resurrection" by engaging in diversionary war tactics. Their domestic circumstances were dire (and in Van Buren's and Lincoln's cases, close advisers did in fact urge the president to manufacture or exploit foreign policy crises for domestic political gain). They all resisted. This is not because these presidents were "above" politics, or because they thought that when it comes to foreign policy, partisan politics should stop at the water's edge. Each chose foreign policies that were generally consistent with the interests of their parties (or faction, in Washington's case), as did most of the presidents considered here. Where expansionism did serve presidents' electoral ends—as in the cases of Monroe, McKinley, and Bush—leaders used it largely as a means to divide the electorate and their domestic opponents, rather than to manufacture political consensus.

Because strategic politicians must attend to the broad interests of their domestic coalitions, it is not surprising that *Innenpolitik* theories that link foreign policy choice to interests of domestic groups perform better than diversionary war theories. Yet here, too, national leaders weigh geopolitical as well as partisan pressures. This is why Van Buren put a stop to Democratic pressure to assist Canadians rebelling against British rule—the risk of foreign policy failure was too great.[7] It also explains why Lincoln resisted Republican demands to get tough with London for selling ships to the Confederacy when these ships were wreaking havoc on northern commerce. Similarly, Roosevelt parried pressure from progressive Democrats who were eager to steer clear of European affairs when it became too risky to ignore Hitler's ambitions. Leaders do think about how foreign policy can help them domestically, as *Innenpolitikers* suggest. But as strategic politicians, they also have strong incentives to

---

of courts and parties" (Skowronek, 1982). The federal government was relatively weak and decentralized. McKinley and Hoover held office during an era when the federal government's powers were expanding—when its capacity to extract national resources was growing (and its ability to respond more directly to international pressures and opportunities was increasing) (Zakaria, 1998).

[7] Annexation fever risked an unnecessary war with London at an otherwise peaceful time and threatened to further weaken Van Buren's party.

avoid foreign policies that threaten to generate failures or crises that will hurt them politically.[8]

Our model of grand-strategy choice also sheds light on theories of *Ideapolitik* (Legro, 2005). It illuminates the circumstances under which leaders will invoke some strategic narratives and not others. Leaders like Monroe, McKinley, and Bush who hold power when security is plentiful and expansionism pays well domestically are the ones who are most likely to invoke grandiose arguments about national greatness, "manifest destiny," and spreading civilization. There is little geopolitical risk, and substantial partisan advantage, in doing so. By contrast, leaders who need security on the cheap (presidents like Washington, Lincoln, and Roosevelt during the 1930s) are more likely to stress the limits of national power, the need to keep ends and means in balance, and the dangers of foreign adventurism.

Our analysis also indicates that simple "median-voter" models of domestic influence on foreign policy should be viewed with caution. As Robert Putnam (1988, 458) argues, how states respond to international constraints (opportunities) depends greatly on what he calls "the fixed costs of [domestic] coalition-building." Because leaders' hold on power depends on a particular "support coalition," to use Putnam's term, two leaders facing similar international circumstances (e.g., a rising geopolitical challenger) may respond in very different ways. As we have seen, one leader may respond assertively by investing heavily in military power—by pursing an "internal balancing" strategy. A leader with a different support coalition might find it too costly or even impossible to respond by ratcheting up the state's militarily capabilities and may thus have to rely on cheaper diplomatic means. A "median voter" analysis will wash out the difference between these two situations, providing unreliable predictions (or no prediction) about what type of grand strategy a leader will favor.[9]

---

[8] This does not mean that leaders always succeed in avoiding foreign policy failure. History is full of examples of political leaders who in an effort to stave off foreign policy failure sowed the seeds of their eventual downfall. Lyndon Johnson's effort to preempt domestic attack for not doing enough to prevent failure in South Vietnam is perhaps the most costly example in modern American history. In Johnson's case, the president recognized the trade-off but decided that not doing enough to keep the South Vietnamese regime propped up would be worse, domestically, than doing too much. On Johnson's view of the domestic risks of military intervention and nonintervention, see, for example, his telephone conversation with Senator Richard Russell (Georgia), Johnson's longtime colleague and former political mentor (Miller Center, 1964).

[9] Some analysts implicitly assume that U.S. grand strategy during the Cold War was shaped by "median voter" logic. As noted earlier, presidents of both political parties relied on "internal balancing" to check Soviet power. Yet the median voter masks a deeper structural property of the Cold War era: a party system where the core constituencies of

In each of the cases examined in this book, presidential choice had a great deal to do with presidents' international and domestic political circumstances—their place in "political time," to borrow Stephen Skowronek's (1997) apt phrase. It had very little to do with presidents' personality traits, governing styles, or foreign policy backgrounds. Classic "first image" distinctions between pragmatists and crusaders, "extroverts" and "introverts," and experience and inexperience are poor predictors of the *type* of grand strategy (the mix of ambition and cost) leaders prefer. Historians generally consider Washington, McKinley, and Clinton to be pragmatists. Yet their foreign policies differed markedly, both in ambition and in cost (they occupy different cells in figure 2.2). Similarly, Lincoln, Truman, and Bush all came to the presidency with no diplomatic experience to speak of. This had little bearing on their choice of foreign policy approach. The same can be said of presidents who were well versed in foreign affairs: Monroe, Van Buren, and Roosevelt are examples. Their experience made them no more likely to favor ambitious grand strategy than others. What we have seen is that political leaders who are placed in similar strategic situations (on both the domestic and international fronts) behave in broadly similar ways: they chose the same *type* of grand strategy.[10]

Presidents' choices are also much less sensitive to "time in office" than popular wisdom holds. Second-term presidents are often thought to be uniquely autonomous from domestic political pressures because they do not face the demands of reelection yet. When viewed together, the cases examined in this book indicate that two-term presidents are no more likely to buck their partisans and "play to the history books" than first-termers. Eight of the twelve chief executives we have considered served more than one term: Washington, Monroe, McKinley, Roosevelt, Truman, Reagan, Clinton, and Bush.[11] Only Roosevelt and, arguably, Rea-

---

the two parties overlapped to a significant degree (Trubowitz, 1998). One consequence is that national-level politics was uncharacteristically bipartisan for much of the Cold War (Trubowitz and Mellow, 2005; Kupchan and Trubowitz, 2007).

[10] This does not mean that leaders are completely interchangeable, or that political skill does not matter. George Washington, Abraham Lincoln, and Franklin Roosevelt held office when the pressures and cross-pressures of geopolitics and party politics were acute. Lesser leaders, I argue, would have responded similarly: they would have gravitated toward scenario III in figure 2.2. Whether they would have been as successful as Washington and Lincoln in warding off foreign dangers, or as deft as Roosevelt in responding to changing international circumstances, is another matter and lies beyond the scope of our model. The model of executive choice predicts that leaders will choose foreign policies strategically and that, as the parameters of geopolitics and party politics change, their foreign policies will adjust accordingly. Even if the model could predict perfectly on this front (and it cannot), it would not tell us when one grand strategy will succeed and another fail. That depends as much on other states' responses as it does on leaders' choices.

[11] Washington, Monroe, Reagan, Clinton, and Bush all served two full terms. McKinley was reelected in November 1900 and served until his death the following September.

gan adopted second-term positions that might be interpreted as putting their personal legacy before partisan interests.[12] Monroe, Clinton, and Bush were no more likely to buck their partisans in the second term. Washington's foreign policies were, if anything, more in tune with Federalist sentiment in his second term. An assassin's bullet cut McKinley's presidency short early in his second term, so we do not have the evidence needed to call this case. Still, it seems unlikely that McKinley would have abandoned expansionist policies that encountered little international resistance and paid off handsomely at the ballot box.[13]

The model of executive choice that is developed here stresses how geopolitics and party politics, working in tandem, influence the formulation of grand strategy. One limitation of our model is that it does not capture the full complexity of these interactive effects.[14] Geopolitics can shape party politics, as it did in the 1930s. As the crisis in Europe deepened, it became easier for Democrats to back Roosevelt's efforts to aid Britain and, as the party in power, harder for Democrats *not* to do so politically. Increasingly, Republicans found themselves on the political defensive. The Japanese attack at Pearl Harbor silenced Republican opposition. Party politics can also affect *foreign leaders'* calculations. George Washington spoke directly to this issue in his Farewell Address, warning that sound statecraft required "the country's presenting a united face to an outside world only too happy to divide it" (Elkins and McKitrick, 1993, 497). The intensifying rivalry between the Federalists and the Republicans, Washington warned, would leave the country vulnerable to foreign mischief and "divide and conquer" stratagems.

In attempting to tease out the full complexities of the interactions between geopolitics and party politics, scholars are cautioned not to lose

---

Roosevelt, of course, was reelected three times, occupying the presidency from March 1933 to April 1945. Truman, who was Roosevelt's vice-president in 1945, served out the rest of FDR's term and was elected president in 1948.

[12] Yet even in the Roosevelt and Reagan cases, it is not obvious that legacy actually trumped partisanship in the second term. Roosevelt did distance himself from the brand of isolationism that many progressive Democrats favored. In doing so, however, he aligned himself more closely with interests in the Democratic Party (e.g., urban-industrial interests; southern planters) that preferred a more proactive approach to check the spread of economic nationalism in Europe. In Reagan's case, some conservative Republicans attacked him in his second term for supporting Soviet leader Mikhail Gorbachev's domestic reforms and for pursing arms control agreements with the Soviet leader. Whether Reagan's actions were driven by concerns about his personal legacy is unclear. Reagan, apparently, was aware that his efforts to work with Gorbachev would anger hard-liners in the Republican Party (Reeves, 2006, 294).

[13] William Jennings Bryan and the Democrats made opposition to expansionism the core issue in the 1900 presidential campaign, and they lost.

[14] For a discussion of "second order" interactive effects, see Trubowitz and Seo (2010).

sight of the basic findings of the present analysis. Geopolitics cannot be reduced to gaming party politics in other countries: the foreign policies one state adopts cannot be seen as only, or even mostly, a response to party (coalition) dynamics in other states. Meanwhile, party preferences are rooted in domestic politics and the forces that shape it: debates over economic development agendas, electoral competition, the rise and fall of social movements, and so on. Geopolitics alone cannot explain, for example, why the Republican Party in the U.S. preferred expansionism during McKinley's presidency, or conversely, the party's preference for a less ambitious and costly foreign policy under Hoover. Republicans in late 1890 America saw expansionism as a powerful antidote to the threat of agrarian populism ("Bryanism"), just as many Republicans in the early 1930s saw isolationism and protectionism as a means to fend off Democratic charges of incompetence and indifference to the hardships and suffering caused by the Great Depression. Electoral politics had as much to do with Republican efforts to raise tariff barriers under Hoover as it did with the Republicans' drive to open new markets in Latin America and East Asia during McKinley's presidency.

Another limitation of our model is that it does not make good predictions about variation *within* broad grand-strategy types. The model does well at predicting (postdicting) the *type* or range of grand strategies that a rational leader will be willing to authorize, mobilize resources for, and invest his or her own political capital in. It rests on the distinction between the four broad "types" of grand strategy that are depicted in the cells of figure 2.2. Our independent variables make a prediction about which "cell" of figure 2.2 the leader will choose, not about the strategy variant within that cell. For example, given the geopolitical and domestic political constraints George Washington confronted, the only type of strategy that was rational (i.e., that promised to protect his position as president) was a satisficing one that offered security on the cheap. Yet Washington's choice of appeasement over other cost-saving strategies such as buckpassing, bandwagoning, or neutralism depended on contingencies that lie beyond the scope of our model. In Washington's case these contingencies included the absence of another state that Washington could safely buckpass to and the infeasibility of neutrality because of America's dependence on trade.

To explain why one particular variant of a broad grand strategy is selected over another, we need a finer-grained model than the one developed here. The theoretical challenge is to amend the model in ways that do not violate its core assumption: that grand strategy is a means by which national leaders strive to maintain or strengthen their hold on executive power. It is not difficult to add variables, but there is little theoretical purchase in doing so if these do not predict differences in strategies that are otherwise similar in purpose and cost.

SECONDARY POWERS AND NONDEMOCRACIES

The model here is based on general principles about balance-of-power politics, domestic coalition building, and political choice. It travels beyond the American case because the tension inherent in leaders' dual role as statesmen and party or coalition leaders is present in regimes of all types. I have sought to show why these tensions are especially intense in democracies like the United States, but the same pressures and choices face leaders of nondemocracies as well.

Consider, for example, the case of China's current grand strategy consisting of what Fravel (2008) calls military policies of internal control, "peripheral denial" (perimeter defense), and limited force-projection, along with a good neighbor "diplomacy of reassurance." While analysts disagree sharply about China's future ambitions and whether it will emerge as a revisionist power, most China watchers still view the international goals of Chinese leader Hu Jintao as relatively conservative and nonexpansionist.[15] Although some see his foreign policy of "peaceful development" as a principled commitment to cooperation in East Asia and beyond, our theory of grand strategy's determinants suggests that Hu's strategy is a doubling down on the Chinese Communist Party's thirty-year effort to promote high rates of economic growth at a time when China faces no clear and present *external* threat to its security.[16] As Hu himself put it in 2008, in this "important period of strategic opportunity" China needs "to do everything possible in foreign affairs to meet the needs of the domestic political economy" (Li, 2009, 45).[17]

Hu's grip on political power and the party's tenuous domestic legitimacy rest on a base of delivering economic well-being ("butter") to its

---

[15] The literature here is substantial. I have relied on the following: A. Goldstein (2005); Shambaugh (2004–5); Lieberthal (2007); Shirk (2007); Johnston (2008); Medeiros (2009); and Ross (2009a; 2009b). For good summaries of scholarly debate about China's grand strategy and its implications for the United States see Christensen (2006).

[16] As A. Goldstein (2005, 28) notes, in the current period China's "periphery is arguably less threatened by great powers than at any time since the early nineteenth century." Many Chinese analysts share this view. They see the country's security environment as relatively benign—the risk of major war is generally thought to be low—and favorable for continued domestic growth and development. For an account of Chinese views, see Medeiros (2009, 19–44). Because most of that growth has benefited the country's coastal provinces disproportionately, Hu has sought to promote more regionally equitable development, albeit not as quickly as his supporters had hoped or many analysts had expected. On geographic growth patterns and regional political effects in China, see Hurst (2009).

[17] Some Chinese foreign policy analysts saw the U.S. undertaking in Iraq in 2003 as an opportunity for China. As one Chinese foreign policy expert suggested to me, China would gain geopolitical slack as the U.S. was tied down "trying to swallow a porcupine" in Iraq. Interview by author at Renmin University, March 2003.

citizens in the form of jobs, roads, housing, and high growth rates.[18] Among other things, this performance constraint gives Hu and his backers in the party "inner circle" strong incentive not to overreach in foreign policy, to invest (as they have) in cheaper defensive military capabilities (e.g., "internal control," "perimeter defense," "access denial"), and to limit spending for power projection to well-defined areas, including Taiwan (Swaine, 2006; Fravel, 2008; Ross, 2009a).[19] This logic also helps explain why Beijing has been less belligerent in managing territorial disputes with its neighbors than many *Realpolitik* or *Innenpolitik* scholars might have predicted (Fravel, 2007–8).

China's rapid ascendancy has made it a test case for realist theories that predict that as nations become richer, their external ambitions increase as well. And on the domestic front, China's widening income gap, intensifying regional disparities, and mounting internal strife would seem to be a recipe for the kinds of external "scapegoating," saber rattling, and diversionary wars that *Innenpolitik* theories predict. Yet neither set of predictions has panned out. What we see instead is a China that has relied increasingly on multilateral diplomacy and regional institutions (e.g. ASEAN, Shanghai-Cooperation Organization), both as a means to ease China's integration into East and Southeast Asia (Qin and Wei, 2008) and as a mechanism to allow China to project power cheaply (Yan, 2006). China's "charm offensive" in Southeast Asia and elsewhere reflects similar calculations (Kurlantzick, 2007), as does its more mercantile use of economic carrots to secure access to resources in Central Asia and sub-Saharan Africa that are needed to sustain China's economic development (I. Taylor, 2008).

Under Hu Jintao, authoritarian China has acted as our model of grand strategy's determinants would predict. China is punching below its weight: it is pursuing a strategy of "underextension" (scenario IV in figure 2.2). Geopolitical slack and pressing domestic needs make an ambitious expansionist grand strategy both unnecessary and unwise: unnecessary, because China faces no compelling international threat; and unwise, because such a strategy would likely invite a powerful American-led response.[20] China's leaders face difficult challenges at home, but they

[18] For a useful discussion of guns-versus-butter issues in Chinese leadership circles and among the Chinese public more broadly, see Frazier (2006).

[19] Beijing has increased spending on the Chinese military in recent years and is likely to continue doing so. However, much of China's defense spending and military apparatus is aimed at access denial, perimeter defense, and securing domestic stability rather than projecting power abroad, a point that is often lost in Western media accounts (Fravel, 2008; Ross, 2009a).

[20] Meanwhile, for the foreseeable future, Chinese leaders can count on the United States to keep Japan from launching a major military build-up under the U.S.-Japanese

do not yet face powerful, constraining, geopolitical cross-pressures. They have the luxury of putting domestic development first (Lieberthal, 2007).[21] As well-known analyst Wang Jisi puts it, China judges the success of its foreign policies on the basis of whether they ensure the smooth implementation of domestic initiatives (Li, 2009, 39).

This logic also generates a robust explanation for why China has chosen not to actively balance against American power.[22] Some analysts have argued that the explanation lies in America's huge power advantages (making it impossible for China to compete), but this does not account for China's conservative approach close to home, or its general tendency to tamp down saber-rattling. Others have argued that the Chinese believe that U.S. intentions in East Asia, Central Asia, and elsewhere are benign, but this seems to suggest that neither *Innenpolitik* nor realist calculations weigh on Chinese strategists. The answer that emerges from the logic we have pursued in this book is that the Chinese are not actively balancing against U.S. power because they have strong incentives not to do so. The configuration of geopolitical slack (security is plentiful) and domestic preference (butter over guns) facing China's rulers today makes "butter over guns" the Chinese leadership's best option. As long as these twin conditions hold, the current grand strategy is likely to persist, no matter who succeeds Hu Jintao at China's helm.

If Hu Jintao's China has punched below its weight, the same cannot be said of Vladimir Putin's Russia. The last decade has witnessed a resurgence of Russian power. Drift and vacillation had characterized Russian foreign policy during Boris Yeltsin's presidency in the 1990s. Initially content to let Russia be a junior partner of the West, Yeltsin later tried to push back against U.S. power over the war in Kosovo and NATO expansion. Putin has been far more disciplined in designing post–Cold War grand strategy for Russia.[23] Instead of searching for ways to accommodate, or alternatively, balance against, Washington, Putin sought to re-

---

security alliance and to shoulder a large part of the burden of maintaining stability on the Korean peninsula.

[21] This has also made it easier for Chinese leaders to hew closely to Deng Xiaoping's preferred path of selective engagement and incremental change in foreign affairs. Deng, the architect of China's dynamic "socialist market economy," cautioned party leaders against assuming the responsibilities (and costs) of international leadership. On Deng's impact on Chinese foreign policy making, see Yahuda (1993).

[22] It also helps explain why U.S. calls for China to become a "responsible stakeholder" in the prevailing international order have not fared well. On this point, see Mann (2010) and Shambaugh (2010). The phrase is Robert Zoellick's, U.S. trade representative during George W. Bush's administration.

[23] The literature on Russian grand strategy under Putin is large. I have relied heavily on the following: Lynch (2001); Wohlforth (2003); D. McDonald (2007); Wallander (2007); and Tsygankov (2008).

focus Russian statecraft by capitalizing on areas of comparative strategic advantage. In particular, Putin looked for ways to redefine Russia's relationship with Western markets and reassert Russian power by establishing a "sphere of influence" in the so-called Near Abroad—the republics in the Caucuses and Central Asia that emerged from the dissolution of the Soviet Union in 1991.[24] Since taking power in 2000, Putin has sought to leverage Russia's energy wealth and geopolitical position to gain greater control over Eurasian oil, gas, and minerals and over the terms on which Europe and Asia gain access to these natural resources (Olcott, 2004; Wallander, 2007; Stent, 2008; Mankoff, 2009).[25] This has meant larger budgets for Russia's conventional military forces; more forceful diplomacy in dealing with neighbors such as Ukraine, Belarus, and Turkmenistan; and greater willingness to use military force to check the rise of countries embracing Western-style democratization and liberalization, as in Putin's 2008 intervention in Georgia.[26]

Putin's "international assertiveness" (Tsygankov, 2008) is a textbook example of how international and domestic pressures can combine to produce an expansionist grand strategy, or more accurately, to make expansionism a grand strategy that is hard for a statesman to resist. Scenario II in figure 2.2 describes Putin's circumstances.[27] Internationally, Putin had geopolitical slack. As Allen Lynch (2001, 10) observes, Putin took office at a time when the international environment was relatively "permissive." Because geopolitical circumstance did not demand a status quo defensive strategy against the West, Russia did not pursue an active balancing strategy (Wohlforth, 2003). Under Yeltsin, the main threats to Russian security had been *internal*, not external. Russian GDP fell by 50 percent in the 1990s (Vinhas de Souza, 2008, 15), producing an economic recession that fueled political disaffection. There were calls from some

---

[24] Some analysts have interpreted Russian grand strategy under Putin as a form of balancing ("soft balancing") against the United States. See, for example, Joffe (2002); Paul (2004); and Pape (2005). For a critique of the soft-balancing argument, see Brooks and Wohlforth (2005).

[25] Putin became acting president in 1999 when Yeltsin resigned abruptly. Putin was elected president in 2000 and reelected in 2004. Because the Russian Constitution does not allow individuals to run for three consecutive presidential terms, Putin orchestrated the election of his protégé, Dmitry Medvedev. After Medvedev's election, he took up the post of prime minister.

[26] On this critical point, there is little disagreement among Russia watchers. However, Russian experts disagree sharply over the sustainability of the assertive foreign policies initiated by Putin. For a review of this debate, see Tsygankov (2009).

[27] I consider Putin's outward push to create a sphere of influence to be analogous to Monroe's offensive push in the Western Hemisphere. "Sphere of influence" per se is not necessarily a revisionist strategy. It can also be designed to preserve the status quo. We read Putin's strategy as revisionist.

quarters of Russian elite opinion for foreign policy retrenchment and withdrawal (Lynch, 2001).

The balance of constraint and opportunity shifted under Putin. After a decade of economic trauma and hardship, Russia experienced a period of stunning growth, easing many of the internal pressures that had accumulated under Yeltsin and making it possible for Putin to ratchet up military spending and consider a more expansive menu of international options.[28] Meanwhile, the pro-American "color revolutions" in Georgia (2003), Ukraine (2004), and Kyrgyzstan (2005) and mounting Islamic unrest in Central Asia posed new external challenges *and* opportunities (Tsygankov, 2008; Oliker et al., 2009, 93–104). Democratization and Islamic radicalization did not constitute a serious geopolitical threat to Russian security or to Putin's hold on power, but they did politicize the regional environment and aggravate Russian worries about the possibility of strongly pro-Western states or of "failed states" on their borders.[29] Globally, the geopolitical environment remained permissive as the United States, especially, sought Russian support in its war on terrorism and turned its attention to the wars in Iraq and Afghanistan.

Putin focused Russian attention and resources on managing the rapidly evolving situations in the Near Abroad. He had every domestic incentive to do so. Stabilizing these areas not only offered greater control over the pipelines, energy flows, and ultimately the profits that enabled Putin to build up huge currency reserves and spread largesse to partisan supporters in Russia (Gaddy and Ickes, 2009).[30] It also offered investment opportunities for Russian companies and extractive industries, now flush with capital. Putin used disputes with Ukraine, Belarus, and Georgia

---

[28] Military spending has increased dramatically under Putin, even if this is not fully reflected in its share of GDP. Barany (2008) estimates that military spending between 2000 and 2008 increased by nearly 500 percent, with growth rates in the military budget averaging 10 percent and in some years reaching as high as 20 percent.

[29] There was a possibility that Ukraine and Georgia might join NATO. Russian frustration over having swallowed two rounds of NATO expansion meant that Putin could not easily dismiss such a possibility. On the question of Russia's relationship to NATO, Putin has been far less consistent and more tactical than strategic. During the past decade, Putin has zigzagged between conflicting positions, saying at times that he wants to end Russia's observer status in Brussels and arguing on other occasions that Russia should become a full member of NATO.

[30] Putin used a large share of the windfall generated by the resource boom to retire the government's foreign debt and then to build reserves. In January 2005 Russia paid off its debts to the International Monetary Fund—a hangover from the Yeltsin era—and began accumulating funds in a newly created oil stabilization fund and in foreign exchange reserves. Between 2000 and mid-2008, Russia's foreign currency reserves increased from US$8.5 to US$600 billion. Only China and Japan had larger reserves. For a discussion of these developments and their impact on the structure of the Russian economy, see Gaddy and Ickes (2009).

over gas prices and payments to gain leverage over these governments.[31] He modernized specialized airborne units and counterguerilla forces for fighting in the Caucuses and strengthened bilateral military ties with friendly Central Asian nations (Oliker et al., 2009). And the Kremlin's coordinated air, ground, and sea operations against Georgia in 2008 successfully curbed the rise of a government that many had seen as a pro-Western beachhead in the region.[32]

The financial and political support of Russia's oil and gas companies was critical to solidifying Putin's grip on power. They benefited enormously from an expansionist grand strategy targeted on the Near Abroad. Under Putin, these companies earned more than $650 billion more from exports than they had in the previous eight years under Yeltsin (Gaddy and Ickes, 2009, 1). The Russian government also had money to burn. Putin hammered into place a system that allowed the Kremlin to collect windfall earnings from exporters in the form of taxes, and government coffers overflowed with the surge in energy profits.[33] With popularity ratings as high as 80 percent (Treisman, 2008), Putin was able to rapidly expand the size of his electoral base under the banner of "United Russia" and to consolidate control over the Duma, the lower house of Russia's parliament (Remington, 2008). He appealed to great powerdom to legitimate his one-party autocracy (D. McDonald, 2007).

At a time of geopolitical slack and rapid economic growth, foreign policies that extended Russian power in the Near Abroad offered concrete results for Putin in the form of strategic, economic, and domestic political advantage. A grand strategy of "hard" or "soft" balancing against the United States, by contrast, could have been financed only by resources that Putin needed to consolidate power at home (Wohlforth, 2003). Russian leaders had few incentives to make such a choice at a time when their country did not face a pressing geostrategic threat. What serves Putin's domestic interests is paying international dividends at the level of great power politics as well. At a time when the United States under Barack Obama is looking to scale back costly commitments, a Russian strategy that distinguishes carefully between the expansionism in the Near Abroad and a status quo orientation in global geopolitics writ large comports well with Obama's international priorities and domestic needs.

---

[31] Ukraine's interest in joining NATO gave Russia another occasion to rap its knuckles.

[32] Putin succeeded in achieving his tactical ends in South Ossetia and in sending a strong signal about what Russia would tolerate in the Near Abroad. But the Russian military's performance was anything but a model of efficiency. Indeed, the episode appears to have finally convinced the military high command that serious internal reforms are essential if it is to be able to sustain Putin's grand strategy (Barany, correspondence, May 2010).

[33] Between 2000 and 2008, federal revenues increased from $24.9 billion to $383 billion (or from roughly 15 percent to nearly 22 percent of GDP) (see Vinhas de Souza, 2008).

BARACK OBAMA AND GRAND STRATEGY

The arrival of the Obama administration has produced a shift in U.S. grand strategy that is in line with our model's expectations. In contrast to George W. Bush, who had strong incentives to exploit American primacy for partisan gain, Obama is choosing a strategy of retrenchment (scenario IV in figure 2.2.). This is apparent from Obama's rhetoric and the actions he has already taken. In contrast to Bush, Obama has emphasized the centrality of international cooperation and acknowledged the emergence of a more level global playing field, while at the same time seeking to rein in the country's military commitments (Kupchan and Trubowitz, 2010). While offering hope and inspiration to a world bereft of international leadership, Obama has spoken plainly at home about the limits of American power and the importance of keeping the U.S. effort proportional to the interests at stake in any particular situation. As he noted in a much-anticipated speech at West Point in December 2009, "I refuse to set goals that go beyond our responsibility, our means, or our interests. And I must weigh all of the challenges that our nation faces. ... That's why our troop commitment in Afghanistan cannot be open-ended—because the nation that I'm most interested in building is our own" (Obama, 2009b). This is the rhetoric of retrenchment.

We see signs of retrenchment in Obama's commitment to bring down U.S. force levels in Iraq and in the decision to set a withdrawal date for Afghanistan.[34] It is evident in his efforts to generate cost savings in the Pentagon's budget (Wirls, 2010, 194–95) and to pressure Europe, China, and others to shoulder a greater share of the international security burden (e.g., in containing Iran's nuclear ambitions).[35] Signs of retrench-

[34] To be sure, as a wartime president, Obama has substantially expanded the size of the U.S. operation in Afghanistan. Nonetheless, he is committed to the steady withdrawal of U.S. forces from Iraq. When he unfurled his new strategy for Afghanistan, which included dispatching an additional 30,000 U.S. troops, he made clear that the mission would be of limited duration, announcing that the coalition would begin handing over operations to Afghan forces during the summer of 2011. On the political significance of Obama's West Point speech, see also Mandelbaum (2010, 1–3).

[35] In both areas, so far, Obama's record has fallen short of expectations. Though the 2010 Pentagon budget that Obama approved was well below amounts requested by the military services, the budget still allowed for more than 3 percent growth over George Bush's last defense budget (Congressional Budget Office, 2010). Current forecasts do suggest that defense spending is likely to taper off in the years ahead. Because the Pentagon's budget is heavily driven by changes in personnel "end strength," the depth of future cuts will depend greatly on whether U.S. troops return on schedule from Iraq and Afghanistan (and on how strongly the Republican majority in the 112th House of Representatives pushes to maintain current defense spending levels). Obama's record in fostering international partnership is also mixed. For an early assessment of Obama's diplomatic initiatives, see T. Wright (2010).

ment are also evident in Obama's decision to pull back from the Bush administration's efforts to negotiate free trade agreements. Obama wants to focus more attention on enforcing U.S. trade laws and World Trade Organization rights and less attention on an activist negotiating agenda (Schott, 2009). The same is true of the administration's efforts to "reset" (improve) the strategic relationship with Russia, revive America's commitment to international institutions and multilateralism, and look to diplomacy rather than coercion to resolve disputes with unfriendly regimes.[36] These diplomatic initiatives have boosted America's standing in the world (American Political Science Association, 2010) in no small part because they contrast so sharply with Bush's combative approach to international institutions.[37] Yet Obama's heavy reliance on cheaper diplomatic means serves his domestic purposes too.

Obama has strong incentives to prioritize domestic needs. He came into office facing the worst economic crisis since the Great Depression. Many of his party's core constituencies (e.g., labor) were hit especially hard. Meanwhile, popular frustration over Bush's $700 billion bailout of Wall Street strengthened the Democrats' resolve to do something for Main Street. The economic crisis solidified the Democrats long-standing preference for butter over guns, and as table 6.1 indicates, this has meant strong support on Capitol Hill for Obama's efforts to bring commitments and costs back into line.[38] While many Democrats disapproved of

---

[36] Whereas the Bush administration shunned engagement with belligerent regimes, Obama has reached out to Iran, North Korea, Cuba, Syria, and Burma. Coercion is still an option in dealing with these countries, but U.S. policy is now predicated on the assumption that engagement is the preferred course (Kupchan and Trubowitz, 2010).

[37] Obama has sought an international agreement to limit greenhouse gas emissions; he signed a new START treaty with Russia; he issued a Nuclear Posture Review that narrows the conditions under which the United States might use nuclear weapons, committed his administration to push for Senate ratification of the Comprehensive Nuclear-Test-Ban Treaty, and outlined a vision of a world free of nuclear weapons; and he approved U.S. participation as an observer in meetings at the ICC. Obama (2009b) is committed to transforming the Group of Eight (G8) into the G-20 and told the United Nations General Assembly last September that, "The United States stands ready to begin a new chapter of international cooperation."

[38] Stabilizing Afghanistan includes votes on Obama's increased troop deployment and proposed withdrawal date, as well as votes on related issues of military and economic aid to Pakistan. Votes for Obama's strategy were coded as support for the U.S. war in Afghanistan. Cutting defense includes roll call votes on the Pentagon's budget, as well as votes to cut (or increase) funding for specific programs such as missile defense. Votes to reduce spending were coded as votes to slow defense spending. Support for diplomacy includes votes on the Department of State's budget as well as Republican efforts to reduce funding for specific aid and development programs (e.g., Peace Corps). I have included only votes where the Obama administration's policy preferences were known or where the proposed amendment was clearly unfriendly to the administration.

TABLE 6.1.
Democratic and Republican support for Barack Obama's foreign policies, 2009

	Stabilize Afghanistan		Cut Defense		Support Diplomacy	
	Party support	Party cohesion	Party support	Party cohesion	Party support	Party cohesion
Democrats	90%	80%	91%	83%	94%	89%
Republicans	2%	96%	25%	89%	15%	85%

Roll call voting in the U.S. House of Representatives from the first session of the 111th Congress: Number of roll call votes: stabilize Afghanistan (9); cut defense (19); support diplomacy (13).

Obama's decision to send more troops to Afghanistan, they have nevertheless backed his plan for stabilizing Afghanistan and neighboring Pakistan, rejecting more costly Republican schemes for combating the Taliban and terrorism in the region. Democratic support for Obama's efforts to scale back defense spending and rely more heavily on diplomacy and foreign aid is also solid. The differences between Democrats and Republicans in each of these areas could not be starker.[39]

None of this predicts that Obama will slavishly follow a linear path toward retrenchment: tactical adjustments are to be expected. This is because retrenchment is not without risk. Foreign leaders may find it in their interest to act more assertively to fill any resulting geopolitical vacuums. Meanwhile, skittish allies in Asia and elsewhere could find it prudent to realign their interests. Republicans could seize setbacks on either front to make political hay. We should not be surprised to see Obama maneuver geopolitically in one theater to offset likely losses from retrenchment in another; to tighten relations in one region of the world (e.g., Southeast Asia) while downsizing the nation's presence in another (Central Asia). What seems unlikely (and would be evidence against the argument advanced here) is that Obama will assume major new strategic commitments or ratchet up Pentagon spending. If domestic renewal, rather than foreign ambition, is driving U.S. statecraft today, then we should expect the nation's interests to be defined more narrowly and its commitments and capabilities adjusted accordingly.

Although Obama often evokes comparisons with Lincoln, his international circumstances more closely resemble those of Martin Van Buren or Herbert Hoover. Like Van Buren and Hoover, Obama has geopolitical

[39] Deep partisan divisions over foreign policy are also evident in public opinion polls. See Kupchan and Trubowitz (2010).

slack. The threat of terrorism remains, but today the United States does not face a geopolitical challenger, and the risk of a sudden shift in the distribution of international power is low. This is reflected in Obama's National Security Strategy (NSS), one-quarter of which is devoted to domestic policies and goals such as strengthening the economy and rebuilding the nation's infrastructure (M. Taylor, 2010). "Our national security," cautions Obama, "begins at home" (2010, 9). The party has taken advantage of the slack in the international system to invest resources at home. While some Democrats worry about Republican accusations that they are too soft on defense (a holdover from Cold War era politics), Democrats have strongly backed Secretary of Defense Robert Gates's efforts to close what he calls the "spigot of defense funding opened by 9/11" (Wirls, 2010, 194). More recently, they backed his plan to trim an additional $100 billion from the Pentagon's budget (Shanker and Drew, 2010).[40] The party has rallied behind Obama's ambitious and expensive plan to overhaul the nation's health care system and the $800 billion economic stimulus package, seeing it as a way to shift the guns-versus-butter balance. At a time when Obama and the Democrats have strong incentives to prioritize domestic needs, a grand strategy aimed at scaling back commitments and reducing costs is what we would expect of this president, given the model of grand strategy determinants developed in this book.

• • •

Five hundred years ago, Niccolò Machiavelli captured the essence of statecraft. He wrote of leaders caught in a vortex of competing and often conflicting pressures: some external, the others internal. Good statecraft, Machiavelli advised, requires an understanding of *both* geopolitics and domestic politics, and how they interact. Machiavelli's analysis of statecraft remains fresh today. Leaders who make grand strategy are cross-pressured by international and domestic imperatives. They must manage these competing pressures if they are to succeed and survive in office. Choices about grand strategy are not as scripted or straightforwardly determined by geopolitical circumstance as much analysis in the *Realpolitik* school would have us believe. Nor are leaders always as free in-

---

[40] In sharp contrast to George W. Bush's NSS of 2002 and 2006, Obama's NSS views the "threat" of terrorism as less consequential than other longer-term international challenges (e.g., nuclear proliferation, dependence on fossil fuels) and the more immediate challenge of "rebuilding the economy." The Obama's NSS also defines the threat of terrorism more narrowly than Bush's, focusing on "al-Qa'ida and its affiliates" (Obama, 2010, 4) as opposed to state-sponsored terrorism at large. Obama's NSS makes no mention of Bush's doctrine of "preemptive war" and attaches comparatively little weight to "democracy promotion," a key feature of Bush's ambitious foreign policy agenda.

ternationally to respond as they please to domestic contingency, as many who subscribe to *Innenpolitik* seem to suggest. If we are to develop useful—parsimonious yet valid—models about how grand strategy is made, we need to move beyond these polar opposites in the study of statecraft. The way forward lies in finding ways to combine the insights of these two traditions of analysis.

Doing so helps us better understand what is happening in American statecraft today. In an era of unipolarity, America enjoys preponderant power and its leaders have a level of "geopolitical slack" that was inconceivable a few short decades ago. The challenge facing leaders who have geopolitical slack is to decide what to do with the room for maneuver they enjoy. Should they seize the moment and look for ways to strengthen their state's power and, at the risk of antagonizing other states, seek to widen their power advantages? Or should these leaders be content to maintain the international status quo and focus more attention on solving problems at home? I have argued that under international conditions like those the United States is experiencing today, when leaders have geopolitical slack, the answer will turn heavily on domestic politics: on whether a leaders' party prefers guns over butter, or vice versa. What distinguishes our era in American statecraft from the Cold War is the wide scope of choice leaders have in defining the general thrust of grand strategy. How they make that choice will depend, as in earlier eras, on their calculations about how to respond to domestic political incentives and geopolitical constraints (opportunities) in a way that is most likely to guarantee their own political success and that of the domestic coalitions they lead.

References

Abramowitz, Alan I., and Kyle Saunders. "Why Can't We All Just Get Along? The Reality of a Polarized America." *Forum: A Journal of Applied Research in Contemporary Politics* 3, no. 2 (2005): Article 1. http://www.bepress.com /forum/vol3/iss2/art1.

Abramowitz, Michael. "Bush Says 'America Loses' under Democrats." *Washington Post*, October 30, 2006.

Adams, Donald R., Jr. "American Neutrality and Prosperity, 1793–1808: A Reconsideration." *Journal of Economic History* 40, no. 4 (1980): 713–37.

Alberts, Sheldon. "Candidates Address 'Security Moms': Bush Warns Kerry Would 'Invite Disaster.'" *Gazette*, October 19, 2004.

American Political Science Association. *U.S. Standing in the World: Causes, Consequences, and the Future.* Washington, D.C.: American Political Science Association, 2010.

Ammon, Harry. *James Monroe: The Quest for National Identity.* Charlottesville: University of Virginia Press, 1990.

Anderson, Stuart. "1861: Blockade vs. Closing the Confederate Ports." *Military Affairs* 41, no. 4 (1977): 190–94.

Art, Robert J. "The United States, the Balance of Power, and World War II: Was Spykman Right?" *Security Studies* 14, no. 3 (2005): 365–406.

Axelrod, Robert. *The Evolution of Cooperation.* New York: Basic Books, 1984.

Bailey, Thomas A. *A Diplomatic History of the American People.* 3rd ed. New York: Appleton-Century-Crofts, 1942.

Barany, Zoltan. "Resurgent Russia? A Still-Faltering Military." *Policy Review*, no. 147 (2008): 39–51.

Barness, Richard W. "John C. Calhoun and the Military Establishment, 1817–1825." *Wisconsin Magazine of History* 50, no. 1 (1966): 43–53.

Barnett, Michael N., and Jack S. Levy. "Domestic Sources of Alliances and Alignments: The Case of Egypt, 1962–73." *International Organization* 45, no. 3 (1991): 369–95.

Barone, Michael. "The 49 Percent Nation." *National Journal*, June 9, 2001, 1710–16.

Bates, Robert H. *Markets and States in Tropical Africa.* Berkeley: University of California Press, 1981.

Bauer, K. Jack. "Naval Shipbuilding Programs 1794–1860." *Military Affairs* 29, no. 1 (1965): 29–40.

Beinhart, Peter. "When Politics No longer Stops at the Water's Edge: Partisan Polarization and Foreign Policy." In *Red and Blue Nation? Consequences and Correction of America's Polarized Politics*, vol. 2, edited by Pietro S. Nivola and David W. Brady, 151–67. Washington, D.C.: Brookings Institution, 2008.

Bell, Rudolph M. *Party and Faction in American Politics: The House of Representatives, 1789–1801.* Westport, Conn.: Greewood Press, 1973.

Bemis, Samuel Flagg. *A Diplomatic History of the United States*. New York: Henry Holt, 1942.

———. *Jay's Treaty: A Study in Commerce and Diplomacy*. New Haven: Yale University Press, 1962.

———. "The United States and the Abortive Armed Neutrality of 1794." *American Historical Review* 24, no. 1 (1918): 26–47.

Bensel, Richard F. *Sectionalism and American Political Development: 1880–1980*. Madison: University of Wisconsin Press, 1984.

———. *Yankee Leviathan: The Origins of Central State Authority in America, 1859–1877*. New York: Cambridge University Press, 1990.

Berinsky, Adam J. *In Time of War: Understanding American Public Opinion from World War II to Iraq*. Chicago: University of Chicago Press, 2009.

Binkley, Wilfred E. *American Political Parties: Their Natural History*. 2nd ed. New York: Alfred A. Knopf, 1947.

Black, Earle, and Merle Black. *Divided America: The Ferocious Power Struggle in American Politics*. New York: Simon and Schuster, 2007.

Block, Fred. "Economic Instability and Military Strength: The Paradoxes of the 1950 Rearmament Decision." *Politics and Society* 10, no. 1 (1980): 35–58.

Bourne, Kenneth. *Britain and the Balance of Power in North America, 1815–1908*. Berkeley and Los Angeles: University of California Press, 1967.

Bowman, Albert Hall. *The Struggle for Neutrality: Franco-American Diplomacy during the Federalist Era*. Knoxville: University of Tennessee Press, 1974.

Braeman, John. "Power and Diplomacy: The 1920's Reappraised." *Review of Politics* 44, no. 3 (1982): 342–69.

Brands, H. W. *Traitor to His Class: The Privledged Life and Radical Presidency of Franklin Delano Roosevelt*. New York: Doubleday, 2008.

Brauer, Kinley J. "Civil War Diplomacy." In *Encyclopedia of American Foreign Policy*, edited by Alexander DeConde, Richard Dean Burns, and Frederik Logevall, 193–206. New York: Scribner, 2002.

———. "The Slavery Problem in the Diplomacy of the American Civil War." *Pacific Historical Review* 46, no. 3 (1977): 436–69.

Brewer, John. *The Sinews of Power: War, Money, and the English States, 1688–1783*. London: Unwin Hyman, 1989.

Bright, Charles. "Class Interest and State Policy in the British Response to Hitler." In *German Nationalism and the European Response, 1880–1945*, edited by Carole Fink, Isabel Hull, and MacGregor Knox, 207–46. Norman: University of Oklahoma Press, 1985.

Brodie, Bernard. *Strategy in the Missile Age*. Princeton: Princeton University Press, 1965.

Brooks, Stephen G., and William C. Wohlforth. "Hard Times for Soft Balancing." *International Security* 30, no. 1 (2005): 72–108.

Brownstein, Ronald. *The Second Civil War: How Extreme Partisanship Has Paralyzed Washington and Polarized America*. New York: Penguin, 2007.

Brzezinski, Zbigniew. *Second Chance: Three Presidents and the Crisis of American Superpower*. New York: Basic Books, 2007.

Buel, Richard, Jr. *Securing the Revolution: Ideology in American Politics, 1789–1815*. Ithaca, N.Y.: Cornell University Press, 1972.

Bueno de Mesquita, Bruce, Alastair Smith, Randolph M. Siverson, and James D. Morrow. *The Logic of Political Survival.* Cambridge, Mass.: MIT Press, 2003.

Burnham, Walter Dean. *Critical Elections and the Mainsprings of American Politics.* New York: W. W. Norton, 1970.

Burns, James MacGregor. *Roosevelt: The Lion and the the Fox.* New York: Harcourt Brace, 1956.

Burns, James MacGregor, and Susan Dunn. *George Washington.* New York: Henry Holt, 2004.

Burns, James MacGregor, and Georgia J. Sorenson. *Dead Center: Clinton-Gore Leadership and the Perils of Moderation.* New York: Scribner, 1999.

Busby, Joshua W., and Jonathan Monten. "Without Heirs? Assessing the Decline of Establishment Internationalism in U.S. Foreign Policy." *Perspectives on Politics* 6, no. 3 (2008): 451–72.

Butfoy, Andrew. "The Rise and Fall of Missile Diplomacy? President Clinton and the 'Revolution in Military Affairs' in Retrospect." *Australian Journal of Politics and History* 52, no. 1 (2006): 98–114.

Cain, P. J., and A. G. Hopkins. "The Political Economy of British Expansion Overseas, 1750–1914." *Economic History Review* 33, no. 4 (1980): 463–90.

Campbell, Charles S. *From Revolution to Rapprochement: The United States and Great Britain, 1783–1900.* New York: John Wiley and Sons, 1974.

Campbell, Duncan Andrew. *Unlikely Allies: Britain, America and the Victorian Origins of the Special Relationship.* London: Hambledon, 2007.

Carroll, Francis M. *A Good and Wise Measure: The Search for the Candian-American Boundary, 1783–1842.* Toronto: University of Toronto Press, 2001.

Casey, Steven. *Cautious Crusade: Franklin D. Roosevelt, American Public Opinion, and the War against Nazi Germany.* New York: Oxford University Press, 2001.

Chan, Steve, and Alex Mintz. *Defense, Wealth, and Growth.* London: Routledge, 1992.

Chollet, Derek, and James Goldgeier. *America between the Wars: From 11/9 to 9/11.* New York: Public Affairs, 2008.

Choucri, Nazli, and Robert C. North. *Nations in Conflict: National Growth and International Violence.* San Francisco: W. H. Freeman, 1975.

Christensen, Thomas J. "Fostering Stability or Creating a Monster? The Rise of China and U.S. Policy toward East Asia." *International Security* 31, no. 1 (2006): 81–126.

———. *Useful Adversaries: Grand Strategy, Domestic Mobilization, and Sino-American Conflict, 1947–1958.* Princeton: Princeton University Press, 1996.

Christensen, Thomas J., and Jack Snyder. "Chain Gangs and Passed Bucks: Predicting Alliance Patterns in Multipolarity." *International Organization* 44, no. 2 (1990): 137–68.

Clarfield, Gerard. "Protecting the Frontiers: Defense Policy and the Tariff Question in the First Washington Administration." *William and Mary Quarterly* 32, no. 3 (1975): 443–64.

Cobden, Richard. *The Political Writings of Richard Cobden.* 2 vols. London: William Ridgway, 1868.

Cohen, Eliot A. "The Strategy of Innocence? The United States, 1920–1945." In *The Making of Strategy: Rulers, States, and War*, edited by Williamson

Murray, MacGregor Knox, and Alvin Bernstein, 428–65. Cambridge: Cambridge University Press, 1994.

———. *Supreme Command: Soldiers, Statesmen, and Leadership in Wartime.* New York: Anchor Books, 2002.

Cohen, Warren I. *America's Response to China: A History of Sino-American Relations.* 4th ed. New York: Columbia University Press, 2000.

Cole, Donald B. *Martin Van Buren and the American Political System.* Princeton: Princeton University Press, 1984.

Cole, Wayne S. *An Interpretive History of American Foreign Relations.* Homewood, Ill.: Dorsey Press, 1968.

———. *Roosevelt and the Isolationists,1932–45.* Lincoln: University of Nebraska Press, 1983.

Coleman, John J. "Clinton and the Party System in Historical Perspective." In *The Postmodern Presidency: Bill Clinton's Legacy in U.S. Politics,* edited by Steven E. Schier, 145–66. Pittsburgh: University of Pittsburgh Press, 2000.

Coombs, Jerald A. *The Jay Treaty: Political Battleground of the Founding Fathers.* Berkeley: University of California Press, 1970.

Congressional Budget Office. *Long-Term Implications of the Fiscal Year 2010 Defense Budget.* Washington, D.C.: CBO, January 2010.

Copeland, Dale C. *The Origins of Major War.* Ithaca, N.Y.: Cornell University Press, 2000.

Cox, Michael. *U.S. Foreign Policy after the Cold War: Superpower without a Mission?* London: Royal Institute of International Affairs, 1995.

Craig, Campbell, and Fredrik Logevall. *America's Cold War: The Politics of Insecurity.* Cambridge, Mass.: Harvard University Press, 2009.

Craig, Gordon A. "Roosevelt and Hitler: The Problem of Perception." In *Deutsche Frage and europaisches Gleichgewicht,* edited by Klaus Hildebrand and Reiner Pommerin, 169–94. Cologne: Bohlau Verlag, 1985.

Crichlow, Scott. "Lincoln, Seward, and the United Kingdom." *White House Studies* 5, no. 3 (2005): 411–22.

Crook, D. P. *The North, the South, and the Powers: 1861–1865.* New York: John Wiley and Sons, 1974.

Cunningham, Nobel E., Jr. *The Presidency of James Monroe.* Lawrence: Unversity Press of Kansas, 1996.

Curtis, James C. *The Fox at Bay: Martin Van Buren and the Presidency, 1837–1841.* Lexington: University Press of Kentucky, 1970.

Dallek, Robert. *Franklin D. Roosevelt and American Foreign Policy, 1932–1945.* Oxford: Oxford University Press, 1979.

Dangerfield, George. *The Era of Good Feelings.* New York: Harcourt, Brace and World, 1952.

Dassel, Kurt, and Eric Reinhardt. "Domestic Strife and the Initiation of Violence at Home and Abroad." *American Journal of Political Science* 43, no. 1 (1999): 56–85.

Davis, Lance, and Robert Huttenback. *Mammon and the Pursuit of Empire: The Political Economy of British Imperialism, 1860–1912.* Cambridge: Cambridge University Press, 1986.

DeConde, Alexander. *Entangling Alliance: Politics and Diplomacy under George Washington.* Durham: Duke University Press, 1958.

———. "Herbert Hoover and Foreign Policy: A Retrospective Assessment." In *Herbert Hoover and the Historians,* edited by Mark M. Dodge, 87–116. West Branch, Iowa: Herbert Hoover Presidential Library Association, 1989.

———. *Herbert Hoover's Latin-American Policy.* Stanford: Stanford University Press, 1951.

Degler, Carl N. "The Ordeal of Herbert Hoover." *Yale Review* 52 (1963): 563–83.

DeRouen, Karl, Jr. "Presidents and the Diversionary Use of Force: A Research Note." *International Studies Quarterly* 44, no. 2 (2000): 317–39.

Desch, Michael C. *When the Third World Matters: Latin America and United States Grand Strategy.* Baltimore: Johns Hopkins University Press, 1993.

Destler, I. M. "Foreign Economic Policy Making under Bill Clinton." In *Making U.S. Foreign Policy in the Post-Cold War World,* edited by James M. Scott, 89–107. Durham: Duke University Press, 1998.

Deudney, Daniel. "The Philadelphian System: Sovereignty, Arms Control, and Balance of Power in the American States-Union." *International Organization* 49, no. 2 (1995): 191–228.

Divine, Robert A. *The Illusion of Neutrality.* Chicago: University of Chicago Press, 1962.

D'Lugo, David, and Ronald Rogowski. "The Anglo-German Naval Race and Comparative Constitutional 'Fitness.'" In *The Domestic Bases of Grand Strategy,* edited by Richard Rosecrance and Arthur A. Stein, 65–95. Ithaca, N.Y.: Cornell University Press, 1993.

Doenecke, Justus D. "The Anti-interventionism of Herbert Hoover." *Journal of Libertarian Studies* 8, no. 2 (1987): 311–40.

———. *Storm on the Horizon: The Challenge to American Intervention, 1939–1941.* Lanham, Md.: Rowman and Littlefield, 2000.

Donald, David Herbert. *Lincoln.* New York: Simon and Schuster, 1996.

Downs, George W., and David M. Rocke. "Conflict, Agency, and Gambling for Resurrection: The Principal-Agent Problem Goes to War." *American Journal of Political Science* 38, no. 2 (1994): 362–80.

Doyle, Michael W. "Politics and Grand Strategy." In *The Domestic Bases of Grand Strategy,* edited by Richard Rosecrance and Arthur Stein, 22–47. Ithaca, N.Y.: Cornell University Press, 1993.

Drew, Elizabeth. "The Enforcer." *New York Review of Books,* May 1, 2003.

Driggs, Don W. "The President as Chief Educator on Foreign Affairs." *Western Political Quarterly* 11, no. 4 (1958): 813–19.

Dueck, Colin. *Reluctant Crusaders: Power, Culture, and Change in American Grand Strategy.* Princeton: Princeton University Press, 2006.

Edsall, Thomas B. *Building Red America: The New Conservative Coalition and the Drive for Permanent Power.* New York: Basic Books, 2006.

Ehrhart, Robert C. "The Politics of Military Rearmament, 1935–1940: The President, the Congress, and the United States Army." Ph.D. dissertation, University of Texas at Austin, 1975.

Eisinger, Robert M. "Gauging Public Opinion in the Hoover White House: Understanding the Roots of Presidential Polling." *Presidential Studies Quarterly* 30, no. 4 (2000): 643–61.

Elkins, Stanley, and Eric McKitrick. *The Age of Federalism: The Early American Republic, 1788–1800.* New York: Oxford University Press, 1993.

Ellis, Joseph J. *His Excellency: George Washington.* New York: Alfred A. Knopf, 2004.

Farnham, Barbara Rearden. *Roosevelt and the Munich Crisis: A Study of Political Decision-Making.* Princeton: Princeton University Press, 1997.

Fausold, Martin L. *The Presidency of Herbert C. Hoover.* Lawrence: University Press of Kansas, 1985.

Ferling, John. *The Ascent of George Washington: The Hidden Political Genius of an American Icon.* New York: Bloomsbury Press, 2009.

Ferrell, Robert, H. *American Diplomacy in the Great Depression: Hoover-Stimson Foreign Policy, 1929–1933.* New Haven: Yale University Press, 1957.

Flexner, James Thomas. *Washington: The Indispensble Man.* Boston: Little, Brown, 1974.

Finnemore, Martha. *The Purpose of Intervention: Changing Beliefs about the Use of Force.* Ithaca, N.Y.: Cornell University Press, 2004.

Fischer, Fritz. *War of Illusions: German Policies from 1911 to 1914.* New York: Alfred A. Knopf, 1975.

Foner, Eric. *Free Soil, Free Labor, Free Men: The Ideology of the Republican Party before the Civil War.* New York: Oxford University Press, 1970.

Fordham, Benjamin O. *Building the Cold War Consensus: The Political Economy of U.S. National Security Policy, 1949–1951.* Ann Arbor: University of Michigan Press, 1998.

Fravel, M. Taylor. "China's Search for Military Power." *Washington Quarterly* 31, no. 3 (2008): 125–41.

———. "Power Shifts and Escalation: Explaining China's Use of Force in Territorial Disputes." *International Security* 32, no. 3 (2007–8): 44–83.

Frazier, Mark W. "Pensions, Public Opinion, and the Graying of China." *Asia Policy* 1 (2006): 43–68.

Freidel, Frank. *Franklin D. Roosevelt: Rendezvous with Destiny.* Boston: Little, Brown, 1990.

Friedberg, Aaron L. "The Future of U.S.-China Relations: Is Conflict Inevitable?" *International Security* 30, no. 2 (2005): 7–45.

———. *In the Shadow of the Garrison State: America's Anti-Statism and Its Cold War Grand Strategy.* Princeton: Princeton University Press, 2000.

———. "The Political Economy of American National Strategy." *World Politics* 41, no. 3 (1989): 387–406.

———. *The Weary Titan: Britain and the Experience of Relative Decline, 1895–1905.* Princeton: Princeton University Press, 1988.

Frieden, Jeffry A. "Actors and Preferences in International Relations." In *Strategic Choice and International Relations*, edited by David A. Lake and Robert Powell, 39–76. Princeton: Princeton University Press, 1999.

———. "Sectoral Conflict and U.S. Foreign Economic Policy, 1914–1940." *International Organization* 42, no. 1 (1988): 59–60.

Fry, Joseph A. *Dixie Looks Abroad: The South and U.S. Foreign Relations, 1789–1973*. Baton Rouge: Lousiana State University Press, 2002.

Fukuyama, Francis. *The End of History and the Last Man*. New York: Free Press, 1992.

Gaddis, John Lewis. *Strategies of Containment: A Critical Appraisal of American National Security Policy during the Cold War*. 2nd ed. New York: Oxford University Press, 2005.

———. *Surprise, Security, and the American Experience*. Cambridge, Mass.: Harvard University Press, 2004.

Gaddy, Clifford G., and Barry W. Ikes. "Putin's Third Way." *National Interest Online*. Washington, D.C., January 21, 2009. http://nationalinterest.org/article/putins-third-way-2958.

Garofano, John. "Tragedy or Choice in Vietnam? Learning to Think Outside the Archival Box: A Review Essay." *International Security* 26, no. 4 (2002): 143–68.

Gaubatz, Kurt. "Election Cycles and War." *Journal of Conflict Resolution* 35, no. 2 (1991): 212–44.

Gelb, Leslie. "Vietnam: The System Worked." *Foreign Policy* 3 (1971): 140–67.

Gellman, Irwin F. *Good Neighbor Diplomacy: United States Policies in Latin America, 1933–1945*. Baltimore: Johns Hopkins University Press, 1979.

Gelpi, Christopher. "Democratic Diversions: Governmental Structure and the Externalization of Domestic Conflict." *Journal of Conflict Resolution* 41, no. 2 (1997): 255–82.

Gerring, John. *Party Ideologies in America, 1828–1996*. Cambridge: Cambridge University Press, 1998.

Gifford, Brian. "Why No Trade-Off between 'Guns and Butter'? Armed Forces and Social Spending in the Advanced Industrial Democracies, 1960–1993." *American Journal of Sociology* 112, no. 2 (2006): 473–509.

Gilpin, Robert. *War and Change in World Politics*. Princeton: Princeton University Press, 1981.

Glaser, Charles L. *Rational Theory of International Politics: The Logic of Competition and Cooperation*. Princeton: Princeton University Press, 2010.

Goble, Hannah, and Peter M. Holm. "Breaking Bonds? The Iraq War and the Loss of the Republican Dominance in National Security." *Political Research Quarterly* 62, no. 2 (2009): 215–29.

Goemans, Hein E. *War and Punishment: The Causes of War Termination and the First World War*. Princeton: Princeton University Press, 2000.

Goldgeier, James M. "NATO Expansion: The Anatomy of a Decision." *Washington Quarterly* 21, no. 1 (1997): 85–102.

Goldin, Claudia, and Frank Lewis. "The Economic Costs of the American Civil War: Estimates and Implications." *Journal of Economic History* 35, no. 2 (1975): 229–326.

———. "The Post-Bellum Recovery of the South and the Cost of the Civil War: Comment." *Journal of Economic History* 38, no. 2 (1978): 487–92.

Goldstein, Avery. *Rising to the Challenge: China's Grand Strategy and International Security*. Stanford: Stanford University Press, 2005.

Goldstein, Gordon M. *Lessons in Disaster: McGeorge Bundy and the Path to War in Vietnam*. New York: Henry Holt, 2008.

Gould, Lewis L. *The Spanish-American War and President McKinley*. Lawrence: University Press of Kansas, 1982.

Gourevitch, Peter. *Politics in Hard Times: Comparative Responses to International Economic Crises*. Ithaca, N.Y.: Cornell University Press, 1986.

———. "The Second Image Reversed: The International Sources of Domestic Politics." *International Organization* 32, no. 4 (1978): 881–912.

Graebner, Norman A. "Abraham Lincoln: Conservative Statesman." In *The Enduring Lincoln*, edited by Norman A. Graebner, 67–94. Urbana: University of Illinois Press, 1959.

———. *Foundations of American Power: A Realistic Appraisal from Franklin to McKinley*. Wilmington, Del.: Scholarly Resources, 1985.

Grassmuck, George L. *Sectional Biases in Congress on Foreign Policy*. Baltimore: Johns Hopkins University Press, 1951.

Greenberg, Stanley B. *Middle Class Dreams: Politics and Power of the New American Majority*. New York: Times Books, 1996.

Greene, Fred. "The Military View of American National Policy, 1904–1940." *American Historical Review* 66, no. 2 (1961): 354–77.

Grenville, John A. S., and George Berkeley Young. *Politics, Strategy, and American Diplomacy: Studies in Foreign Policy, 1873–1917*. New Haven: Yale University Press, 1966.

Griffin, Larry J., Joel A. Devine, and Michael Wallace. "Monopoly Capital, Organized Labor, and Military Expenditures in the United States, 1949–1976." *American Journal of Sociology* 88 (1982): S113–53.

Haas, Mark L. *The Ideological Origins of Great Power Politics, 1789–1989*. Ithaca, N.Y.: Cornell University Press, 2005.

Hagan, Kenneth J. *This People's Navy: The Making of American Sea Power*. New York: Free Press, 1991.

Haglund, David G. *Latin America and the Transformation of U.S. Strategic Thought, 1936–1940*. Albuquerque: University of New Mexico Press, 1984.

Halberstam, David. *War in a Time of Peace: Bush, Clinton, and the Generals*. New York: Simon and Shuster, 2001.

Hall, John A., and G. John Ikenberry. *The State*. Minneapolis: University of Minnesota, 1989.

Harper, John Lamberton. *American Machiavelli: Alexander Hamilton and the Origins of U.S. Foreign Policy*. New York: Cambridge University Press, 2004.

Harris, John F. *The Survivor: Bill Clinton in the White House*. New York: Random House, 2005.

Harris, William V. *War and Imperialism in Republican Rome: 327–70 B.C.* New York: Oxford University Press, 1985.

Hart, Gary. *James Monroe*. New York: Henry Holt, 2005.

Hearden, Patrick, J. *Roosevelt Confronts Hitler: America's Entry into World War II*. DeKalb: Northern Illinois University Press, 1987.

Hechter, Michael, and William Brustein. "Regional Modes of Production and Patterns of State Formation in Western Europe." *American Journal of Sociology* 85, no. 5 (1980): 1061–94.

Heinrichs, Waldo. *Threshold of War: Franklin D. Roosevelt and American Entry into World War II*. New York: Oxford University Press, 1988.

Henriques, Peter H. *Realistic Visionary: A Portrait of George Washington.* Charlottesville: University of Virginia Press, 2006.

Heo, Uk. *The Political Economy of Defense Spending around the World.* Lewiston, N.Y.: Edwin Mellen, 1999.

Herring, George C. *From Colony to Superpower: U.S. Foreign Relations since 1776.* New York: Oxford University Press, 2008.

Hicks, Alexander, and Joya Misra. "Political Resources and the Growth of Welfare in Affluent Capitalist Democracies, 1960–1982." *American Journal of Sociology* 99, no. 3 (1993): 668–710.

Hobson, J. A. *Imperialism: A Study.* London: Allen and Unwin, 1902, repr. 1938.

Hockett, Homer C. *Political and Social Growth of the United States, 1492–1852.* Rev. ed. New York: Macmillan, 1933.

———. "Western Influences on Political Parties to 1825: An Essay in Historical Interpretation." *Ohio State University Bulletin,* August 1917, 9–157.

Hogan, Michael J. "Foreign Policy, Partisan Politics, and the End of the Cold War." In *The End of the Cold War: Its Meaning and Implications,* edited by Michael J. Hogan, 229–43. New York: Cambridge University Press, 1992.

Holcombe, Randall G. "The Growth of the Federal Government in the 1920s." *CATO Journal* 16, no. 2 (1996): 175–99.

Holt, Michael F. *Political Parties and American Political Development: From the Age of Jackson to the Age of Lincoln.* Baton Rouge: Lousiana State University Press, 1992.

Hooks, Gregory. "Military and Civilian Dimensions of America's Regional Policy, 1972–1994." *Armed Forces and Society* 29, no. 2 (2003): 227–51.

Horsman, Reginald. "The Dimensions of an 'Empire for Liberty': Expansion and Republicanism, 1775–1825." *Journal of the Early Republic* 9, no. 1 (1989): 1–20.

Huber, Evelyne, and John D. Stephens. *Development and Crisis of the Welfare State: Parties and Policies in Global Markets.* Chicago: University of Chicago Press, 2001.

Huntington, Samuel P. "The Clash of Civilizations." *Foreign Affairs* 72, no. 3 (1993): 22–49.

———. "Coping with the Lippmann Gap." *Foreign Affairs* 66, no. 3 (1988): 453–77.

Hurst, William. *The Chinese Worker after Socialism.* New York: Cambridge University Press, 2009.

Ikenberry, G. John. *After Victory: Institutions, Strategic Restraint, and the Rebuilding of Order after Major Wars.* Princeton: Princeton University Press, 2001.

———. "Is American Multilateralism in Decline?" *Perspectives on Politics* 1, no. 3 (2003): 533–50.

Ikenberry, G. John, Michael Mastanduno, and William C. Wohlforth. "Introduction: Unipolarity, State Behavior, and Systemic Consequences." *World Politics* 61, no. 1 (2009): 1–27.

Jacobson, Gary C. *A Divider, Not a Uniter: George W. Bush and the American People.* New York: Pearson Longman, 2007.

James, Scott, C. *Presidents, Parties, and the State: A Party System Perspective on Democratic Regulatory Choice, 1884–1936*. New York: Cambridge University Press, 2000.

Jenkins, Brian. *Britain and the War for the Union*. Montreal: McGill-Queen's University Press, 1980.

Jervis, Robert. "The Compulsive Empire." *Foreign Policy* 137 (July–August 2003): 82–87.

———. "Cooperation under the Security Dilemma." *World Politics* 30, no. 2 (1978): 167–214.

———. *The Logic of Images in International Relations*. Princeton: Princeton University Press, 1970.

———. *Perception and Misperception in International Politics*. Princeton: Princeton University Press, 1976.

———. "Unipolarity: A Structural Perspective." *World Politics* 61, no. 1 (2009): 188–213.

Jervis, Robert, and Jack Snyder, editors. *Dominoes and Bandwagons: Strategic Beliefs and Great Power Competition in the Eurasian Rimland*. New York: Oxford University Press, 1991.

Joffe, Josef. "Defying History and Theory: The United States as the 'Last Superpower.'" In *America Unrivaled: The Future of the Balance of Power*, edited by G. John Ikenberry, 155–80. Ithaca, N.Y.: Cornell University Press, 2002.

Johnson, Paul M., and Robert A. Wells. "Soviet Military and Civilian Resource Allocation 1951–1980." *Journal of Conflict Resolution* 30, no. 2 (1986): 195–219.

Johnston, Alastair Iain. *Cultural Realism: Strategic Culture and Grand Strategy in Chinese History*. Princeton: Princeton University Press, 1995.

———. *Social States: China in International Institutions, 1980–2000*. Princeton: Princeton University Press, 2008.

Jonas, Manfred. *Isolationism in America, 1935–1941*. Ithaca, N.Y.: Cornell University Press, 1966.

Jones, Dorothy V. *License for Empire: Colonialism by Treaty in Early America*. Chicago: University of Chicago Press, 1982.

Jones, Howard. *Abraham Lincoln and a New Birth of Freedom: The Union and Slavery in the Diplomacy of the Civil War*. Lincoln: University of Nebraska Press, 1999.

———. *Union in Peril: The Crisis over British Intervention in the Civil War*. Chapel Hill: University of North Carolina Press, 1992.

Judis, John. "Turd Blossom: Karl Rove's Dreams Go Down the Toilet." *New Republic*, August 20, 2007.

Kagan, Donald, and Frederick W. Kagan. *While America Sleeps: Self-Delusion, Military Weakness, and the Threat to Peace Today*. New York: St. Martin's Griffin, 2000.

Kahler, Miles. *Decolonization in Britain and France: The Domestic Consequences of International Relations*. Princeton: Princeton University Press, 1984.

Kamlet, Mark S., and David C. Mowery. "Influences on Executive and Congressional Budgetary Priorities, 1953–1981." *American Political Science Review* 81, no. 1 (1987): 155–78.

Katzenstein, Peter J. "Introduction: Domestic and International Forces and Strategies of Foreign Economic Policy." *International Organization* 31, no. 4 (1977): 587–606.

———. *The Culture of National Security: Norms, Identity, and World Politics.* New York: Columbia University Press, 1996.

Katzenstein, Peter J., and Robert O. Keohane, eds. *Anti-Americanisms.* Ithaca, N.Y.: Cornell University Press, 2007.

Katznelson, Ira. "Flexible Capacity: The Military and Early American Statebuilding." In *Shaped by War and Trade: International Influences on American Political Development*, by Ira Katznelson and Martin Shefter, 82–110. Princeton: Princeton University Press, 2002.

Kaufmann, Chaim. "Threat Inflation and the Failure of the Marketplace of Ideas: The Selling of the Iraq War." *International Security* 29, no. 1 (2004): 5–48.

Kehr, Eckart. *Battleship Building and Party Politics in Germany, 1894–1901: A Cross Section of the Political, Social, and Ideological Preconditions of German Imperialism.* Translated by Pauline R. Anderson and Eugene N. Anderson. Berkeley: University of California Press, 1930, repr. 1977.

Kennedy, Paul. *The Rise and Fall of Great Powers: Economic Change and Military Conflict from 1500 to 2000.* New York: Vintage Books, 1987.

———. *Strategy and Diplomacy, 1870–1945.* London: Allen & Unwin, 1981.

Keohane, Robert O. *After Hegemony: Cooperation and Discord in the World Political Economy.* Princeton: Princeton University Press, 1984.

———. "Associative American Development, 1776–1860: Economic Growth and Political Disintegration." In *The Antinomies of Interdependence: National Wealth and the International Division of Labor*, by John Gerhard Ruggie, 43–90. New York: Columbia University Press, 1983.

Keohane, Robert O., and Joseph S. Nye. *Power and Interdependence.* Boston: Little, Brown, 1977.

Khong, Yuen Foong. *Analogies at War: Korea, Munich, Dien Bien Phu, and the Vietnam Decisions of 1965.* Princeton: Princeton University Press, 1992.

Kier, Elizabeth. *Imagining War: French and British Military Doctrine between the Wars.* Princeton: Princeton University Press, 1997.

Kindleberger, Charles P. *The World in Depression, 1929–1939.* Berkeley: University of California Press, 1973.

Kirshner, Jonathan. *Appeasing Bankers: Financial Caution on the Road to War.* Princeton: Princeton University Press, 2007.

Klein, Joe. *The Natural: The Misunderstood Presidency of Bill Clinton.* New York: Doubleday, 2002.

Kleppner, Paul. *The Third Electoral System, 1853–1892.* Chapel Hill: University of North Carolina Press, 1979.

Klingberg, Frank L. "The Historical Alternation of Moods in American Foreign Policy." *World Politics* 4, no. 2 (1952): 239–73.

Knorr, Klaus. *The War Potential of Nations.* Princeton: Princeton University Press, 1956.

Koh, Harold Hongju. *The National Security Constitution: Sharing Power after the Iran-Contra Affair.* New Haven: Yale University Press, 1990.

Kohn, Richard H. *Eagle and Sword: The Federalists and the Creation of the Military Establishment in America, 1783–1802.* New York: Free Press, 1975.

Krasner, Stephen D. *Defending the National Interest: Raw Materials Investments and U.S. Foreign Policy.* Princeton: Princeton University Press, 1978.

Krebs, Ronald R., and Jennifer K. Lobasz. "Fixing the Meaning of 9/11: Hegemony, Coercion, and the Road to War in Iraq." *Security Studies* 16, no. 3 (2007): 409–51.

Kupchan, Charles A. *Vulnerability of Empire.* Ithaca, N.Y.: Cornell University Press, 1994.

Kupchan, Charles A., and Peter L. Trubowitz. "Dead Center: The Demise of Liberal Internationalism in the United States." *International Security* 32, no. 2 (2007): 7–44.

———. "The Illusion of Liberal Internationalism's Revival." *International Security* 35, no. 1 (2010): 95–109.

Kurlantzick, Joshua. *Charm Offensive: How China's Soft Power Is Transforming the World.* New Haven: Yale University Press, 2007.

Kurth, James. "America's Grand Strategy: A Pattern of History." *National Interest* 43 (1999): 3–19.

Labs, Eric J. "Do Weak States Bandwagon?" *Security Studies* 1, no. 3 (1992): 383–416.

LaFeber, Walter. *The American Search for Opportunity, 1865–1913.* Cambridge: Cambridge University Press, 1993.

Lake, David A. *Power, Protection, and Free Trade: International Sources of U.S. Commercial Strategy, 1887–1939.* Ithaca, N.Y.: Cornell University Press, 1988.

Lake, David A., and Robert Powell, eds. *Strategic Choice and International Relations.* Princeton: Princeton University Press, 1999.

Lamborn, Alan C. "Power and the Politics of Extraction." *International Studies Quarterly* 27 (1983): 125–46.

———. *The Price of Power: Risk and Foreign Policy in Britain, France, and Germany.* Boston: Unwin, Hyman, 1991.

Langer, Gary, and Jon Cohen. "Voters and Values in the 2004 Election." *Public Opinion Quarterly* 69, no. 5 (2005): 744–59.

Layne, Christopher. "Kant or Cant: The Myth of the Democratic Peace." *International Security* 19, no. 2 (1994): 5–49.

———. *The Peace of Illusion: American Grand Strategy from 1940 to the Present.* Ithaca, N.Y.: Cornell University Press, 2006.

———. "Security Studies and the Use of History: Neville Chamberlain's Grand Strategy Revisited." *Security Studies* 17, no. 3 (2008): 397–437.

Leffler, Melvin P. "Bush's Foreign Policy." *Foreign Policy* 144 (September–October 2004): 22–28.

———. *The Elusive Quest: America's Pursuit of European Stability and French Security, 1919–1933.* Chapel Hill: University of North Carolina Press, 1979.

Legro, Jeffrey W. *Rethinking the World: Great Power Strategies and International Order.* Ithaca, N.Y.: Cornell University Press, 2005.

Legro, Jeffrey W., and Andrew Moravcsik. "Is Anybody Still a Realist?" *International Security* 24, no. 2 (1999): 5–55.

Lemann, Nicholas. "The Controller: Karl Rove Is Working to Get George Bush Reelected, but He Has Bigger Plans." *New Yorker*, May 12, 2003.

Lenin, Vladimir I. *Imperialism, the Highest Stage of Capitalism*. New York: International Publishers, 1939.

Levi, Margaret. *Of Rule and Revenue*. Berkeley: University of California Press, 1988.

Levy, Jack S. "The Diversionary Theory of War: A Critique." In *Handbook of War Studies*, edited by Manus I. Mildarsky, 259–88. London: Unwin, Hyman, 1989.

Li, Mingjiang. "Domestic Sources of China's Soft Power Approach." *China Security* 5, no. 2 (2009): 34–49.

Lian, Bradley, and John R. Oneal. "Presidents, the Use of Military Force, and Public Opinion." *Journal of Conflict Resolution* 37, no. 2 (1993): 277–300.

Lieberman, Peter. *Does Conquest Pay? The Exploitation of Occupied Industrial Societies*. Princeton: Princeton University Press, 1996.

Lieberthal, Kenneth. "How Domestic Forces Shape the PRC's Grand Strategy and International Impact." In *Domestic Political Change and Grand Strategy*, edited by Ashley J. Tellis and Michael Wills, 29–66. Seattle: National Bureau of Asian Research, 2007.

Light, Paul C. "The President's Agenda: Notes on the Timing of Domestic Choice." *Presidential Studies Quarterly* 11, no. 1 (1985): 67–82.

Lindsay, James M. "The New Apathy: How an Uninterested Public Is Reshaping Foreign Policy." *Foreign Affairs* 79, no. 5 (September–October 2000): 2–8.

Little, Richard. "British Neutrality versus Offshore Balancing in the American Civil War: The English School Strikes Back." *Security Studies* 16, no. 1 (2007): 68–95.

Livermore, Shaw. *The Twilight of Federalism*. Princeton: Princeton University Press, 1962.

Lobell, Steven E. *The Challenge of Hegemony: Grand Strategy, Trade, and Domestic Politics*. Ann Arbor: University of Michigan Press, 2003.

Lobell, Steven E., Norrin M. Ripsman, and Jeffrey W. Taliaferro, eds. *Neoclassical Realism, the State, and Foreign Policy*. New York: Cambridge University Press, 2009.

Logevall, Frederik. "Party Politics." In *Encyclopedia of American Foreign Policy*, edited by Alexander DeConde, Richard Dean Burns, and Frederik Logevall, 99–111. New York: Scribner, 2002.

Long, David F. "The Board of Navy Commissioners." In *In Peace and War: Interpretations of American Naval History, 1775–1984*, edited by Kenneth J. Hagan, 63–78. Westport, Conn.: Greenwood Press, 1984.

Lovin, Clifford R. "Herbert Hoover, Internationalist, 1919–1923." *Prologue* 20, no. 4 (1988): 449–72.

Luttwak, Edward N. *The Grand Strategy of the Byzantine Empire*. Cambridge, Mass.: Harvard University Press, 2009.

———. *The Grand Strategy of the Roman Empire: From the First Century AD to the Third*. Baltimore: Johns Hopkins University Press, 1976.

Lynch, Allen C. "The Realism of Russia's Foreign Policy." *Europe-Asia Studies* 53, no. 1 (2001): 7–31.

MacDonald, C. A. *The United States, Britain, and Appeasement, 1936–1939*. New York: St. Martin's Press, 1981.

Machiavelli, Niccolò. *The Prince*. New York: Bantam Books, 1966.

Mahin, Dean B. *One War at a Time: The International Dimensions of the Civil War.* Washington, D.C.: Potomac Books, 1999.

Mandelbaum, Michael. *The Frugal Superpower: America's Global Leadership in a Cash-Strapped Era.* New York: Public Affairs, 2010.

Mankoff, Jeffrey. *Russian Foreign Policy: The Return of Great Power Politics.* Lanham, Md.: Rowman and Littlefield, 2009.

Mann, James. *About Face: A History of America's Curious Relationship with China, from Nixon to Clinton.* New York: Vintage, 2000.

———. "Behold China." *New Republic,* March 17, 2010. http://www.tnr.com /article/world/behold-china.

———. *Rise of the Vulcans: The History of Bush's War Cabinet.* New York: Viking Books, 2004.

Marks, Frederick W., III. "Six between Roosevelt and Hitler: America's Role in the Appeasement of Nazi Germany." *Historical Journal* 28, no. 4 (1985): 969–82.

———. *Wind over Sand: The Diplomacy of Franklin Roosevelt.* Athens: University of Georgia Press, 1988.

Markusen, Ann, Peter Hall, Scott Campbell, and Deitrick Sabina. *The Rise of the Gunbelt: The Military Remapping of Industrial America.* New York: Oxford Univesity Press, 1991.

Martin, Lisa L. "Self-Binding: How America Benefits from Multilateralism—And the Costs We Bear by Going It Alone in a Risky New Century." *Harvard Magazine* 107, no. 1 (2004): 33–36.

Martis, Kenneth C. *The Historical Atlas of Political Parties in the United States Congress, 1789–1989.* New York: Macmillan, 1989.

Mastanduno, Michael. "U.S. Foreign Policy and the Pragmatic Use of International Institutions." *Australian Journal of International Affairs* 59, no. 3 (2005): 317–33.

Mastanduno, Michael, David A. Lake, and G. John Ikenberry. "Toward a Realist Theory of State Action." *International Studies Quarterly* 33, no. 4 (1989): 457–74.

Mattern, Susan P. *Rome and the Enemy: Imperial Strategy in the Principate.* Berkeley and Los Angeles: University of California Press, 1999.

May, Ernest. *Imperial Democracy: The Emergence of America as a Great Power.* New York: Harcourt Brace Jovanovich, 1961.

———. *The Making of the Monroe Doctrine.* Cambridge: Cambridge University Press, 1975.

Mayer, Arno J. *Dynamics of Counterrevolution in Europe.* New York: Harper and Row, 1971.

McCormick, Richard P. *The Second American Party System: Party Formation in the Jacksonian Era.* Chapel Hill: University of North Carolina Press, 1966.

McDonald, David. "Domestic Conjunctures, the Russian State, and the World Outside, 1700–2006." In *Russian Foreign Policy in the Twenty-first Century and the Shadow of the Past,* edited by Robert Legvold, 145–203. New York: Columbia University Press, 2007.

McDonald, Forrest. *The Presidency of George Washington.* Lawrence: University Press of Kansas, 1974.

McDonald, Patrick J. *The Hidden Hand of Peace: Capitalism, the War Machine, and International Relations Theory*. Cambridge: Cambridge University Press, 2009.

McKee, Oliver, Jr. "The Next Speaker." *North American Review* 232, no. 2 (1931): 135–40.

McKitrick, Eric, L. "Party Politics in the Union and Confederate War Efforts." In *The American Party Systems*, edited by William Nisbet Chambers and Walter Dean Burnham, 11–51. Oxford: Oxford University Press, 1967.

McNair, Elizabeth S., James C. Murdoch, Chung-Ron Pi, and Todd Sandler. "Growth and Defense: Pooled Estimates for the NATO Alliance, 1951–1988." *South Economic Journal* 62, no. 3 (1995): 846–60.

McPherson, James M. *Battle Cry of Freedom: The Civil War Era*. New York: Oxford University Press, 1988.

Mearsheimer, John J. "Hollow Victory." *foreignpolicy.com*. November 2, 2009. http://www.foreignpolicy.com/.

———. *The Tragedy of Great Power Politics*. New York: Norton, 2001.

Medeiros, Evan S. *China's International Behavior: Activism, Opportunism, and Diversification*. Santa Monica: Rand Corporation, 2009.

Mellow, Nicole. *The State of Disunion: Regional Sources of Modern American Partisanship*. Baltimore: Johns Hopkins University Press, 2008.

Melman, Seymour. *After Capitalism: From Managerialism to Workplace Democracy*. New York: Alfred A. Knopf, 2001.

Mercer, Jonathan. *Reputation and International Politics*. Ithaca, N.Y.: Cornell University Press, 1996.

Milkis, Sidney M. "The Presidency and Political Parties." In *The Presidency and the Political System*, edited by Michael Nelson, 341–82. Washington, D.C.: Congressional Quarterly Press, 2005.

Miller Center. Lyndon Johnson to Richard Russell, 10:55 a.m., 27 May 1964, Tape WH6405.10, Citations # 3519, #3520, and #3521, Recordings of Telephone Conversations—White House Series, Lyndon B. Johnson Library. Transcript by the Presidential Recordings Program, Miller Center of Public Affairs, University of Virginia, Charlottesville. http://tapes.millercenter.virginia.edu/clips/1964_0707_russell/.

Millett, Alan R., and Peter Maslowski. *For the Common Defense: A Military History of the United States of America*. New York: Free Press, 1984.

Milward, Alan S. *War, Economy and Society, 1939–1945*. London: Allen, Lane, 1977.

Mintz, Alex, and Chi Huang. "Guns versus Butter: The Indirect Link." *Journal of Political Science* 35, no. 3 (1991): 738–57.

Morgan, Clifton T., and Kenneth Bickers. "Domestic Discontent and the External Use of Force." *Journal of Conflict Resolution* 36, no. 1 (1992): 25–52.

Morgan, Howard Wayne. *William McKinley and His America*. Syracuse, N.Y.: Syracuse University Press, 1963.

Morgenthau, Hans. *Politics among Nations: The Struggle for Peace and Power*. New York: Alfred A. Knopf, 1948.

Morrow, James D. "Arms versus Allies: Trade-Offs in the Search of Stability." *International Organzation* 47, no. 2 (1993): 208–33.

Mueller, John. "Simplicity and Spook: Terrorism and the Dynamics of Threat Exaggeration." *International Studies Perspectives* 6, no. 2 (2005): 208–34.

Narizny, Kevin. *The Political Economy of Grand Strategy.* Ithaca, N.Y.: Cornell University Press, 2007.

Neale, Robert G. *Great Britain and the United States Expansion: 1989–1900.* East Lansing: Michigan State University Press, 1966.

Neustadt, Richard E. *Presidential Power and the Modern Presidents: The Politics of Leadership from Roosevelt to Reagan.* Rev. ed. New York: Free Press, 1990.

Newton, Scott. *Profits of Peace: The Political Economy of Anglo-German Appeasement.* Oxford: Clarendon, 1996.

Nielsen, George Raymond. "The Indispensable Institution: The Congressional Party during the Era of Good Feelings." Ph.D. dissertation, University of Iowa, 1968.

Nincic, Miroslav. *Democracy and Foreign Policy: The Fallacy of Political Realism.* New York: Columbia University Press, 1992.

Ninkovich, Frank. *The Wilsonian Century: U.S. Foreign Policy since 1900.* Chicago: University of Chicago Press, 1999.

Nordlinger, Eric A. *Isolationism Reconfigured: American Foreign Policy for a New Century.* Princeton: Princeton University Press, 1995.

North, Douglass C. *The Economic Growth of the United States, 1790–1860.* New York: Prentice-Hall, 1961.

Obama, Barack. "National Security Strategy." *White House.* May 2010. http://www.whitehouse.gov/sites/default/files/rss_viewer/national_security_strategy.pdf.

———. "President in Address to the Nation on the Way Forward in Afghanistan and Pakistan." *White House.* December 1, 2009a. http://www.whitehouse.gov/the-press-office/remarks-president-address-nation-way-forward-afghanistan-and-pakistan.

———. "Speech to the United Nations' General Assembly." *www.nytimes.com.* September 23, 2009b. http://www.nytimes.com/2009/09/24/us/politics/24prexy.text.html.

O'Connor, John. *The Fiscal Crisis of the State.* New York: St. Martin's Press, 1973.

Offner, Arnold A. *American Appeasement: United States Foreign Policy and Germany, 1933–1938.* Cambridge: Cambridge University Press, 1969.

Offner, John L. "McKinley and the Spanish-American War." *Presidential Studies Quarterly* 34, no. 1 (2004): 50–61.

———. *An Unwanted War: The Diplomacy of the United States and Spain over Cuba, 1895–1898.* Chapel Hill: University of North Carolina Press, 1992.

OhUallacháin, Breandán. "Regional and Technological Implications of the Recent Buildup in American Defense Spending." *Annals of the Association of American Geographers* 77, no. 2 (1987): 208–23.

Olcott, Martha Brill. *The Energy Dimension in Russian Global Strategy: Vladimir Putin and the Geopolitics of Oil.* Monograph, James Baker III Institute for Public Policy. Houston: Rice University, 2004.

Oliker, Olga, Keith Crane, Lowell H. Schwartz, and Catherine Yusupov. *Russian Foreign Policy: Sources and Implications.* Santa Monica: Rand Corporation, 2009.

Olson, Mancur. *Rise and Decline of Nations*. New Haven: Yale University Press, 1982.

Osgood, Robert E. *Ideals and Self-Interest in America's Foreign Policy*. Chicago: University of Chicago Press, 1953.

Ostrom, Charles, and Brian Job. "The President and the Political Use of Force." *American Political Science Review* 80, no. 2 (1986): 541–66.

Owen, John M. *Liberal Peace, Liberal War: American Politics and International Security*. Ithaca, N.Y.: Cornell University Press, 2000.

Pampel, Fred C., and John B. Williamson. "Welfare Spending in Advanced Industrial Democracies, 1950–1980." *American Journal of Sociology* 93, no. 6 (1988): 1424–56.

Pape, Robert A. "Soft Balancing against the United States." *International Security* 30, no. 1 (2005): 7–45.

Paret, Peter, Gordon A. Craig, and Felix Gilbert. *Makers of Modern Strategy: From Machiavelli to the Nuclear Age*. Princeton: Princeton University Press, 1986.

Patrick, Stewart. "Multilateralism and Its Discontents: The Causes and Consequences of American Ambivalence." In *Multilateralism and U.S. Foreign Policy: Ambivalent Engagement*, edited by Stewart Patrick and Shepard Forman, 1–44. Boulder: Lynne Rienner, 2002.

Patterson, James T. *Congressional Conservatism and the New Deal: The Growth of the Conservative Coalition in Congress, 1933–1939*. Lexington: University Press of Kentucky, 1967.

Paul, T. V. "The Enduring Axioms of Balance of Power Theory." In *Balance of Power Revisited: Theory and Practice in the Twenty-first Century*, edited by T. V. Paul, James J. Wirtz, and Michel Fortmann, 1–28. Stanford: Stanford University Press, 2004.

Pelz, Stephan. "Changing International Systems, the World Balance of Power, and the United States, 1776–1976." *Diplomatic History* 15, no. 1 (1991): 47–81.

Pérez, Louis A. *The War of 1898: The United States and Cuba in History and Historiography*. Chapel Hill: University of North Carolina Press, 1998.

Perkins, Dexter. *The Monroe Doctrine, 1823–1826*. 2nd ed. Cambridge: Cambridge University Press, 1955.

Phillips, Kevin. *William McKinley*. New York: Henry Holt, 2003.

Pollack, Sheldon D. *War, Revenue, and State Building: Financing the Development of the American State*. Ithaca, N.Y.: Cornell University Press, 2009.

Posen, Barry. *The Sources of Military Doctrine: Britain, France, and Germany between the World Wars*. Ithaca, N.Y.: Cornell University Press, 1984.

Potter, Philip B. K. "Does Experience Matter? American Presidential Experience, Age, and International Conflict." *Journal of Conflict Resolution* 51, no. 3 (2007): 351–78.

Pratt, Julius W. *Expansionists of 1898: The Acquisition of Hawaii and the Spanish Islands*. Baltimore: Johns Hopkins University Press, 1936.

Press, Daryl G. *Calculating Credibility: How Leaders Assess Military Threats*. Ithaca, N.Y.: Cornell University Press, 2007.

Price, Kevin S., and John J. Coleman. "The Party Base of Presidential Leadership and Legitimacy." In *High Risk and Big Ambition: The Presidency of George W.*

Bush, edited by Steven E. Schier, 55–76. Pittsburgh: University of Pittsburgh Press, 2004.

Prucha, Francis Paul. *The Sword of the Republic: The United States Army on the Frontier, 1783–1846*. London: Macmillian, 1969.

Putnam, Robert D. "Diplomacy and Domestic Politics: The Logic of Two-Level Games." *International Organization* 42 (1988): 427–60.

Qin, Yaqing. "International Factors and China's External Behavior: Power, Interdependence, and Institutitons." In *China's 'New Diplomacy': Tactical or Fundamental Change*, edited by Puline Kerr, Stuart Harris, and Qin Yaqing, 33–54. New York: Palgrave, 2008.

Qin, Yaqing, and Wei Lin. "Structures, Processes and the Socialization of Power: East Asian Community Building and the Rise of China." In *China's Assent: Power, Security, and the Future of International Politics*, edited by Robert Ross and Zhu Feng, 115–38. Ithaca, N.Y.: Cornell University Press, 2008.

Quandt, William B. "The Electoral Cycle and the Conduct of Foreign Policy." *Political Science Quarterly* 101, no. 5 (1986): 825–37.

Quester, George H. "The Wilson Presidency, the U.S. Navy, and Homeland Defense." *White House Studies* 4, no. 2 (2004): 137–48.

Ransom, Roger L. "EH.Net Encyclopedia." *EH.Net*. 2001. www.eh.net/encyclopedia/content/ransom.civil.war.ut.php.

Rathbun, Brian. "A Rose by Any Other Name: Neoclassical Realism as the Logical and Necessary Extension of Structural Realism." *Security Studies* 17, no. 2 (2008): 294–321.

Rawley, James A. *The Politics of Union: Northern Politics during the Civil War*. Lincoln: University of Nebraska Press, 1980.

———. *Turning Points of the Civil War*. 2nd ed. Lincoln: University of Nebraska Press, 1989.

Reeves, Richard. *President Reagan: The Triumph of Imagination*. New York: Simon and Schuster, 2006.

Reid, Brian Holden. "Power, Sovereignty, and the Great Republic: Anglo-American Diplomatic Relations in the Era of the Civil War." *Diplomacy and Statecraft* 14, no. 3 (2003): 45–76.

Remington, Thomas. "Patronage and the Party of Power: President-Parliament Relations under Vladimir Putin." *Europe-Asia Studies* 60, no. 6 (2008): 959–87.

Remini, Robert V. "New York and the Presidential Election of 1816." In *Political Parties in American History*, vol. 1: *1789–1828*, edited by Winfred E. A. Bernhard, 416–30. New York: C. P. Putnam's Sons, 1973.

Reynolds, David. *From Munich to Pearl Habor: Roosevelt's America and the Origins of the Second World War*. Chicago: Ivan R. Dee, 2001.

Riker, William H. *The Art of Political Manipulation*. New Haven: Yale University Press, 1986.

Ripsman, Norrin M., and Jack S. Levy. "Wishful Thinking or Buying Time? The Logic of British Appeasement in the 1930s." *International Security* 33, no. 2 (2008): 148–81.

Rock, Stephen R. *Appeasement in International Politics*. Lexington: University Press of Kentucky, 2000.

Rose, Gideon. "Neoclassical Realism and Theories of Foreign Policy." *World Politics* 51, no. 1 (1998): 144–77.

Rosecrance, Richard, and Arthur A. Stein. "Beyond Realism: The Study of Grand Strategy." In *The Domestic Bases of Grand Strategy*, edited by Richard Rosecrance and Arthur A. Stein, 3–21. Ithaca, N.Y.: Cornell University Press, 1993.

Rosenau, James N. "Toward the Study of National-International Linkages." In *Linkage Politics: Essays on the Convergence of National and International Systems*, edited by James N. Rosenau, 43–63. New York: Free Press, 1969.

Rosenberg, Emily S. *Spreading the American Dream: American Economic and Cultural Expansion: 1890–1945*. New York: Hill and Wang, 1982.

Ross, Robert S. "China's Naval Nationalism: Sources, Prospects, and the U.S. Response." *International Security* 34, no. 2 (2009a): 46–81.

———. *Chinese Security Policy: Structure, Power, and Politics*. New York: Routledge, 2009b.

Rottinghaus, Brandon. "Limited to Follow: The Early Public Opinion Apparatus of the Herbert Hoover White House." *American Politics Research* 31, no. 5 (2003): 540–56.

Russett, Bruce M. "Who Pays for Defense?" *American Political Science Review* 63, no. 2 (1969): 412–26.

Samuels, Richard J. *"Rich Nation, Strong Army": National Security and the Technological Transformation of Japan*. Ithaca, N.Y.: Cornell University Press, 1996.

———. *Security Japan: Tokyo's Grand Strategy for East Asia*. Ithaca, N.Y.: Cornell University Press, 2007.

Scattschneider, E. E. *The Semisovereign People: A Realist's View of Democracy in America*. New York: Holt, Reinhart, and Winston, 1960.

Schelling, Thomas C. *The Strategy of Conflict*. Cambridge, Mass.: Harvard University Press, 1960.

Schick, Allen. *The Federal Budget: Politics, Policy, Process*. Rev. ed. Washington, D.C.: Brookings Institution, 2000a.

———. "'A Surplus, If We Can Keep It': How the Federal Budget Surplus Happened." *Brookings Review* 18, no. 1 (2000b): 36–39.

Schlesinger, Arthur M., Jr. *Imperial Presidency*. New York: Houghton Mifflin, 1973.

Schott, Jeffrey J. "Trade Policy and the Obama Administration." *Business Economics* 44, no. 3 (2009): 150–53.

Schroeder, John H. *Shaping a Maritime Empire: The Commercial and Diplomatic Role of the American Navy, 1829–1861*. Westport, Conn: Greenwood Press, 1985.

Schroeder, Paul W. "Historical Reality vs. Neo-Realist Theory." *International Security* 19, no. 1 (1994a): 108–48.

———. *The Transformation of European Politics, 1763–1848*. New York: Oxford University Press, 1994b.

Schuessler, John M. "The Deception Dividend: FDR's Undeclared War." *International Security* 34, no. 4 (2010): 133–65.

Schumpeter, Joseph A. *Imperialism and Social Classes*. 1919. Translated by Heinz Norden. New York: Meridian Books, 1955.

Schwarz, Jordan A. *The Interregum of Despair: Hoover, Congress, and the Depression*. Urbana: University of Illinois Press, 1970.

Schweller, Randall L. *Deadly Imbalances: Tripolarity and Hitler's Strategy of World Conquest*. New York: Columbia Unversity Press, 1997.

Schweller, Randall L. *Unanswered Threats: Political Constraints on the Balance of Power.* Princeton: Princeton University Press, 2006.

Shambaugh, David. "Beijing: A Global Leader with 'China First' Policy." *Yale Global,* June 30, 2010. http://yaleglobal.yale.edu/content/beijing-global -leader-china-first-policy.

———. "China Engages Asia: Reshaping the Regional Order." *International Security* 29, no. 3 (2004–5): 64–99.

Shanker, Thom, and Christopher Drew. "Pentagon Faces Growing Pressure to Trim Budget." *New York Times,* July 22, 2010. http://www.nytimes.com /2010/07/23/us/politics/23budget.html?_r=1&scp=1&sq=Pentagon%20Faces %20Growing%20Pressures%20to%20Trim%20Budget&st=cse.

Shapiro, Robert Y., and Yaeli Block-Elkon. "Political Polarization and the Rational Public." In *Power and Superpower: Global Leadership and Exceptionalism in the 21st Century,* edited by Morton H. Halperin, Jeffrey Laurenti, Peter Rundlet, and Spencer P. Boyer, 49–68. New York: Century Foundation Press, 2007.

Sharp, James Roger. *American Politics in the Early Republic: The New Nation in Crisis.* New Haven: Yale University Press, 1993.

Shefter, Martin. "War, Trade, and U.S. Party Politics." In *Shaped by War and Trade: International Influences on American Political Development,* edited by Ira Katznelson and Martin Shefter, 113–33. Princeton: Princeton University Press, 2002.

Shirk, Susan L. *China: Fragile Superpower.* New York: Oxford University Press, 2007.

Shoch, James. *Trading Blows: Party Competition and U.S. Trade Policy in a Globalizing Era.* Chapel Hill: University of North Carolina Press, 2001.

Silbey, Joel H. "The Incomplete World of American Politics, 1815–1829: Presidents, Parties and Politics in 'The Era of Good Feelings.'" *Congress & the Presidency* 11, no. 1 (1984): 1–17.

———. *Martin Van Buren and the Emergence of American Popular Politics.* Lanham, Md.: Rowman and Littlefield, 2002.

———. *Storm over Texas: The Annexation Controversy and the Road to Civil War.* New York: Oxford University Press, 2005.

Silva, Mark. "Cheney Back on the Campaign Trail as GOP's 'Attack Dog.'" *Chicago Tribune,* August 18, 2006.

Skeen, C. Edward. "Calhoun, Crawford, and the Politics of Retrenchment." *South Carolina Historical Magazine* 73, no. 3 (1972): 141–55.

Skidmore, David. "Understanding the Unilateralist Turn in U.S. Foreign Policy." *Foreign Policy Analysis* 1, no. 2 (2005): 207–28.

Skowronek, Stephen. *Building a New American State: The Expansion of National Administrative Capacities, 1877–1920.* Cambridge: Cambridge University Press, 1982.

———. *The Politics Presidents Make: Leadership from John Adams to Bill Clinton.* Cambridge, Mass.: Harvard University Press, 1997.

———. *Presidential Leadership in Political Time: Reprise and Reappraisal.* Lawrence: University Press of Kansas, 2008.

Slater, Jerome. "The Domino Theory and International Politics: The Case of Vietnam." *Security Studies* 3, no. 2 (1993): 186–224.

Small, Melvin. *Democracy and Diplomacy: The Impact of Domestic Politics on Foreign Policy, 1789–1994.* Baltimore: Johns Hopkins University Press, 1996.

Smith, Carlton B. "Congressional Attitudes toward Military Preparedness during the Monroe Administration." *Military Affairs* 40, no. 1 (1976): 22–26.

Smith, Joe Patterson. "A United States of North America—Shadow or Substance? 1815–1915." *Canadian Historical Review* 26, no. 2 (1945): 109–18.

Snyder, Jack. *Myths of Empire: Domestic Politics and International Ambition.* Ithaca, N.Y.: Cornell University Press, 1991.

Snyder, Jack, Robert Y. Shapiro, and Yaeli Bloch-Elkon. "Free Hand Abroad, Divide and Rule at Home." *World Politics* 61, no. 1 (2009): 155–87.

Sofka, James R. "American Neutral Rights Reappraised: Identity or Interest in the Foreign Policy of the Early Republic?" *Review of International Studies* 26 (2000): 599–622.

———. "The Eighteenth Century International System: Parity or Primacy?" *Review of International Studies* 27 (2001): 147–63.

Solingen, Etel. *Regional Orders at Century's Dawn: Global and Domestic Influences on Grand Strategy.* Princeton: Princeton University Press, 1998.

Sprout, Harold, and Margaret Sprout. *The Rise of American Naval Power, 1776–1918.* Princeton: Princeton University Press, 1944.

Spykman, Nicholas John. *America's Strategy in World Politics: The United States and the Balance of Power.* New York: Harcourt, Brace, 1942.

Steele, Brent J. "Ontological Security and the Power of Self-Identity: British Neutrality and the American Civil War." *Review of International Studies* 31 (2005): 519–40.

Stein, Arthur A. "Domestic Constraints, Extended Deterrence, and the Incoherence of Grand Strategy: The United States, 1938–1950." In *The Domestic Bases of Grand Strategy*, edited by Richard Rosecrance and Arthur A. Stein, 96–123. Ithaca, N.Y.: Cornell University Press, 1993.

Stent, Angela E. "Restoration and Revolution in Putin's Foreign Policy." *Europe-Asia Studies* 60, no. 6 (2008): 1089–1106.

Stokes, Donald E. "Spatial Models of Party Competition." *American Political Science Review* 57, no. 2 (1963): 368–77.

Stoler, Mark A. *Allies and Adversaries: The Joint Chiefs of Staff, the Grand Alliance, and U.S. Strategy in World War II.* Chapel Hill: University of North Carolina Press, 2000.

Stoll, Richard J. "The Guns of November: Presidential Reelections and the Use of Force, 1947–1982." *Journal of Conflict Resolution* 28, no. 3 (1982): 231–46.

Stout, Cushing. *The American Image of the Old World.* New York: Harper and Row, 1963.

Strahan, Randall, Vincent G. Moscardelli, Moshe Haspel, and Richard S. Wike. "The Clay Speakership Revisited." *Polity* 32, no. 4 (2000): 561–93.

Strauss, Barry S. *Athens after the Pelopennesian War: Class, Faction and Policy, 403–386 B.C.* Ithaca, N.Y.: Cornell University Press, 1986.

Stuart, Reginald C. *War and American Thought: From the Revolution to the Monroe Doctrine.* Kent: Kent State University Press, 1982.

Suskind, Ron. *The One Percent Doctrine: Deep Inside America's Pursuit of Its Enemies since 9/11.* New York: Simon and Schuster, 2006.

Swaine, Michael D. "China's Regional Military Posture." In *Power Shift: China and Asia's New Dynamics*, edited by David Shambaugh, 266–86. Berkeley: University of California Press, 2006.

Symonds, Graig L. *Lincoln and His Admirals.* New York: Oxford University Press, 2008.

Tannenwald, Nina. "The Nuclear Taboo: The United States and the Normative Basis of Nuclear Non-Use." *International Organization* 53, no. 3 (1999): 433–468

Tarar, Ahmer. "Diversionary Incentives and the Bargaining Approach to War." *International Studies Quarterly* 50, no. 1 (2006): 169–88.

Taylor, Ian. *China's New Role in Africa.* Boulder: Lynne Reinner, 2008.

Taylor, Miles E. "Obama's National Security Strategy under the Microscope." *World Politics Review*, June 1, 2010. http://www.worldpoliticsreview.com/articles/5656/obamas-national-security-strategy-under-the-microscope.

Temin, Peter. *The Jacksonian Economy.* New York: W. W. Norton, 1969.

Thurow, Lester C. *Head to Head: The Coming Economic Battle among Japan, Europe, and America.* New York: Warner, 1993.

Tompson, William. "Putting Yukos in Perspective." *Post-Soviet Affairs* 21, no. 2 (2005): 159–81.

Trachtenberg, Marc. *The Craft of International History.* Princeton: Princeton University Press, 2006.

———. "Making Grand Strategy: The Early Cold War Experience in Retrospect." *SAIS Review* 19, no. 1 (1999): 33–40.

Trask, David F. *The War with Spain in 1898.* Lincoln: University of Nebraska Press, 1981.

Treisman, Daniel. "The Popularity of Russian Presidents." Unpublished manuscript, University of California, Los Angeles, 2008.

———. "Rational Appeasement." *International Organization* 58, no. 2 (2004): 345–73.

Trubowitz, Peter. *Defining the National Interest: Conflict and Change in American Foreign Policy.* Chicago: University of Chicago Press, 1998.

———. "Déjà Vu: Political Struggles over American Defense Policy." In *Downsizing Defense*, edited by Ethan Kapstein, 61–78. Washington, D.C.: CQ Press, 1993.

———. "Geography and Strategy: The Politics of American Naval Expansion." In *The Politics of Strategic Adjustment: Ideas, Institutions, and Interests*, edited by Peter Trubowitz, Emily O. Goldman, and Edward Rhodes, 105–38. New York: Columbia University Press, 1999.

Trubowitz, Peter, and Nicole Mellow. "Going Bipartisan: Politics by Other Means." *Political Science Quarterly* 120 (2005): 433–53.

Trubowitz, Peter, and Jungkun Seo. "Partisan Ambition and Scapegoat Theory: U.S.-China Relations in Political Perspective." Unpublished manuscript, University of Texas at Austin, 2010.

Tsygankov, Andrei P. "Does Russia Have a Grand Strategy?" New York: International Studies Association, February 2009.

———. "Russia's International Assertiveness: What Does It Mean for the West?" *Problems of Post-Communism* 55, no. 2 (2008): 38–55.

Turner, Frederick Jackson. *Rise of the New West, 1819–1829*. New York: Harper and Brothers, 1906.

Van Alstyne, Richard. *The Rising American Empire*. New York: Quadrange, 1960.

Van Evera, Stephen. *Causes of War: Power and the Roots of Conflict*. Ithaca, N.Y.: Cornell University, 1999.

Vinhas de Souza, Lúcio. *A Different Country: Russia's Economic Resurgence*. Brussels: Centre for European Policy Studies, 2008.

Wallander, Celeste A. "Russia: The Domestic Sources of a Less-Than-Grand Strategy." In *Domestic Political Change and Grand Strategy*, edited by Ashley J. Tellis and Michael Wills, 139–75. Seattle: National Bureau of Asian Research, 2007.

Wallander, Celeste A., and Robert O. Keohane. "Risk, Threat, and Security Institutions." In *Imperfect Unions: Security Institutions over Time and Space*, by Helga Haftendorn, Robert O. Keohane, and Celeste A. Wallander, 21–47. New York: Oxford University Press, 1999.

Wallerstein, Immanuel. *The Capitalist World Economy*. Cambridge: Cambridge University Press, 1979.

Walt, Stephen M. *The Origin of Alliances*. Ithaca, N.Y.: Cornell University Press, 1987.

———. *Over-Achievers and Under-Achievers*. April 21, 2009. http://walt.foreign-policy.com/posts/2009/04/21/over_achievers_and_under_achievers.

———. "Two Cheers for Clinton's Foreign Policy." *Foreign Affairs* 79, no. 2 (2000): 63–79.

———. "Why Alliances Endure or Collapse." *Survival* 39, no. 1 (1997): 156–79.

Waltz, Kenneth N. *Foreign Policy in Democratic Politics: The American and British Experience*. Boston: Little, Brown, 1967.

———. *Theory of International Politics*. New York: Random House, 1979.

Watson, Harrry L. *Liberty and Power: The Politics of Jacksonian America*. New York: Farrar, Straus and Giroux, 1990.

Watson, Richard L., Jr. "Congressional Attitudes toward Military Preparedness, 1829–1835." *American Historical Review* 34, no. 4 (1948): 611–36.

Weatherford, M. Stephen. "After the Critical Election: Presidential Leadership, Competition and the Consolidation of the New Deal Realignment." *British Journal of Political Science* 32, no. 2 (2002): 221–57.

Weaver, Kent R. "The Politics of Blame Avoidance." *Journal of Public Policy* 6, no. 4 (1986): 371–439.

Weber, Jennifer L. *Copperheads: The Rise and Fall of Lincoln's Opponents in the North*. New York: Oxford University Press, 2006.

Weeks, William Earl. *John Quincy Adams and American Global Empire*. Lexington: University Press of Kentucky, 1992.

Wheeler, Everett L. "Methodological Limits and the Mirage of Roman Strategy: Part I." *Journal of Military History* 57, no. 1 (1993): 7–41.

Whelan, Frederick G. *Hume and Machiavelli: Political Realism and Liberal Thought*. Lanham, Md.: Lexington Books, 2004.

Whitaker, Arthur P. *The United States and the Independence of Latin America*. New York: W. W. Norton, 1964.

Widmer, Ted. *Martin Van Buren*. New York: Henry Holt, 2005.

Wilentz, Sean. *The Rise of American Democracy: Jefferson to Lincoln*. New York: W. W. Norton, 2005.

Williams, T. Harry. *Lincoln and the Radicals*. 3rd ed. Madison: University of Wisconsin Press, 1969.

Wills, Garry. "The Clinton Principle." *New York Times Magazine*, January 19, 1997.

———. "The Would-Be Progressives." *New York Review of Books*, July 11, 1996.

Wilson, Joan Hoff. *Herbert Hoover: Forgotten Progressive*. New York: Harper Collins, 1975.

Wilson, John R. M. *Herbert Hoover and the Armed Forces: A Stude of Presidential Attitudes and Policy*. New York: Garland, 1993.

———. "The Quaker and the Sword: Herbert Hoover's Relations with the Military." *Military Affairs* 38, no. 2 (1974): 41–47.

Wilson, Major L. *The Presidency of Martin Van Buren*. Lawrence: University Press of Kansas, 1984.

Wilson, Woodrow. *Congressional Government*. 15th ed. Boston: Houghton Mifflin, 1900.

Winks, Robin W. *Canada and the United States: The Civil War Years*. 4th ed. Baltimore: Johns Hopkins University Press, 1998.

Wirls, Daniel. *Irrational Security: The Politics of Defense from Reagan to Obama*. Baltimore: Johns Hopkins University Press, 2010.

Witte, John F. *The Politics and Development of the Federal Income Tax*. Madison: University of Wisconsin Press, 1985.

Wohlforth, William C. *The Elusive Balance: Power and Perceptions during the Cold War*. Ithaca, N.Y.: Cornell University Press, 1993.

———. "Russia's Soft Balancing Act." In *Strategic Asia, 2003–4: Fragility and Crisis*, edited by Richard J. Ellings, Aaron L. Friedberg, and Michael Wills, 165–80. Seattle: National Bureau of Asian Research, 2003.

Wolanin, Thomas R. *Presidential Advisory Commissions: Truman to Nixon*. Madison: University of Wisconsin Press, 1975.

Wolfers, Arnold. *Discord and Collaboration: Essays on International Politics*. Baltimore: Johns Hopkins University Press, 1962.

Wood, Gordon S. *Empire of Liberty: A Histoy of the Early Republic, 1789–1815*. New York: Oxford University Press, 2009.

Woodward, C. Vann. "The Age of Reinterpretation." *American Historical Review* 66, no. 1 (1960): 1–19.

Wright, John D. *The Oxford Dictionary of Civil War Quotations*. New York: Oxford University Press, 2006.

Wright, Thomas. "Strategic Engagement's Record." *Washington Quarterly* 33, no. 3 (2010): 35–60.

Yahuda, Michael. "Deng Xiaoping: The Statesman." *China Quarterly* 135 (1993): 551–72.

Yan, Xuetong. *Analysis of China's National Interests.* Edited by Monte R. Bullard. Translated by Jun Meng. Prod. Center for Nonproliferation Studies. Monterey, 2008.

———. "The Rise of China and Its Power Status." *Chinese Journal of International Politics* 1 (2006): 5–33.

Zakaria, Fareed. "The Reagan Strategy of Containment." *Political Science Quarterly* 105 (1990): 373–95.

———. *From Wealth to Power: The Unusual Origins of America's World Role.* Princeton: Princeton University Press, 1998.

Zelizer, Julian. *Arsenal of Democracy: The Politics of National Security—From World War II to the War on Terrorism.* New York: Basic Books, 2009.

Ziegler, Paul R. *Palmerston.* London: Palgrave, 2003.

Index

Adams, Charles Francis, 63n52
Adams, Henry, 63n52
Adams, John, 84
Adams, John Quincy, 81–83, 86–87, 90
Adams-Onís Treaty (1819). *See* Transcontinental Treaty
Afghanistan, 109n, 124nn37 and 40; war in, 18n13, 100, 101n41, 103, 143, 145, 146n38, 147
Africa, 51, 61, 70, 71, 125n40, 131, 140
alliances: as external balancing, 12, 33n28; limits of offensive, 12n4
Al Qaeda, 148n40
American System of Henry Clay, 84–85
annexation. *See* expansionism
Antiballistic Missile Treaty (1972), 100. *See also* missile defense
APEC. *See* Asia-Pacific Economic Cooperation
appeasement: Innenpolitik views of, 45–46; Realpolitik views of, 41, 44, 45; strategy of, 5, 13, 14, 15, 22, 29, 31, 35, 41, 43, 44–76, 138
Argentina, 81
Armed Neutrality League, 49
ASEAN. *See* Association of Southeast Asian Nations
Asia, 12, 28, 65, 90, 96–98, 101, 104, 107, 116, 126, 131, 138–39, 141–42, 147
Asia-Pacific Economic Cooperation (APEC), 122
Association of Southeast Asian Nations, 140
Australia, 101n41
Austria, 47, 81
Austria-Hungary, 92
autarky. *See* isolationism

Bahrain, 101n41
"bait and bleed": strategy of, 11. *See also* bloodletting; divide and rule
balancing: determinants of, 32–33; straegies of, 8, 11, 11n, 12–13, 31, 40, 43, 49, 130–32, 141, 144
bandwagoning: methods of, 13n5; strategy of, 13, 15, 35, 44n2, 49n16, 138

Bank of England, 111
Bank of the United States, 111
Barbary states, 51–52
Battle of Antietam (1862), 62n51
Battle of Bull Run (1862): Second, 58n38
Belarus, 142, 143
Belgium, 109
Berlin Wall, 99n36, 121
binding: strategy of, 12, 12n3, 15, 131n
blackmail: strategy of, 5, 11, 14
blame: its effect on grand strategy, 32–37, 129, 135n8; politics of, 3, 17–19, 20, 21, 22n. *See also* specific case studies
bloodletting: strategy of, 11. *See also* "bait and bleed"; divide and rule
Blue-Orange War Plan, 118
Boer War, 96n29
Bosnia, 107n, 124
Boxer Rebellion, 97n32
Braeman, John, 118
Brazil, 92–93, 127
Britain, 5, 17, 25, 47, 60n47, 70, 75n74; and United States, 1, 27, 45, 46–64, 66, 68, 69n65, 70–84, 86, 92–93, 96, 109, 112, 134n7, 137. *See also* Civil War (U.S.); Napoleonic wars; War of 1812; World War II
British Guiana, 92n25
Bryan, William Jennings, 94, 137n13. *See also* Populist movement
Bryanism. *See* Populist movement
buckpassing: strategy of, 13, 14, 15, 22, 29, 31, 35, 41, 43, 44n2, 55, 65, 71–74, 138
Bulgaria, 69n64
Bundy, McGeorge, 18n14
Burma, 146n36
Burns, James MacGregor, 50, 74
Bush, George W., 141n22, 145; and democracy promotion, 99n36; electoral politics and, 103–4; expansionism as a partisan wedge for, 28, 98, 101–4, 105; expansionist strategy of, 41, 43, 78, 97–104, 134–135, 136, 148n40; fiscal policy of, 100n39; and geopolitical slack, 20, 39, 97, 100, 103, 104; guns